SEVENTH EDITION

COURSE DESIGN

A Guide to Curriculum Development for Teachers

GEORGE J. POSNER
Cornell University

ALAN N. RUDNITSKY
Smith College

PEARSON

Boston   New York   San Francisco
Mexico City   Montreal   Toronto   London   Madrid   Munich   Paris
Hong Kong   Singapore   Tokyo   Cape Town   Sydney

To Adrienne, Sue, Becky, Prema, Robin, Kim, Emma, Regan,
Maggie, and Hannah

Series Editor: Traci Mueller
Series Editorial Assistant: James P. Neal III
Marketing Manager: Krista Groshong
Production Editor: Judy Fiske
Editorial Production Service: Nesbitt Graphics, Inc.
Composition and Manufacturing Buyer: Andrew Turso
Electronic Composition: Nesbitt Graphics, Inc.
Cover Administrator: Joel Gendron

For related titles and support materials, visit our online catalog at www.ablongman.com.

Between the time Website information is gathered and then published, it is not unusual for some sites to have closed. Also, the transcription of URLs can result in typographical errors. The publisher would appreciate notification where these errors occur so that they may be corrected in subsequent editions.

Library of Congress Cataloging-in-Publication Data

Posner, George J.
    Course design : a guide to curriculum development for teachers / George J. Posner, Alan
N. Rudnitsky -- 7th ed.
        p.   cm.
    Includes bibliographical references and index.
    ISBN 0-205-45766-5
    1. Curriculum planning. 2. Education, Secondary -- Curricula. 3. Education,
 1. Elementary -- Curricula. I. Rudnitsky, Alan N. II. Title.

LB2806.15.P67 2006
375'.001--dc22   2005046977

Printed in the United States of America

16   15

CONTENTS

CHAPTER SEVEN

Developing General Teaching Strategies   164

CHAPTER EIGHT

Planning a Course Evaluation   196

Epilogue   219

FIGURES AND TABLES

FIGURES

TABLES

PREFACE

Course Design: A Guide to Curriculum Development for Teachers, Seventh Edition, attempts to bridge theory and practice in curriculum development. Intended primarily for teachers and teachers in training, it presents the concepts and skills of curriculum development and shows how to apply them to actual course planning. The overriding goal of the book is to assist the reader in becoming a flexible and, at the same time, systematic curriculum planner by developing a greater awareness of the important decisions to be made and the alternative courses of action available at each decision point.

Course Design has four principal functions: (1) as a textbook for graduate and undergraduate courses in curriculum development and instructional design or as a supplement to a "methods" course, (2) as a basis for in-service workshops for classroom teachers, (3) as material for individual teachers desiring to increase their professional competence, and (4) as a self-instructional "lab" portion of courses in curriculum development or instructional design. In our curriculum development courses, we typically supplement much of the theoretical content by having students develop a course or unit in step-by-step fashion. Students are then able to receive feedback as their work progresses, as well as see other students' work.

We begin *Course Design* with a set of guidelines for developing an actual course. By working through this book, you will produce a design for an actual course. We guide you through this process by providing relevant design theory, frequent exercises, representative examples, a glossary of terms, bibliographic references, and finally, sample course designs completed by students. The combination of theory and the process of actually designing a course makes *Course Design* a unique approach to learning curriculum development skills.

These materials have been used in beginning curriculum development courses for many years at Cornell University and Smith College. Those enrolled in the courses have been primarily undergraduate and graduate students who plan to teach in public schools, two-year colleges, and nonformal educational settings. The students have designed a wide variety of courses whose diverse subject matter includes beekeeping, propaganda analysis, creative writing, communication media, advanced algebra, developmental psychology, ecology, reading for parents of nonreaders, and hockey. Many refinements and revisions included in the seventh edition have come as a result of student comments and the student-developed course designs.

HIGHLIGHTS OF THE SEVENTH EDITION

1. We have added new material and references, put greater emphasis on planning for meaningful learning and understanding, and further highlighted and made explicit the cognitive orientation of *Course Design*'s approach.

2. We have added a much expanded section on national and state standards, standards-based reform, and how standards fit into the course design process.

3. We have added an expanded section on multiple intelligences.

Every time we use this book we think of changes that would improve it. In addition, reviews conducted by our editor at Allyn & Bacon supplied us with valuable suggestions for strengthening the text. We are fortunate to have had the opportunity to obtain the advice of competent and knowledgeable reviewers:

Cindy Arnold, Bethel College
Joslen Letscher, University of Detroit/Mercy
Mona C. Majdalani, University of Wisconsin/Eau Claire
Helena Mariella-Walrond, Bethune-Cookman College
David McCrory, West Virginia University

...and to be able to use this advice for the continuing refinement of what we believe to be a basically sound approach.

A book such as this comes into existence through a process of evolution. The sources of ideas are difficult to identify because they are numerous and have been incorporated into our general orientation to curriculum development. The intellectual source of much of the book is the theoretical work of Mauritz Johnson. Although he did not participate directly in the preparation of the manuscript, Johnson's clarity of thought about curriculum and instruction has been both an inspiration and a conceptual guide. Graduate and undergraduate students at Cornell University and Smith College contributed innumerable significant suggestions and many of the examples provided. Colleagues at Cornell and Smith have provided many useful suggestions used to improve the book. We wish to thank the following individuals for their generous permission, allowing us to include their course planning work as examples in *Course Design:*

Michelle Chang, "Immigration: A Social Studies Unit for Sixth Graders"
Elizabeth Clark, "The Inuit of North Alaska"
Susan D'Agostino, "Symmetry"
Leanne Dineen, "World Geography"
Susan M. Etheredge, "A Metric Measurement Unit for Grades One and Two"
Bernadette Gaffney, "The Rocky Shore Ecosystem"
Erika Hollander, "Native American Culture"
Marion Johnson, "Modern Dance"
Megan Kennedy, "Geology"
Kevin Kinneavy, "Coordinate Geometry"
Alyssa Krawczyk, "Sylvia Plath"
Jeff Lydon, "Essay Writing Story"
Kerry Nappi, "Colonial America: Social Studies Curriculum for Grade 5"
Kelly Nerbonne, "Rivers"
Anne Marie O'Reilly, "Wonders of the Forest Community"

Laura Rochat, "The Sounds of Poetry"
Donna Taylor, "An Introduction to Black-and-White Photography: From
    Snapshot to Art Form" ("The Camera")
Margaret Timmerman, "A Survey of Western Art"

These substantial contributions are greatly appreciated; any errors or short-comings are the authors' alone.

GETTING ORIENTED

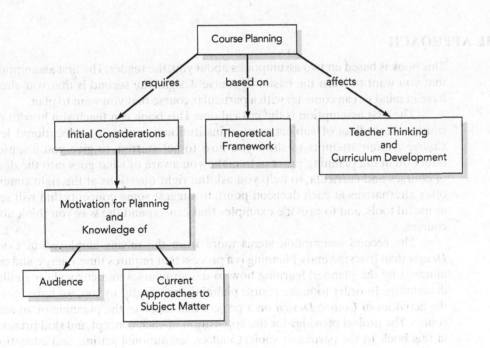

After completing this chapter, you should be able to:

1. Understand the theoretical framework underlying the course planning process and that the most important effect of good planning is on the subsequent thinking of the planner/teacher.

2. Know that the process of course planning presented here is intended to be modified and adapted by teachers when they engage in actual planning.

3. Understand the format of a course planning project and why a project has been selected as a focal point for learning the concepts and skills of course planning.

4. Understand the distinction between processes and products of planning.

5. Understand the distinction between curricular and instructional matters.

6. Understand the following terms and their interrelationship: *value, educational goal, curriculum, instructional plan, instruction, actual learning outcome,* and *evaluation* (see the Glossary for definitions).

7. Know the three basic needs for course design and be able to perform the preliminary research necessary to begin planning.

8. Generate an initial list of ideas for your course.

THE APPROACH

This book is based on two assumptions about you, the reader. The first assumption is that you want to learn the basics of course design. The second is that you already have in mind or can come up with a particular course that you want to plan.

The first assumption is the critical one. This book can teach you how to plan courses, regardless of subject matter, institutional setting, or educational level. *Course Design* attempts to show you how to get started, to give you a sense of direction in the planning process, to make you aware of what goes into the design of courses and curricula, to help you ask the right questions at the right times, to offer alternatives at each decision point, to suggest some concepts that will serve as useful tools, and to provide examples that can expand the way you think about courses.

The second assumption stems more from the means employed in *Course Design* than from the ends. Planning is a process that requires time, energy, and commitment by the planner; learning how to design courses and curricula is similarly demanding. In order to make course planning meaningful to you, we have focused the activities of *Course Design* on a project that involves the planning of an actual course. The project provides for the application of each concept and skill presented in this book to the particular subject matter, institutional setting, and educational level that interest you.

Focusing the learning activities of this book on your own project has important pedagogical value. If you want to learn the concepts and skills of course planning but do not have a particular course in mind, we suggest that you decide on a course in a familiar subject area that can serve as a focus.

Keep in mind that the project is primarily a means to an end. The skills and concepts of course planning are primary, and the project is intended to help you acquire them. The steps followed in working through the book do teach how to plan courses, but, given the time constraints usually present, the approach may appear at times too detailed and systematic for actual course planning. This is to be expected. The approach has been designed to teach course planning but not necessarily to guide the course planning process once the skills and concepts have been learned. Learning long division serves as a useful analogy: When we learn long division, we may learn a series of specific steps to follow. But once we learn the process, we skip steps and generally divide in a more flexible and intuitive way than when we were learning it.

It is too much to expect a single approach to curriculum development to work always and for everyone. Factors such as audience, setting, subject matter, and grade level place their own particular constraints on teachers. You should feel free to modify our general approach to suit your particular circumstance.

Planning at the *elementary school* level has unique constraints. Fundamentally, elementary teachers tend to plan in unit-sized rather than course-sized sections. Elementary school units vary in scope and duration, but typical units may last from two to six weeks and cover topics such as fractions, time, punctuation, myths and fairy tales, animals in winter, oceans, the Revolutionary War, and elections, to name a few.

The emphasis on unit planning is not to suggest that this is the only kind of educational planning elementary teachers can or should do. On the contrary, elementary teachers need to engage in a broader form of planning in which they consider their overall program. Units should be planned in context with other units. Units in a particular content area are preceded and followed by other units; typically, these units are related. The sequence of units is something that should be planned, not simply allowed to happen haphazardly or because textbooks sequence their material in a particular way. In addition, units in one content area are taught concurrently with units in other content areas. Teachers should consider which units work particularly well together, which units conflict or are difficult to teach at the same time, and which units may depend on learning in another content area. In any case, steps that may not at first seem appropriate for elementary unit planning can prove crucial for planning that is broader in scope.

The following suggestions may prove helpful for elementary teachers:

1. Intended learning outcomes are likely to be fewer in number. Try to teach a few important ideas and skills well rather than cover too many intended learnings.

2. Some suggested course planning steps such as formulating central questions and sequencing and organizing a course's units may not be appropriate. We suggest that you think about all the course planning steps and consider various alternatives, but do not become a slave to them.

At times we single out and focus on the concerns of elementary teachers, particularly with regard to curriculum organization (Chapter 5) and teaching strategies (Chapter 7). Appendixes A, C, and D provide three extensive sample elementary unit plans. At all times, we hope you will use our suggestions with flexibility and imagination. You will not find a prescription in this text for the one right way to develop curricula or the way all curricula should look.

You may need to modify our general approach because different projects have different needs and requirements and thus will have different emphases. Teachers who have taught topics for a long time but have never really considered what particular learnings they were seeking will likely put greater emphasis on clarifying their intended learning outcomes. Teachers wishing to introduce totally new types of courses will have to concentrate on the courses' justification and thus emphasize the rationale. Teachers planning interdisciplinary courses will have to think carefully about how ideas from different disciplines are related. This will likely require a more complex course outline (see Chapter 2)—perhaps an outline for content from each discipline. Do not think that every component of the design process you encounter in the book requires equal emphasis and attention. Flexibility and adaptation will help make your project more meaningful.

THE PROJECT

If you complete each course planning step in this book, you will finish with the following products:

1. A *rationale* for the course, including the overall educational goals.

2. A *curriculum plan* describing intended learning outcomes for the course, prioritized according to importance, to be expressed in formats that may include the following:

    a. lists of statements and paragraphs
    b. maps of major ideas
    c. a story or narrative expressing the course's "theme"
    d. flowcharts of skills

3. An *instructional plan* describing what each unit is about, how it fits into the overall organization of units, what learning outcomes each unit is intended to accomplish, and what general teaching strategies could be used in each unit to accomplish the intended learning outcomes.

4. An *evaluation plan* describing behavioral indicators for each high-priority intended learning outcome (main effects), together with a list of some unintended, undesirable learning outcomes (side effects) to be on the lookout for.

You will make other products along the way, such as course introductions, course outlines, and central questions. For the purposes of this book, these are considered instrumental products, used mainly to improve the major components listed above. Instructors using this text in class may or may not require that these instrumental products be part of a final project.

In the appendixes you will find four completed course designs that might give you some idea of our aim.

SOME GUIDELINES FOR GETTING STARTED

Now that you have an idea what this book is about, you can start planning a course as a focal point for learning the basics of curriculum development. Decide on a course you want to plan. In making your decision, consider the following points: (1) Your course may run as long as a whole year or it may be as short as a four-week "mini-course." (2) Choose a course for which you know the subject matter well. It is difficult to plan something that is unfamiliar to you. (3) Create a course to answer some educational need, whether it be a learner or a societal need, a "felt" or an "unfelt" need. (4) Don't be afraid to create a unique course; you may want to give a traditional course a different emphasis, combine diverse subject matter, or adjust a course usually taught to one audience so that it can be taught to a different (for example, older, more heterogeneous, more "turned off") audience.

Motivation for Planning

When you begin to plan a course you may have any number of ideas, resources, or restrictions fixed in your mind. You may have received a mandate from an administrative source (for example, the state education department) specifying goals or requiring a certain level of student achievement. An existing course may not be producing satisfactory results. Students may not be taking with them the math they need for next year's work. You may want to implement a new teaching technique and may find the existing course inappropriately organized for such a technique. A school may provide a new language laboratory, a nature trail, a computer terminal, or sophisticated audiovisual equipment that will extend the capabilities of teachers, and courses will have to be created or re-created to use these new resources. Courses at a two-year college may not be attracting students, and new courses may be needed to lure them. Courses previously considered appropriate for a particular kind of student may have to be redesigned as the student population becomes more mature or more heterogeneous. A new middle school may require courses specifically designed for its population and institutional purposes.

All settings for course planning provide "givens" that affect the start of the planning process, and these should be made explicit from the beginning if the course planning process is to proceed in an open and systematic manner, rather than according to some hidden agenda.

Audience for the Course

Right at the outset, and indeed all the way through the planning process, a guiding principle should be to consider the students at every stage. It is necessary to consider carefully their maturity, needs, interests, abilities, and knowledge. Educating *all* students is and has always been a significant challenge. The increasing diversity of the school population and educators' recognition of the importance of considering diversity when planning and teaching have added to the complexity of the challenge. The term *diversity* encompasses a wide range of individual and group factors. These include learning styles, cultural and language backgrounds, gender, social class, and an enormous spectrum of special needs. Consideration of these issues should have an impact on curriculum and instruction. The nature of the impact can range from choice of content and examples to instructional methods to assessment.

If you are unfamiliar with the characteristics and background of your intended audience, you will have some preliminary work to do before beginning to plan the course. The following resources may help you learn about your audience:

1. Texts in educational psychology covering both the psychology of human learning and human development.

2. Texts and other sources that examine issues of diversity, multicultural education, and working with students with special needs.

3. Observations or practice teaching at a local school or college with a student population similar to yours.

4. Interviews with teachers who have taught students similar to yours.

We will have more to say about understanding your students in subsequent chapters.

Current Approaches to the Subject

Another requisite for course planning is a thorough understanding of the subject matter. One part of this understanding is an ability to identify and explain the key concepts and skills in the subject. Another is a thorough knowledge of the details of the subject. Still another is a familiarity with current curricular approaches to the subject matter. This thorough understanding is not easily obtained. Extensive reading, thoughtful writing, and even hands-on experience are typically required. Certainly, reading a single textbook is not sufficient, since such an approach seriously limits your awareness of alternative viewpoints and does not allow for the development of sufficient depth in the subject. If you are unfamiliar with the current approaches, you may want to do some preliminary work before you begin course planning. The following suggestions may be useful:

1. Collect as many current textbooks and syllabi in the subject as you can. Skim through each of them and study their contents pages in particular in order to get an idea of what is currently being taught in the subject.

2. Try to find out (from texts, teachers, or syllabi) what the students usually study in the subject or related subjects before they get to your course. Also try to determine what they may study in the subject after they complete your course.

3. Talk with teachers in your subject in order to identify topics, approaches to the subject, resources, exercises, and activities that seem to have the potential for stimulating interest.

Course planning begins with and is based on three things: (1) a clearly recognized motivation or source; (2) a recognition of the capacities, needs, and interests of the students; and (3) a familiarity with current approaches to the subject matter.

QUESTIONS FOR DISCUSSION: GETTING STARTED

1. In what general area do you want to plan a course (civics, English, dance, filmmaking, reading, gardening, biology, ecology)?

2. Make a list of courses you have taken (or taught) specifically in this or a related area. How might those courses differ from the courses you want to plan? How might they be similar?

3. Do you have something special in mind for your course (a new technique, a special audience, new equipment)? Describe.

4. What are five questions an interested party might ask about your course?

Course Planning Step 1.1   Write a brief paragraph describing your course. With these initial thoughts in mind, it may be helpful to get an overview of *Course Design* before proceeding further with your project.

A FRAMEWORK FOR COURSE DESIGN*

Any systematic approach to course planning must be considered within the context of a theoretical framework. At the least, such a framework must identify important aspects of the planning process and must show how these aspects are interrelated. In the broadest sense, the theoretical approach to course planning developed here can be considered rational. What makes the approach rational is that there are reasons for what is planned to take place in the classroom. The reasons are based on what we want students to learn. Thus, the underlying premise of this conceptual framework is that conceiving of and clarifying what students should learn is the foundation for course planning. This section presents such a framework.

*Much of the following discussion has been adapted from Johnson (1967). We encourage you to read his paper for a deeper understanding of the conceptual farmework underlying this book.

The basic concept such a framework must deal with is *curriculum*. There are almost as many definitions of curriculum as there are writers, and we do not claim that any one definition is correct. Nevertheless, certain conceptual distinctions are useful in course planning, and certain definitions of curriculum make these distinctions important. One such distinction is that between *processes* and *products* of planning. Another is that between *curricular* and *instructional* matters.

Process–Product

A process consists of one or more events. A product is something produced by a process. Planning is usually a highly complex process, and a plan is the product of that process.

In order to make several points regarding this distinction, let us examine a noneducational but relatively familiar planning situation. A blueprint for a proposed building is a plan developed by an architect or engineer. In the planning (a *process*) the architect considers architectural form, building materials, characteristics of the proposed site, intended use of the building, energy efficiency, and many other factors. The blueprint is the result (a *product*) of the planning and it guides the process of construction. A blueprint specifies what the product of construction should be but does not specify how the process of construction (the construction schedule) should proceed. This analogy illustrates how a plan may (but does not have to) be intended for an anticipated process (for example, construction). Also, a complex process such as building a house may be broken down into discrete component processes, such as preparing blueprints, preparing a construction schedule, and constructing the house according to the blueprint.

Course design similarly has several processes, each producing its own product. Curriculum planning produces an articulation of what students should learn. This product guides the process of instructional planning, which produces an instructional plan, which then serves as a guide for the process of instruction.

Curriculum–Instruction

Instruction is obviously a process—a series of events intended to lead to some learning outcomes. As such, it is analogous to the process of house construction. Instruction consists of all the ways teachers attempt to get learners engaged in content or subject matter. Instructional matters, then, have to do with the nature of the activities and specific content that make up the process of instruction. The process of instruction is guided by a plan analogous to a construction schedule, termed the *instructional plan*.

It is important to distinguish instruction from curriculum. Instruction is a process; curriculum is not. Many (if not most) books on education consider curriculum as consisting of experiences or the activities that engender these experiences. But this usage confuses curriculum with instruction. A more precise view of curriculum is that it is what is taught in school or what is intended to be learned. It does not refer to what is to be *done* in school or what is to *happen* in the learning process. Curriculum represents a set of *intentions,* a set of intended learning outcomes. Consequently, curricular matters have to do with the nature and organization of those things we as course planners want learned in our courses. *Curriculum development* results in a design specifying the desired learnings (the intended learning outcomes); thus, curriculum is analogous to a blueprint or an architectural design. Instructional planning, on the other hand, results in a plan outlining the intended process of instruction; thus, an instructional plan is analogous to a construction schedule. A curriculum and an instructional plan are as different as a design for a new house and a plan giving the steps in its construction. Yet they are related in that a blueprint is a necessary guide for planning a construction schedule.

Curriculum development entails selection and organization of a set of intended learning outcomes. Selecting intended learning outcomes is itself guided by the educational goals to be served. Educational goals should indicate what the learning should lead to, not what it consists of; they describe intended educational results in much the same way curriculum describes intended learning outcomes. (See Chapter 3 for more details on educational goals.) Educational results derive from the complex, interactive, and cumulative effects of actual learning outcomes, intended and unintended, both in school and outside school, in addition to maturation and other forces acting on students. Educational goals describe desired results of the entire educational process. The selection of intended learning outcomes (i.e., curriculum development) represents the best guess as to what needs to be learned to achieve the educational goals. Using our terminology, if a statement is in terms of things to be learned, it is curricular; if it is in terms of attributes of the well-educated person, it is an educational goal; if it is in terms of teaching strategies, it is instructional.

Thus, the *curriculum* indicates *what* is to be learned, the *goals* indicate *why* it is to be learned, and the *instructional plan* indicates *how* to facilitate learning. None of these three planning processes—curriculum development, goal setting, and instructional planning—results in any learning. Only the instruction process and accompanying learner engagement do that.

Figure 1.1 on page 10 depicts the major processes related to course planning and their resulting products. The arrows in the figure should be interpreted as processes, the boxes as products. Moving from left to right on the chart, we answer various implementation questions. How do we implement our values? By aiming at a particular educational goal. How do we implement our educational goal? By having students learn particular things (a particular curriculum). How do we implement our curriculum? By providing particular activities (that is, a particular instructional plan). Moving from right to left, we answer justification questions: Why this instructional plan? Because instructional planning was guided by this curriculum. Why this curriculum? Because we are aiming at this educational goal. And so on.

Notice in Figure 1.1 that an additional process is included—that of evaluation. For the purposes of this book, evaluation planning will consist of specifying a set of

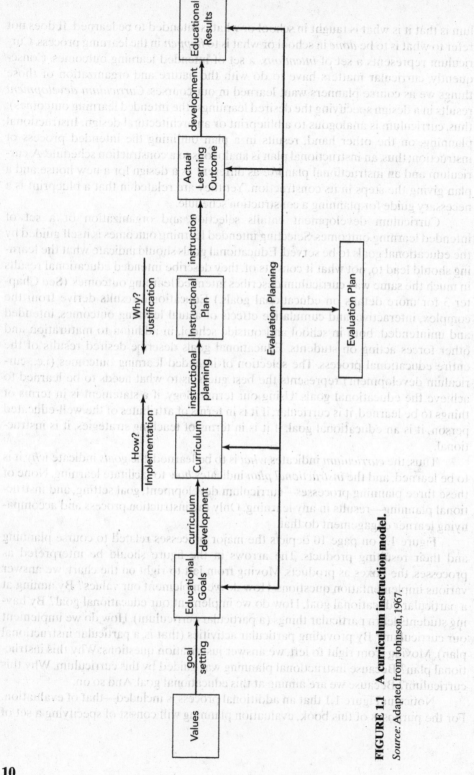

FIGURE 1.1 A curriculum instruction model.
Source: Adapted from Johnson, 1967.

sample indicators that can be used to analyze actual learning outcomes and educational results. The approach used will emphasize evaluation for course improvement rather than for grading individual students.

Although this framework generally clarifies the logical relations among educational products and processes, it also misleads in several significant ways. Perhaps the greatest danger in using this framework is when it is interpreted as a step-by-step guide to course design. At times the framework will function adequately as such a guide, but generally it is counterproductive to assume that this conceptual overview is also a procedural model. For example, it is usually wrong to insist on developing curriculum only after goals and values have been specified. Goals and values do underlie our reason for including particular curricular content, but it is not always necessary to specify those goals and values first. Actually, it is often possible to think more productively about abstract topics (such as goals) after thinking about more concrete matters (such as curricular content and instructional techniques). Therefore, it is important when using the framework to remember that it is a conceptual overview rather than a procedural flowchart of the course design process.

Related to this issue is the assumption by some readers that course design is a fairly straightforward linear process. If anything, we have probably contributed to this belief by depicting a linear framework in Figure 1.1 and by presenting course design in a step-by-step manner. We have obviously oversimplified the process, and you should be careful not to fall into the trap of thinking about course design in a strictly linear manner.

A linear approach is one in which each step is completed before the next one is begun. In course design, no steps are ever completed once and for all. Generally, we move to the next step after making a rough approximation because we realize that we will be in a better position to continue our work on an early step with the insights that a later step provides. A course design evolves as a series of successive approximations. In fact, course designs are never really completed. Rather, we "abandon" further planning for the time being. The same can be said of our course planning steps. There is no reason to insist on any degree of finality to a course planning step so long as we remember that we will be returning to that step at a later time equipped with new ideas and clearer thinking.

With this general framework in mind, it may be useful to specify the relationship between process–products and the corresponding chapters of *Course Design*. Generally speaking, values and educational goals are described in the course's rationale. This component is developed in Chapter 3. Curriculum is described, in part, in the course's statement of intended learning outcomes and the conceptual map(s) for the course. The intended learning outcomes are selected and their organization analyzed in Chapter 2, and they are further refined in Chapter 4. The instructional plan is described in the unit outline of the course developed in Chapters 5, 6, and 7. The approach to evaluation is described in the course's evaluation plan, a component of course design developed in Chapter 8. Figure 1.2 on page 12 summarizes the relationships between the model and components of course design as presented in this book.

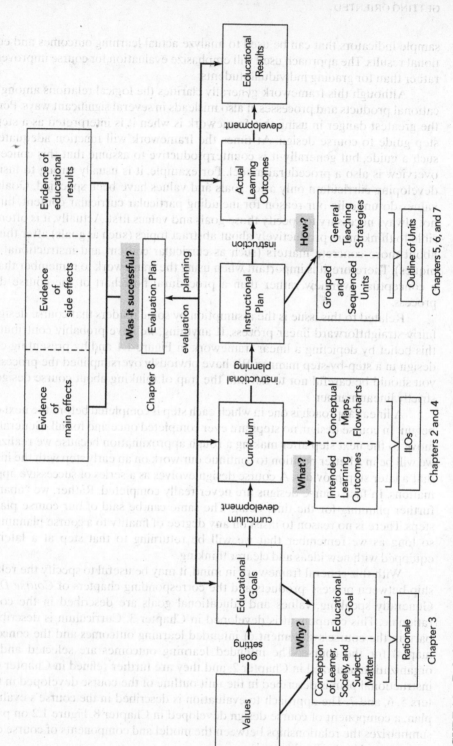

FIGURE 1.2 Relationship between the model and components of *Course Design*.

QUESTIONS FOR DISCUSSION: THE CONCEPTUAL FRAMEWORK

1. What are the advantages and disadvantages of defining curriculum as "an organized set of intended learning outcomes"?

2. Although ends and means are relative, isn't there an ultimate end? What happens when we ask the question "Why?" of an underlying value?

3. What questions (other than "Why?" "What?" "How?" and "Was it successful?") should a course design help to answer?

4. The analogy between curriculum development and the design of houses is not perfect. In what ways does the analogy break down?

5. Do values ever influence curriculum development and instructional planning directly, rather than indirectly through educational goals?

RELATION OF COURSE DESIGN TO CURRICULUM DEVELOPMENT

The premise of this book is that designing a course or (in the case of elementary grades) a unit is a special case of the more general process of curriculum development. While there may be more to the typical curriculum development process than designing courses and units, this latter process requires the use of many key aspects of curriculum development. Curriculum development, like course and unit design, requires careful consideration of the rationale for the curriculum, decisions about what students should be expected to learn, attention to matters of organization and sequence, determination of teaching strategies, and planning for evaluation. These matters are all addressed in this book. While not explicitly among the steps of course planning, there are five other important matters to consider: (1) group deliberation, (2) scope and sequence from year to year, (3) curriculum adaptation, (4) interdisciplinary planning, and (5) teacher thinking. We hope that discussing these matters here will help you understand how the concepts and skills you learn in this book fit into a more comprehensive preparation in curriculum development.

Group Deliberation

Curriculum development is typically done by teams of people working together on a common project. For example, a curriculum committee in elementary mathematics might spend two weeks each summer for three years developing a school district's K–6 mathematics curriculum. The team might consist of one teacher from each grade level, together with the district computer coordinator, a special educator, a librarian, a principal, and the district's director of elementary education. The process by which curriculum development teams produce a curriculum is termed *deliberation*.

Walker (1971, 2003) and Schwab (1970) do address some of these issues. These writers contend that group deliberation is at the heart of curriculum development. Deliberation "treats both ends and means and must treat them as mutually determining one another" (Schwab, 1970, p. 36). Deliberation consists of "formulating decision points, devising alternative choices at these decision points, considering arguments for and against suggested decision points and . . . alternatives, and finally, choosing the most defensible alternative" (Walker, 1971, p. 54). Clearly, this process is less linear than any process delineated step by step can possibly be. We agree with Walker and Schwab that curriculum development can best be described as a "complex and arduous" deliberation task (Schwab, 1970, p. 36). We also recognize the need to provide students with a project-centered approach to curriculum study— one that will help students develop some if not all of the concepts and skills necessary for considering "the most promising alternative actions in light of the best available knowledge" (Walker, 2003, p. 215). In addition, since the logistics of college course work will require many of you to work on your course planning projects individually, rather than in groups, after completing this project you will still need to learn how to apply the concepts and skills learned to group work. To the extent that your instructor provides some opportunity for group discussion of project work, you will learn the difference between developing curricula alone and within a group context. McCutcheon (1995) provides a thorough discussion of deliberation as both an individual ("solo") and a group process.

Beginning in the mid to late 1990s, increasing numbers of teachers have become participants in lesson study (Lewis, Perry, & Hurd, 2004; Watanabe, 2002). Lesson study is aimed at increasing and improving practitioner knowledge (Hiebert, Gallimore, & Stigler, 2002). Lesson study, as the name suggests, focuses on planning and analyzing a lesson or series of lessons. We believe that many of the planning steps and considerations included in *Course Design* will prove applicable and valuable in the context of lesson planning, especially lesson study planning, where the clarity and completeness of the plan are essential.

Curriculum Adaptation

It is unusual for anyone to develop a curriculum from scratch. More generally, school districts and individual teachers adapt an existing curriculum to make it more up to date, multicultural, multimedia, thematic, computer assisted, relevant to students' lives, hands-on, or career oriented (Glatthorn, 1987). Or an existing curriculum may need adaptation in order to bring it into better alignment with state standards or to increase its effectiveness in addressing the needs of certain students, whether they be "at risk" or "gifted and talented." Earlier we discussed many of these motivations for planning as they relate to course design. Here we mention them as a basis for adapting existing curricula, rather than for developing a curriculum from scratch. The point is that although this book approaches curriculum development as a task of course or unit design, this approach might differ from curriculum development work you might face in schools. Although many of the concepts and skills you will learn in this book will be helpful, your work in schools might require you to apply these concepts and skills in a manner that might vary considerably from the apparent linear progression of curriculum development we advocate in this book.

In order to prepare you for this reality, we discuss several instances of it: in Chapter 3 as an issue of "entry point" in planning, in Chapter 5 when we present alternative approaches to forming units in your course, and at other times when we issue warnings about the apparent linearity of the curriculum development process. Similar warnings regarding linearity in planning apply to all of the course planning steps presented in this book. For example, rather than begin to develop general teaching strategies from your intended learning outcomes, you might need to modify intended learning outcomes in order to make them consistent with teaching strategies that emphasize a "hands-on" approach to teaching. Eliot Wigginton (1985) provides a detailed account of how to plan a course in a nonlinear, fluid, but purposeful manner as the planner attempts to "make courses do double duty"; that is, address the state's list of required competencies and the teacher's or the school's own agenda. His description is full of practical wisdom that any curriculum developer may find invaluable.

Interdisciplinary Planning and Differentiated Instruction

Many teachers are attracted to curriculum design because it offers opportunities to develop interdisciplinary units. By drawing on elements of history, science, mathematics, the arts, and literature, teachers are able to provide students with experiences that are richer, more authentic, and more engaging than traditional single-discipline experiences. In addition, these experiences allow students to see how the various disciplines relate to each other, and, in so doing, reduce the fragmentation of the curriculum. Jacobs (1989, 1997, 1998) cites the exponential growth of knowledge, accompanied by increase in specialization, shifting subject-matter boundaries, and fragmentation of the school day as reasons for more interdisciplinary experiences at school. Of course, these arguments are not new. The benefits of embedding knowledge in real-world problems and topics have been proposed by many great educational theorists and practitioners (see, for example, Dewey, 1938).

However, quality implementation of interdisciplinary curriculum has proved difficult. One serious problem occurs when a curriculum draws from different disciplines but consists of disconnected pieces of content, therefore lacking intellectual coherence. (Jacobs, 1989, refers to this as the "potpourri problem.") Another problem occurs when a selected theme is too narrow to support a rigorous learning experience in more than a single discipline (Perkins, 1989).

Problems also occur when educators see discipline-based and interdisciplinary curriculum as mutually exclusive; that is, an either-or choice (the "polarity problem," according to Jacobs, 1989). At one pole (the strict discipline-based pole), students are deprived of potentially rich learning experiences. At the other pole, planners feel compelled to include all disciplines in every unit. This practice prevents students from engaging in in-depth, focused study within a discipline.

Almost all courses or units have relationships or connections to other disciplines; it is far from being an either-or choice. There are many options for thinking about interdisciplinary curriculum, ranging from largely discipline-based units to completely integrated programs (Jacobs, 1989). Among the options within this range are parallel disciplines, interdisciplinary, and integrated-day approaches. A *parallel disciplinary approach* would involve a correspondence between or among content from several disciplines. A historical study of the Industrial Revolution could be accompanied by literature about the conditions of factory work and a scientific study of machines. *Interdisciplinary approaches* bring together an array of disciplines to study a subject or problem. Studying a culture could combine reading, writing, math, science, history, art, and music. *Integrated-day* and completely interdisciplinary programs are more extensive commitments to interdisciplinary work. Integrated-day programs are most often seen in primary school and base all the day's work on a particular theme. Themes change regularly, but the approach is consistent. A completely integrated program is typically problem or theme based. A group might undertake a study of water quality and various disciplines would come into play as required.

Using themes, or *thematic curriculum planning,* is often synonymous with interdisciplinary curriculum planning (Fredericks et al., 1993; Thompson, 1991). Themes are large ideas that integrate the concepts of several disciplines (Martinello & Cook, 1994). Sources for themes include students' common interests, literature and trade books, textbook topics, current events, local sites and community resources, cultural heritage, teacher interest and expertise, objects and artifacts, and abstract concepts. Planners using a thematic approach must guard against themes that may be too narrow and also against those that are too broad and apt to receive superficial treatment (Perkins, 1989). Perkins suggests carefully evaluating the appropriateness and potential of a theme. Among the criteria of a good theme are that it applies to a wide range of subjects, including those beyond the scope specifically included in the unit; discloses fundamental patterns common to many subjects; reveals similarities and contrasts; and fascinates, provokes curiosity and inquiry, and draws students and teachers deeper into the study of the subjects.

The planning process of *Course Design* is well suited to interdisciplinary planning. The steps and decisions that a planner must make are the same whether or not a unit is interdisciplinary. In later chapters we will include suggestions for planners who wish to use the course design process for interdisciplinary planning.

Differentiated instruction is receiving considerable attention from educators (Hall, 2003). The premise of differentiated instruction is to "recognize students' varying background knowledge, readiness, language preferences in learning and interests, and to respond responsively" (Hall, Strangman, & Meyer, 2003, p. 2). Most teachers are aware of this and know that one of their greatest challenges is accommodating these differences. To the extent that the differentiated instruction movement reminds us of this, it provides a worthy service. Advocates of differentiated instruction emphasize that instruction should aim at broad principles, ideas, and understandings for all students rather than focus on minute details and a large number of facts (Tomlinson, 2001). The planning process of *Course Design* helps teachers clarify and focus on meaning and understanding and thus is well suited for teachers intent on pursuing differentiated instruction.

Curriculum Development and Teacher Thinking

The teaching environment, as Clark and Peterson (1986) note, is characterized by complexity, a fast pace, and unpredictability. Teachers must think constantly about managerial concerns, covering the material, how students are doing, what is coming next, and what has transpired, to name a few of the demands. Teachers must respond quickly to a tremendous variety of situations and events (Kindsvatter, Wilen, & Ishler, 1988). In such an environment careful planning can have substantial benefits. However, no instructional plan can anticipate the unexpected. An instructional plan tells teachers what materials to use, what learning activities students should engage in, what sequence these activities should take, and more. But, of course, an instructional plan cannot tell a teacher how to respond to spontaneous classroom interactions. These unpredictable yet commonplace occurrences are essential aspects of instruction and can thus have significant effects on the outcomes of instruction. The ways in which teachers become aware of, interpret, and respond to these events depend to a great extent on what and how they are thinking.

A curriculum is commonly thought of as a guide to instructional planning. If it guided *only* instructional planning, a curriculum would be important but of limited direct significance in day-to-day classroom teaching. However, we have found that the curriculum, or at least the curriculum development process, can also guide teachers in their responses to daily unexpected classroom events. Our experience with *Course Design* is that it has a significant effect on teachers' thinking and on how they act in the classroom. Teachers report that the design process, as a whole, has given them a clear conception of what they want learned, and this conception has directly affected their teaching. Teachers find themselves better able to respond to questions and comments in a focused way, to ask pertinent questions, to react to various types of student errors, and to take advantage of unforeseen teaching opportunities as they arise. As a result of engaging in the design process, teachers have found that their judgments about their own teaching effectiveness become increasingly based on what and how students learn, not just on how smoothly the day went.

A clear conception of what is to be learned in a course is, perhaps, the major goal of *Course Design*. This clear conception is more than statements of outcomes; it is bound up in a design process that includes justification for learnings and how these learnings will be actualized and evaluated. As you work through the various steps of *Course Design,* keep in mind that this process is intended to affect your everyday thinking as well as your planning.

ALIGNMENT WITH STANDARDS

Any lingering doubts about the universality of standards in United States public schools was put to rest in 2002 when the federal government enacted the No Child Left Behind Act. The act requires states to develop and test for standards in reading, language arts, mathematics, science, and English proficiency. States are graded on their performance and these grades are announced with considerable fanfare. Publicly grading towns and even schools are common practices within states. Teachers cannot ignore standards. The challenge is to maintain best practice, teaching for meaningful learning while adhering to the standards.

Standards have been around far longer than 2002. The standards-based reform movement was begun by discipline-based professional organizations. Notable efforts to produce standards that have come from these organizations include Curriculum and Standards for School Mathematics (NCTM, 1989), National Science Education Standards (National Research Council, 1996), and National Standards for History, Basic Edition (National Center for History in the Schools, 1996). These standards have had considerable influence in the creation of state standards. There are strong family resemblances, especially in mathematics and science. At the same time, there are some major differences between state and national standards, in large measure because the achievement of state standards must be measured by paper and pencil tests. Figures 1.3 and 1.4 are examples of national standards.

Content Standard A:

As a result of activities in grades 9–12, all students should develop

- Abilities necessary to do scientific inquiry
- Understandings about scientific inquiry

Content Standard B:

As a result of activities in grades 9–12, all students should develop an understanding of

- Structure of atoms
- Structure and properties of matter
- Chemical reactions
- Motions and forces
- Conservation of energy and increase in disorder
- Interactions of energy and matter

Content Standard C:

As a result of activities in grades 9–12, all students should develop an understanding of

- The cell
- Molecular basis of heredity
- Biological evolution
- Interdependence of organisms
- Matter, energy, and organization in living systems
- Behavior of organisms

FIGURE 1.3 National Science Education Standards: Content Standards Grades 9–12.

Source: Reprinted with permission from *National Science Education Standards,* © 1996 by the National Academy of Sciences, courtesy of the National Academies Press, Washington, DC.

Number and Operations Standard

Instructional programs from prekindergarten through grade 12 should enable all students to—

Understand numbers, ways of representing numbers, relationships among numbers, and number systems

Grades 6–8 Expectations

In grades 6–8, all students should:

- Work flexibly with fractions, decimals, and percents to solve problems;
- Compare and order fractions, decimals, and percents efficiently and find their approximate locations on a number line;
- Develop meaning for percents greater than 100 and less than 1;
- Understand and use ratios and proportions to represent quantitative relationships;
- Develop an understanding of large numbers and recognize and appropriately use exponential, scientific, and calculator notation;
- Use factors, multiples, prime factorization, and relatively prime numbers to solve problems;
- Develop meaning for integers and represent and compare quantities with them.

FIGURE 1.4   Excerpt from NCTM Number and Operations.

Source: Reprinted with permission from *Principles and Standards for School Mathematics,* copyright 2000, by the National Council of Teachers of Mathematics. All rights reserved.

Notice that in both samples, the standards describe what students are expected to learn. However, as both documents contend, a set of standards is not to be mistaken for a curriculum. Consider the following:

> *The Standards is a framework for curriculum development. However, it contains neither a scope-and-sequence chart nor a listing of topics by specific grade level. This is deliberate.... One possible next step is for teachers and mathematics educators to develop curricula based on the standards. (NCTM, 1989, p. 252)*

> *The content standards are not a science curricula.... The components of the science content described can be organized with a variety of emphases and perspectives into many different curricula. The organizational schemes of content standards are not intended to be used as curriculum; instead, the scope, sequence, and coordination of concepts, processes, and topics are left to those who design and implement curricula in science programs. (National Research Council, 1996, pp. 210–213)*

> ### United States History Studies Since Reconstruction
>
> Knowledge and skills.
>
> (1) History. The student understands traditional historical points of reference in U.S. history from 1877 to the present. The student is expected to:
>
> (A) identify the major eras in U.S. history from 1877 to the present and describe their defining characteristics;
>
> (B) apply absolute and relative chronology through the sequencing of significant individuals, events, and time periods; and
>
> (C) explain the significance of the following dates: 1898, 1914–1918, 1929, 1941–1945, and 1957.

FIGURE 1.5 Texas Essential Knowledge and Skills for Social Studies Subchapter C, High School. There are twenty-six more standards in Knowledge and Skills, each with between two and eight statements about what the student is expected to do.

Source: Texas Education Agency, *Texas Essential Knowledge and Skills* (TEKS), http://www.tea.state .tx.us/teks/

> *Content is what students should learn. Curriculum is the way content is organized and emphasized. (NRC, 1996, p. 111)*

As these statements imply, standards provide a guide and a checkpoint for curriculum. Standards tell us the extent to which our curricula cover the content worth covering.

State standards are varied in the way they are written and the way they are organized and presented. There has been no attempt at consensus among state education departments (Marzano & Kendall, 1996). Braden et al. (2000) rated the quality of state standards on a variety of criteria and this too has highlighted the variability of state standards. Eleven states received grades in the A range, eighteen B, sixteen C, four D, and one F. Figures 1.5 through 1.8 on pages 21–25 are examples of state standards (all states had a grade of B+ or better).

The four brief excerpts from state standards presented here illustrate both commonalities and differences among the standards. A common element that we find particularly important is that broad statements of meaning or understanding are translated or transformed into much more specific statements of outcome. In Texas, understanding historical points of reference include being able to state the important or defining event of that particular year.[1] In New York, along with the key idea comes performance indicators, sample test items, student tasks and per-

---

[1] A total of five dates between 1877 and the present. Why 1957 (Sputnik)? Why this date rather than the date that a man walked on the moon, or John F. Kennedy was assassinated, or a score of other contenders? Nor is it clear why or how knowing these dates is linked to understanding. Zenger & Zenger (2002) report that there is no basis in the research literature for the way we develop, place, and align educational standards.

formances. While most performance indicators ask students to do things like describe, investigate, or explain—all observable behavior—they sometimes use the term *understand*—not an observable behavior. Understanding is a problematic performance indicator. California, too, follows broad standards with more specific indicators. California expresses the standards themselves in performance terms (e.g., compare, contrast, relate, analyze). Most performance indicators are even more narrowly focused than the already observable standards. It is thus surprising to find the term *understanding* used as a performance indicator. Massachusetts standards include knowledge and skills. Skills tend to be expressed in performance terms calling for students to consider or recognize. Knowledge employs the word *understand*. Massachusetts, too, translates its learning standards into (what it calls) examples. The examples are all stated as things students will do. Rather than assessment, the "doing" here is more instructional. Presumably, engaging in these activities will result in learning what is called for by the standard. Thus students read, discuss, explain, and describe.

Combine the variation, arbitrariness, ambiguity, and inconsistencies found among every state's standards and it's little wonder teachers have a difficult time working with the standards. How are schools and teachers to make use of these standards? Encouragingly, the American Federation of Teachers (2001) finds the quality of state standards to be improving. The AFT calls for the creation of curriculum including learning continuum, instructional resources and strategies, and lesson plans. Kauffman et al. (2002) report on a study that followed a group of new teachers who have to make use of standards: "*These teachers received little or no guidance about what to teach or how to teach it. Left to their own devices, they struggled day to day to prepare content and materials*" (p. 273).

While it may be an attractive prospect for some, we do not think it is a good thing to supply teachers with detailed daily lesson plans. Such plans are apt to be even more specific, narrower, and focused than even the performance-level statements of the standards. The danger in this is that teachers lose sight of, or worse, never gain sight of the underlying intent of the learning standard. We believe that best practice when it comes to standards entails teachers engaging in a planning process in which they at least clarify and think about the bigger learning picture.

Teachers can choose from a variety of suggested approaches for working with standards. The National Research Council (1999) has a guide for program design in the areas of mathematics and science. The guide does not suggest specific planning steps, but rather, champions principles of clarity and coherence while pointing out some pitfalls to avoid (e.g, too much rote memorization, too much content covered superficially, and the use of mix-and-match instructional modules). This is a useful guide.

There are any number of more step-by-step approaches to planning with standards (see Glatthorn, 1999; Perna & Davis, 2000; Solomon, 1998). While each of these authors offers many valuable suggestions, all the approaches they describe suffer from a serious flaw. They all employ an approach to design that starts with the broadly stated standard, develops more specific and behavioral performance standards, and then uses the most narrowly stated outcome as the basis for designing instruction. Glatthorn (1999) expresses this quite clearly:

Once you have developed your long-term plans for term or year (these are based on standards), you have two choices about the next step. You can use the long-term schedule to begin the development of units—or you can develop the performance tasks. The recommendation here is to identify the performance tasks and then shape the unit so that students can do well when the assessment is made. (p. 67)

For most states, the performance standards are already written; teachers don't have to do that themselves. Teachers can go directly to developing units to teach the

Students will use a variety of intellectual skills to demonstrate their understanding of major ideas, themes, developments, and turning points in the history of the United States and New York.

1. The study of New York State and United States history requires an analysis of the development of American culture, its diversity and multicultural context, and the ways people are unified by many values, practices, and traditions.

Students:

- explore the meaning of American culture by identifying the key ideas, beliefs, and patterns of behavior, and traditions that help define it and unite all Americans.

- interpret the ideas, values, and beliefs contained in the Declaration of Independence and the New York State Constitution and United States Constitution, Bill of Rights, and other important historical documents

This is evident, for example, when students:

▲ explain the ideas embodied in the Declaration of Independence, the United States Constitution, the Bill of Rights, and the New York State Constitution and show how these documents express fundamental and enduring ideas and beliefs

▲ describe how massive immigration, forced migration, changing roles for women, and internal migration led to new social patterns and conflicts; and identify ideas of national unity that developed amidst growing cultural diversity. (Adapted from *National Standards for U.S. History*)

2. Important ideas, social and cultural values, beliefs, and traditions from New York State and United States history illustrate the connections and interactions of people and events across time and from a variety of perspectives.

Students:

- describe the reasons for periodizing history in different ways

- investigate key turning points in New York State and United States history and explain why these events or developments are significant

   understand the relationship between the relative importance of United States domestic and foreign policies over time

- analyze the role played by the United States in international politics, past and present.

FIGURE 1.6 New York Learning Standard 1, History of the United States and New York, Intermediate Level.

Source: New York State Education Department; Curriculum, Instruction & Instructional Technology; Learning Standards; http://www.emsc.nysed.gov/ciai/ls.html

performances. This approach can reasonably be considered teaching to the test. What happens is that teachers and students focus on one or maybe two specific and overt manifestations of understanding. The end result is that understanding vanishes as a sought-after and valued (let alone actual) outcome.

We wish we could offer suggestions that are both comprehensive and easily implemented. We can offer neither. Instead, we offer several principles that underlie the manner in which teachers should use *Course Design* when working with standards (or, for that matter, textbooks or other curriculum specifications). First, teachers must engage in some sort of (planning) process that helps them conceive of what learners should learn. This must be a more substantial process than reading standards written by others and then going directly to instructional planning.

This is evident, for example, when students:

▲ use demographic information, mapping exercises, photographs, interviews, population graphs, church records, newspaper accounts, and other sources to conduct case studies of particular groups in the history of the State or nation and classify information according to type of activity: social, political, economic, cultural, or religious

▲ use a variety of sources to study historic and contemporary events in the United States; investigate different interpretations of the events and identify circumstances of time and place that influence the authors' perspectives (Adapted from *National Standards for U.S. History*)

▲ recognize the reasons for periodizing history and know some designations of historical periods; discuss the usefulness of the following periods:

Three Worlds and Their Meeting in the Americas (Beginnings to 1607)
Colonization, Settlement and Communities (1607 to 1763)
The Revolution and the New Nation (1763 to 1815)
Expansion and Reform (1801 to 1861)
Crisis of the Union: Civil War and Reconstruction (1850 to 1877)
The Development of Modern America (1865 to 1920)
Modern America and the World Wars (1914 to 1945)
Contemporary America (1945 to Present)
(Taken from *U.S. History Framework for the 1994 National Assessment of Educational Progress*)

▲ undertake case studies to research violations of basic civil and human rights and case studies of genocide. Use examples from United States, New York State, and world history. Case studies might include chattel slavery and the Nazi Holocaust. Other civil and human rights violations might focus on the mass starvation in Ireland (1845–1850), the forced relocation of Native American Indians, and the internment of Japanese Americans during World War II.

▲ trace the tension between arguments for United States isolation versus engagement during the following time periods: up to 1941, from 1941–1975, and from 1976 to the present.

STANDARD 1
Key ideas are identified by numbers (1).
Performance indicators are identified by bullets (■).
Sample tasks are identified by triangles (▲).

FIGURE 1.6 (continued)

10.2 Students compare and contrast the Glorious Revolution of England, the American Revolution, and the French Revolution and their enduring effects worldwide on the political expectations for self-government and individual liberty.

1. Compare the major ideas of philosophers and their effects on the democratic revolutions in England, the United States, France, and Latin America (e.g., John Locke, Charles-Louis Montesquieu, Jean-Jacques Rousseau, Simón Bolívar, Thomas Jefferson, James Madison).

2. List the principles of the Magna Carta, the English Bill of Rights (1689), the American Declaration of Independence (1776), the French Declaration of the Rights of Man and the Citizen (1789), and the U.S. Bill of Rights (1791).

3. Understand the unique character of the American Revolution, its spread to other parts of the world, and its continuing significance to other nations.

4. Explain how the ideology of the French Revolution led France to develop from constitutional monarchy to democratic despotism to the Napoleonic empire.

5. Discuss how nationalism spread across Europe with Napoleon but was repressed for a generation under the Congress of Vienna and Concert of Europe until the Revolutions of 1848.

FIGURE 1.7   California History–Social Science Content Standards, Grade Ten; World History, Culture, and Geography: The Modern World. There are eleven more standards with between three and seven more specific statements.

Source: California State Board of Education; Content Standards; http://www.cde.ca.gov/be/st/ss/index.asp

Second, when knowledge is the learning goal, the teacher's conception should highlight understanding. And, finally, instructional planning should be guided by this broad conception of learning rather than by narrow, performance-level statements. In subsequent chapters, we say much more about understanding and how to think more clearly about teaching for understanding. For now, the following anecdote about an all-too-familiar scenario might help clarify what we mean:

> *The daughter of one of the authors asked her father to test her on the material she had been studying. The material was from a tenth-grade biology course and had to do with cells. Her several pages of notes consisted of terms (e.g., cell nucleus, vacuole, mitosis, meiosis) followed by one- or two-sentence definitions. After looking over the notes, Dad asked, "So tell me, what's the story here?" After a moment's silence, Daughter replied, "Dad, I hate it when you ask me about the story. All I have to do is memorize the definitions."*

We're sure the biology teacher, if asked, would say that her intention was to have students understand the structure, function, and reproduction of cells. However, being able to explain the meanings of these terms and identify all the cell components in a diagram is not the same as understanding.

Strand One   History

Learning Standard 2: Historial Understanding. Students will understand the meaning, implications, and importance of historical events, while recognizing the contingency and unpredictability of history—how events could have taken other directions—by studying past ideas as they were thought, and past events as they were lived, by people of the time.

Learning Standard Components (Core Knowledge and Skills)	Examples
Grades 5–8 Students understand how people in the past could believe themselves justified in excluding others from their community or privileges.	Students explain the reasons why the citizens of Athens, under the circumstances of their time, could convict Socrates of impiety and corrupting the young and put him to death. They contrast freedom of religion in the United States with governmentally sanctioned religion in ancient Athens and contemporary theocracies such as Iran; and they discuss current Massachusetts laws and regulations against educational malpractice.

They explain why, in the 18th century, despite the fact that by 1789 the United States was the most democratic large nation in the world, most political leaders believed it was reasonable to exclude women, Native Americans, slaves, and men without property from voting and public office. They discuss the power of the Declaration of Independence to show the injustice of slavery, oppression, and discrimination; and they discuss reasonable contemporary qualifications for voting, including age, citizenship, and absence of felony convictions. |
| Students recognize the contingency of history and how it must be taken into account when passing judgment on people and actions of the past. | They explain references to historical contingency in Lincoln's Second Inaugural Address, and how his words demonstrate both empathy and strict moral judgment.

They explain both the intended and the unintended consequences of Radical Republican activism in the defeated South, early in Reconstruction years. |

FIGURE 1.8   Massachusetts History and Social Studies Curriculum Framework.

Source: Massachusetts Department of Education; History and Social Science Curriculum Framework; http://www.doe.mass.edu

We believe that working through the course planning steps in Chapters 2 through 4 before planning instruction will help teachers make good use of standards and increase the likelihood of students learning with understanding. Whether working from standards or existing curriculum material, teachers teach better because they have thought about, worked with, and assimilated the broad intentions for teaching and learning. Planning instruction aimed at understanding and other high-level outcomes and teaching in ways that make connections among ideas within and outside content areas simply cannot happen when instruction is based on the indicators of learning rather than on the learning itself.

GENERATING INITIAL IDEAS

It is important at the beginning of course planning to have something tangible with which to work. The first step is to create a list of "initial ideas." This list may take virtually any form and may consist of words and phrases or sentences identifying subject matter, content areas, specific facts, teaching techniques, and so on. It may contain the names of specific books; it may list other resources. Anything important to the course should go on an "ideas" list. At this point it is not important that the list be consistent or balanced.

Creating a list of initial ideas is also well suited to beginning interdisciplinary curriculum planning. Initial ideas, in most cases, cut across several disciplines, and this is even more likely if you are starting the planning process with an interdisciplinary unit already in mind. After you generate initial ideas, we recommend that you think about problems, themes, or issues that seem central to the kind of unit you are considering. Doing some thinking about integrating themes should help you identify a context for, or means to tie together, many of your initial ideas; after all, for a curriculum to be interdisciplinary, there must be substantive relations among the disciplines, not simply a collection of ideas that falls into different disciplinary categories. In addition, a theme may suggest connections to other disciplines you have not yet considered and which ought to be further explored during this first phase of planning (Fredericks, Meinback, & Rothlein, 1993; Jacobs, 1989; Martinello & Cook, 1994; Perkins, 1989; Thompson, 1991).

Another planning activity that should assist interdisciplinary planning is generating questions that you think could be explored or answered in your unit. These questions need not be focused and are quite different from central questions (which you will be creating later). These are questions that you think are appropriate for and would be interesting to your students. In turn, this may lead to activities where students generate their own questions. You may want to incorporate this activity into your instructional plan. Having developed a list of questions yourself, you may anticipate many student questions and more readily be able to incorporate and follow students' interests as you teach the unit. In any event, thinking of questions in the manner proposed here can be very revealing of interdisciplinary connections.

Considering themes and questions is likely to be a useful activity for all planners. We do not wish to suggest that only planners of interdisciplinary courses or units should generate a theme and questions. We think these activities are important for interdisciplinary planning, but they are likely to be useful to all planners.

Course Planning Step 1.2   Jot down any and all ideas you have for your course on a list of initial ideas. The following example illustrates the form these initial ideas may take for an environmental science course. Absolutely no restrictions are placed on this list.

the relationships among various environmental systems
respect and care for the environment
forest succession
ecosystems
food chains
producers, consumers, decomposers
field trips to forest, field, pond
Sapsucker Woods Bird Sanctuary
individual project
plant and animal identification
how one affects environment
pollution
niches
become better individuals
blindfolded walk
build terrarium
nature trail

The following example uses a unit on the Industrial Revolution to illustrate some aspects of interdisciplinary planning. The first list represents initial ideas and is followed by some possible themes and then questions.

THE INDUSTRIAL REVOLUTION IN AMERICA

change from agrarian to industrial society
the rise of the great mills and mill towns
factory labor and life
the assembly line
source of power (water, coal)
child labor
industrial centers in the Northeast
Industrial Revolution in England
changes in transportation
the shoe industry
the textile industry

literature of the period
inventions and inventors
steam engine of James Watt
machines
simple machines
concepts in physics (work, energy, force)
dams
visit national historic site in Lowell
use simple machines construction kit
visit the Pro Brush company
look at dams that remain on local rivers

Some possible integrating themes for an Industrial Revolution unit include:

Harnessing Nature for Power   This theme might focus on how the availability of water and coal influenced the way work could be accomplished, leading to the invention of important machines; how these revolutionized manufacturing, the lives of workers, and the lives of consumers.

Several Generations of an American Family   Look at the arrival of immigrants who saved enough to purchase a small farm in New England. Succeeding generations both work on the farm and take on other employment such as clerking and furniture making. The opening of the West and the advent of larger industry affects the viability of farms and craft industry. Follow changes in family and community as more and more people depend on industry for their livelihoods. Perhaps have some move to large city.

The Textile Industry   Examine the preindustrial textile industry: how cloth is made and what kinds of cloth are available, to whom, and at what expense. Look at the supply of raw material. Consider the impact of the textile industry on slavery in the American South. Trace the growth of large textile manufacturers, their influence on garment manufacture, and other side effects. Look at machines, life in the factories, etc.

QUESTIONS FOR AN INDUSTRIAL REVOLUTION UNIT

What was it like to work in a factory?
How much did workers get paid?
Who were the workers?
What kinds of things did factories make?
What besides manufacturing did the Industrial Revolution change?
How were goods supplied before the revolution?
What started the revolution?
Did the revolution end? Why?
Who benefited most from the revolution?
Did anyone suffer from the revolution?
How did the Industrial Revolution affect the environment?

REFERENCES

American Federation of Teachers. (2001). Making standards matter. *American Educator, 25*(4), 30–33, 47–48.

Braden, L., Finn, C., Lerner, L., Munroe, S., Petrilli, M., Raimi, R., Saxe, D., Smith, T., & Strotsky, S. (2000). *The state of state standards 2000.* Washington, DC: Thomas B. Fordham Foundation.

Clark, C., & Peterson, P. (1986). Teacher thought processes. In M. Wittrock (Ed.), *Handbook of research on teaching* (3rd ed.). New York: Macmillan.

Curriculum and Evaluation Standards for School Mathematics, National Council of Teachers of Mathematics, Reston, VA: 1989.

Dewey, J. (1938). *Experience and education.* New York: Macmillan.

Fredericks, A. D., Meinback, A. M., & Rothlein, L. (1993). *Thematic units.* New York: Harper Collins.

Glatthorn, A. A. (1987). *Curriculum leadership.* Glenview, IL: Scott, Foresman.

Glatthorn, A. (1999). *Performance standards & authentic learning.* Larchmont, NY: Eye on Education.

Hall, T. (2003). Differentiated instruction. National Center on Accessing the General Curriculum. Retrieved from http://www.cast.org/ncac/index.cfm?i=2876

Hall, T., Strangman, N., & Meyer, A. (2003). Differentiated instruction and implications for UDL implementation. National Center on Accessing the General Curriculum. Retrieved from http://www.cast.org/ncac/index.cfm?i=4800

Hiebert, J., Gallimore, R., & Stigler, J. (2002). A knowledge base for the teaching profession: What would it look like and how can we get one? *Educational Researcher, 31*(5), 3–15.

Jacobs, H. H. (1989). The growing need for interdisciplinary curriculum content. In Jacobs, H. H. (Ed.), *Interdisciplinary curriculum: Design and implementation.* Alexandria, VA: Association for Supervision and Curriculum Development.

Jacobs, H. H. (1997). *Mapping the big picture: Integrating curriculum and assessment K–12.* Alexandria, VA: Association for Supervision and Curriculum Development.

Jacobs, H. H. (1998). The teacher as designer: Integrating the curriculum. *The International Schools Journal, 18*(1), 22–33.

Johnson, M. (1967). Definitions and models in curriculum theory. *Educational Theory, 17*(2), 127–139.

Kauffman, D., Johnson, S. M., Kardos, S. M., Liu, E., & Peske, H. G. (2002). "Lost at sea": New teachers' experiences with curriculum and assessment. *Teachers College Record, 104*(2), 273–300.

Kindsvatter, R., Wilen, W., & Ishler, M. (1988). *Dynamics of effective teaching.* New York: Longman.

Lewis, C., Perry, R., & Hurd, J. (2004, February). A deeper look at lesson study. *Educational Leadership,* 18–22.

McCutcheon, G. (1995). *Developing the curriculum: Solo and group deliberation.* New York: Longman.

Martinello, M. L., & Cook, G. E. (1994). *Interdisciplinary inquiry in teaching and learning.* New York: Merrill.

Marzano, R., & Kendall, J. (1996). *A comprehensive guide to designing standards-based districts, schools, and classrooms.* Alexandria, VA: ASCD.

National Research Council. (1996). *National science education standards.* Washington, DC: National Academy Press.

National Research Council. (1999). *Designing mathematics and science programs: A guide for using mathematics and science education standards.* National Academy of Sciences. Washington, DC: National Academy Press.

National standards for history: Basic edition. (1996). Los Angeles: National Center for History in the Schools.

Perkins, D. N. (1989). Selecting fertile themes for integrated learning. In Jacobs, H. H. (Ed.), *Interdisciplinary curriculum: Design and implementation.* Alexandria, VA: Association for Supervision and Curriculum Development.

Perna, D., & Davis, J. (2000). *Aligning standards & curriculum for classroom success.* Glenview, IL: Pearson Skylight.

Schwab, J. J. (1970). *The practical: A language for curriculum.* Washington, DC: National Education Association.

Solomon, P. (1998). *The curriculum bridge: From standards to actual classroom practice.* Thousand Oaks, CA: Corwin Press.

Thompson, G. (1991). *Teaching through themes.* New York: Scholastic Professional Books.

Tomlison, T. A. (2001). *How to differentiate instruction in mixed ability classrooms.* (2nd ed.). Alexandria, VA: Association for Supervision and Curriculum Development.

Walker, D. F. (1971). A naturalistic model of curriculum development. *School Review, 80,* 51–65.

Walker, D. F. (2003). *Fundamentals of curriculum: Passion and professionalism.* Mahwah, NJ: Lawrence Erlbaum Associates.

Watanabe, T. (2002, March). Learning from Japanese lesson study. *Educational Leadership,* 36–39.

Wigginton, E. (1985). *Sometimes a shining moment: The Foxfire experience.* Garden City, NY: Doubleday.

Zenger, W. F., & Zenger, S. K. (2002). Why teach certain material at specific grade levels? *Phi Delta Kappan, 84*(3), 212.

final ideas.

CHAPTER TWO

SETTING A DIRECTION

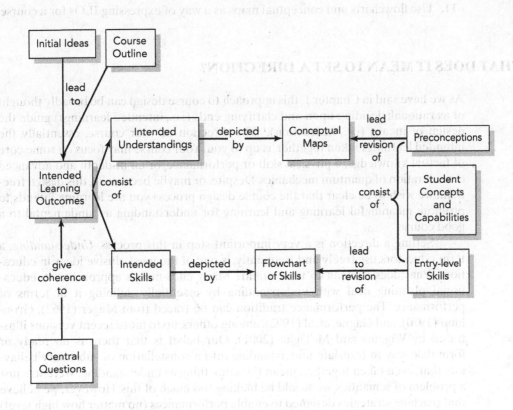

After completing this chapter, you should be able to:

1. **Use graphic organizers to help develop a course.**

2. **Develop a tentative course outline.**

3. **Comprehend the meaning and significance of the intended learning outcome (ILO).**

4. Generate one or more central questions for a course.

5. Distinguish ILOs from teaching strategies, materials, activities, and other initial ideas.

6. Identify ILOs implicit in desirable teaching strategies, materials, activities, and test items.

7. Categorize ILOs into skill and understanding categories.

8. Construct a flowchart for a course or a unit.

9. Construct a conceptual map for a course or a unit.

10. Construct a story for a course or a unit.

11. Use flowcharts and conceptual maps as a way of expressing ILOs for a course.

WHAT DOES IT MEAN TO SET A DIRECTION?

As we have said in Chapter 1, this approach to course design can be broadly thought of as rational; deciding upon and clarifying ends (i.e., intended learnings) guide the design of means (i.e., instruction).[1] The direction of your course, essentially the intended learnings taken together, is up to you. Your course may focus on some core of factual knowledge, a physical skill or performance, or an in-depth and advanced consideration of quantum mechanics. Despite, or maybe because of, this design freedom, we wish to be clear that the course design process you are learning intends to promote meaningful learning and learning for understanding as fundamental to a good course.

Setting a direction is a very important step in this process. *Understanding*, a term educators use freely and frequently, is one of the most elusive ideas in education. What does it mean to understand? Many ends-means approaches to educational planning deal with understanding by essentially defining it in terms of performance. The performance tradition can be traced from Mager (1962), Gronlund (1970), and Gagne, et. al (1992), among others, up to more recent versions illustrated by Wiggins and McTighe (2001). Our belief is that there is no ready or formulaic way to translate understanding into a constellation of subsidiary behaviors that, even taken together, mean the same thing as understanding. Were this just a problem of semantics, we would be making too much of this. However, we believe that teaching strategies designed to enable performances (no matter how high level) too often miss the mark of teaching for understanding. Learners may DO well but not understand. *Course Design* opts for a different, albeit more difficult, approach.

---

[1]This approach to design has also been referred to as backward design (Wiggins & McTighe, 2001). Backward denotes that ends guide means. Among the differences between the design process described in *Course Design* and that described by Wiggins and McTighe (2001) in *Understanding by Design* is the fact that we do not see ends preceding means as backward. We think you will also find other differences.

Understanding needs to be a legitimate intention in and of itself, one that serves the function of directly guiding instruction (with no mediating performance specifications). To accomplish this, understanding still needs to be unpacked and clarified. Doing this means thinking deeply and in a variety of ways about the ideas themselves. It means thinking about the complex set of meanings and relationships inherent in the understandings in which you want your learners to participate. Grappling with what you want learned, first in this chapter as you set a direction and in subsequent chapters when you think about why you want students to learn it and further clarify your intentions, leads to the kind of vision and thoughtfulness teachers must have to plan and teach effectively.

The first step in setting a direction for the course is to elaborate on your list of initial ideas. Graphic organizers can be helpful in accomplishing this step.

GRAPHIC ORGANIZERS

Graphic organizers come in many forms (see Jones, Pierce, & Hunter, 1988/89). When used in interdisciplinary planning, a graphic organizer can help to develop ideas in different disciplinary areas and to explore relationships among these areas. But all kinds of planning could benefit from the use of graphic organizers. Planners should consider graphic organizers as tools to help them elaborate on their initial ideas, thus adding to the shape and substance of their course or unit. Subsequent steps in the course design process will call for the use of conceptual maps and flowcharts. Both are graphic organizers. The following section describes and illustrates several graphic organizers.

Webs

A *web* is a graphic organizer that facilitates considering relationships among ideas and topics. A good starting place for a web is the list of initial ideas. By using a web, you can explore relationships among ideas and add new ideas. While some planners use a web to generate initial ideas, we do not recommend doing so. Having to consider relationships is likely to interfere with the production of ideas. Once a list of initial ideas has been generated, webbing can be very helpful. A web is rather free-form in that the items of a web and the lines connecting items can be placed anywhere. It is easy to see how an open format like this can generate a graphic organizer that is too complex to be useful. One approach that can help you avoid this is to create an initial web, making it as complex as you wish, then refine it by eliminating items that are not particularly important. You can also create several webs that explore different items or different kinds of relationships. Figure 2.1 on page 34 shows a web based on the initial ideas for the Industrial Revolution unit.

Sometimes it is useful to impose some measure of organization on the web. Conceptual maps, described later, are instances of more highly structured webs. The web described and illustrated in Figure 2.2 on page 35 is sometimes referred to as a

FIGURE 2.1   A web.

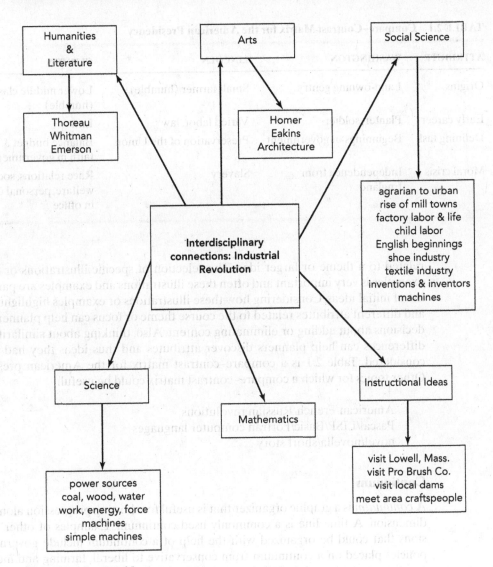

FIGURE 2.2   A spider map.

spider map. It is an example of a more structured web; in this instance, used to show how interdisciplinary areas relate to each other, which disciplines are represented, and which are not. A spider map begins with established connections to a central idea or theme and then builds on this spiderlike organization.

Compare–Contrast Matrix

A *compare–contrast matrix* is another graphic organizer that can assist planners in further elaborating initial ideas. Many courses are aimed at teaching students ideas

TABLE 2.1   Compare–Contrast Matrix for the American Presidency

ATTRIBUTE	WASHINGTON	LINCOLN	CLINTON
Origins	Land-owning gentry	Small farmer (humble)	Lower middle class (humble)
Early career	Planter, soldier	Varied labor, law	Law
Defining task	Beginnings of government	Preservation of the Union	Balance budget & restore faith in government
Moral crisis	Independence from England	Slavery	Race relations, social welfare, personal conduct in office

related to a theme or larger idea. The selection of specific illustrations or content examples is very important and often these illustrations and examples are part of the list of initial ideas. Considering how these illustrations or examples highlight similar and different attributes related to the course theme or focus can help planners make decisions about adding or eliminating content. Also, thinking about similarities and differences can help planners discover attributes and thus ideas they had not yet considered. Table 2.1 is a compare–contrast matrix for the American presidency. Other topics for which a compare–contrast matrix could be useful:

> American/French/Russian revolutions
> Pascal/LISP/Basic/Fortran computer languages
> novel/novella/short story

Continuum

A *continuum* is a graphic organizer that is useful for showing progression along some dimension. A time line is a commonly used continuum. Examples of other dimensions that could be organized with the help of a continuum include governmental policies placed on a continuum from conservative to liberal, farming and industrial practice on a continuum of environmental impact, reasons for moving a professional sports team from one city to another on a continuum of economic benefit.

Problem–Solution Outlines

Many courses or units have themes, ideas, or aspects that can be conceptualized in terms of problems needing solutions. Often instruction can be organized around interesting problems to be attempted or solved. Thinking about problems related to your course or unit at this early stage is very helpful in further elaborating initial ideas. You can state the problem and then list various solutions with pros and cons. Tables 2.2 and 2.3 are examples of problem–solution outlines.

TABLE 2.2 Problem: Achieving Peace in the Middle East

SOLUTION	PROS	CONS
Negotiation	Nonviolent	Time-consuming, all must compromise, no guarantee of success
Military force	Victor achieves objectives	Costly in terms of life, continued human cost, one side loses
Imposed from outside	Probably fair, minimal human cost to enforce	No real stake in keeping peace, may decide to pull out, may not be impartial

Other problems for which this graphic organizer can be helpful include the following: An extremely congested intersection, which could be solved by retiming lights, redesigning the intersection, or building pedestrian walkways. Bottlenecks in transmitting electronic data, which could be solved by improving all physical data pathways (i.e., using fiber-optic cable), building better devices that send and receive information, or compressing the information.

Cycle

A *cycle* is a graphic organizer that illustrates a process or series of events that act or interact in a repeated manner, typically to produce some result or effect. Sometimes the list of initial ideas may include or refer to such a process or series of events. Planners ought to consider their initial ideas to see if a cyclic process or series of events is listed or implied. Using a cycle organizer can help planners flesh out aspects of the process that they may want to include in their course or unit. Figure 2.3 on page 38 illustrates a cycle.

TABLE 2.3 Problem: Balancing the Federal Budget

SOLUTION	PROS	CONS
Grow the economy	No one sacrifices	Based on assumptions
Raise taxes	Generates revenue to maintain existing programs	Stifles economy, may impose hardship on poor
Cut spending	Need not raise taxes	Poor, education, and environment are among nonentitlements and suffer most
Combination of taxes and program cuts	Shared sacrifice	Same programs will suffer, people will not like higher taxes

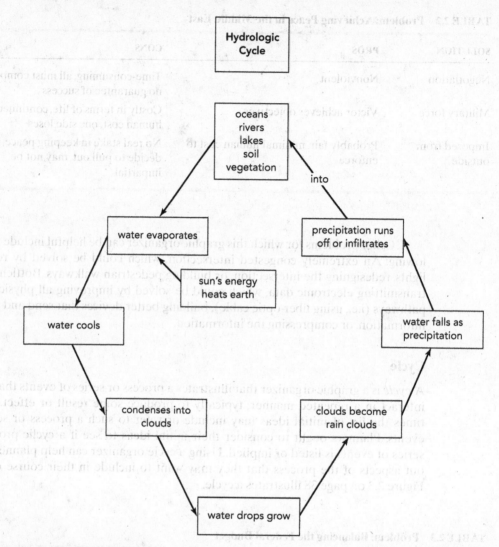

FIGURE 2.3   A cycle.

Causal Interaction Maps

A *causal interaction map* is a graphic organizer that can help planners consider and further develop cause–effect relationships in their course or unit. As is true of the other graphic organizers, using a causal interaction map helps planners take a fresh look at their initial ideas, in this instance in terms of causal relationships (see Figure 2.4). Such relationships can be discovered and/or further developed.

Course Planning Step 2.1   Look at your list of initial ideas, including any themes or questions you may have developed. Think about the various graphic organizers and

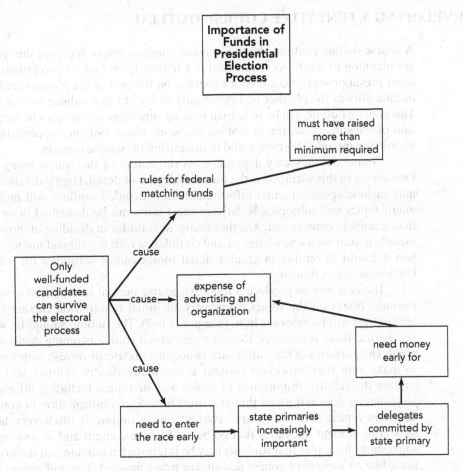

FIGURE 2.4   A causal interaction map.

the kinds of relationships and ideas they highlight. Consider the use of appropriate graphic organizers to help you elaborate on your initial ideas.

Course Planning Step 2.2   Once you have made an initial list of ideas and elaborated those ideas, you should give your course a title. A title may be creative and novel or it may be traditional. A good way to formulate a title is to consider your list of initial ideas and see if an appropriate title emerges. Planners sometimes have a title for a course in their minds at the outset of planning. If this is true in your case and if this title does not conflict with your initial ideas, use it. Another factor in titling your as-yet-incompletely specified idea is considering whether or not these ideas are coherent. This is really the primary purpose of supplying a title at this point. It is the first of many considerations of the relationship of the parts to the whole, a consideration that gives an initial focus for the course.

DEVELOPING A TENTATIVE COURSE OUTLINE

A course outline contains the major ideas, components, or topics of the subject you are planning to teach. As mentioned in Chapter 1, the task of curriculum development presupposes subject-matter expertise on the part of the planner, and a course outline affords the planner an opportunity to lay out that subject matter concisely. This concise outline will be of help in making sure there are no gaps in the presentation of the subject matter, in making decisions about audience appropriateness, in identifying intended learnings, and in organizing the course content.

Course outlines vary depending on the nature of the course being planned. One aspect of this variation is the outline's degree of detail. Highly detailed outlines may include specific factual information. Less detailed outlines will include only major topics and subtopics. Relatively short units can be described in more detail than complete courses can. Another factor to consider in deciding on how much to include is your own knowledge of and confidence with the subject matter. You may find it useful to outline in greater detail topics and/or subtopics for which your knowledge is less thorough.

The best way to produce a tentative course outline is to consult several good resource books on the topics. Some of your initial research on current curricular approaches will be relevant here (see pages 6–7). The outline should be written as you peruse these references. Do not worry about course planning decisions at this point. The purposes of the outline are to acquire, update, or refresh your knowledge; to make sure that important content is not inadvertently omitted; and to make explicit the relative importance of topics and subtopics. Including information in your outline does not mean that you must include the information in your course. Teachers report that the "extra" content on an outline is often very helpful in answering student questions that go beyond lesson content and in coming up with suggestions for topics that students may be interested in pursuing on their own. Outlines, like all aspects of course design, are never finished. You will always find new resources and acquire new information. Outlines should be regularly updated and fleshed out. After you have taught a unit several times, the outline should be quite detailed. The unit outline on the Inuit, included as an example, is an initial outline, prepared before the unit was taught for the first time.

CONTENT OUTLINE—THE INUIT OF NORTH ALASKA

I. Geography
   A. History of glacial ice cap (In Pleistocene times the massive accumulation of water in the glacier ice caused a lowering of the sea level, permitting a few hardy animals to cross the Bering Strait from Asia to America.)
   B. Van Allen belts
      1. Radiation
      2. Aurora borealis

    C. Arctic land mass
       1. Location on a globe
       2. Physical characteristics
          a. Permafrost
          b. Perennially frozen topsoil
          c. Vegetation
       3. Climate
          a. Seasons
          b. Arctic days and nights
          c. Weather
          d. Temperatures
       4. Inhabitants
          a. Mammals
          b. Birds
          c. Insects
    D. Arctic Ocean
       1. Physical characteristics
       2. Inhabitants
          a. Mammals
          b. Fish
II. Ecosystem
    A. The food chain
       1. Producers
       2. Consumers
       3. Decomposers
       4. Niche
    B. Habitats
    C. Adaptations
       1. Plants—Arctic plants must retain enough heat to enable photosynthesis to take place (43°). They do it in the following ways:
          a. Small leathery leaves
          b. Clumping
          c. Hairy leaves and stems
          d. Large root systems to reserve supply of carbohydrates
       2. Animals
          a. Some animals such as the musk ox have adapted long fur.
          b. Some animals have adapted shorter appendages with less surface to radiate away body heat.
          c. Some animals have adapted a thick undercoat.
          d. Some animals have adapted hair that is thicker at the top and traps body heat.
          e. Some animals change the color of their fur. Cells that formerly contained pigment contain air that holds body heat.

III. Humans
    A. Food
        1. Food gathering
            a. Berries
            b. Pemmican
        2. Hunting
            a. Aboriginal technology
                (1). Transportation
                    (a). Umiaks and kayaks
                    (b). Sleds
                        (i). Dogs
                        (ii). Harnesses
                (2). Weapons
                (3). Trading
            b. Western technology
    B. Clothing
        1. Function
            a. Summer dress
            b. Winter dress
        2. Labor intensive vs. cost intensive
    C. Shelter
        1. Sod
        2. Skin
        3. Wood
        4. Snow
        5. Stone
    D. Culture
        1. Language
            a. Storytelling
            b. Poetry
            c. Literature—myths and legends
        2. Art
            a. Masks
            b. Carving
            c. Printmaking
            d. Stitchery
        3. Religion
            a. Magic
            b. Shamans
            c. Amulets
        4. Games

     The exact sequence of the topics in the outline is not particularly important at this stage. Decisions about whether particular content is appropriate for the intended audience need not be made now, unless these decisions are obvious. Of far greater importance is the outline's inclusiveness and that the format adequately represents the relative importance of the subtopics under each topic.

Courses that do not focus on traditional subject matter will require outlines suited to their content. The teaching of reading, writing, typing, or instrumental music, to name a few, are typically performance-oriented courses. A course outline for subjects like these should break down the overall performance into subtopics that can be separately addressed. A reading unit, for example, could be divided into the following subtopics: decoding using phonic cues, decoding using the context, decoding by structural analysis, reading for literal meaning, making inferences for news articles, and so on. Regardless of course type, an outline of the course is the planner's first chance to think systematically about the substantive elements of the subject.

Course Planning Step 2.3   Develop a tentative course outline.

INTENDED LEARNING OUTCOMES (ILOs)

The primary product of this planning phase is a set of *intended learning outcomes,* or learning objectives. An intended learning outcome is a statement of what the student is to learn. It may be a statement about facts, ideas, principles, capabilities, skills, techniques, values, or feelings. A set of ILO statements may be altered, reconsidered, and refined, but it is a foundation for almost every step in course planning.

Since the notion of ILO is crucial to all that follows, let us examine it in more detail. The use of the word *intended* emphasizes control and direction in the educational process. A course may result in many outcomes, and some of them may be quite accidental, whether good or bad. Course planning does not proceed with the hope of accidental learning but with lucid, stateable intentions. The word *learning* is again used advisedly, for it emphasizes that the major purpose of planning a course is to effect student learning. Courses are for students, not for teachers or for testers. A student may learn more or less than a teacher has actually taught. Much of the content taught (for example, the use of examples) may be only instrumental for the learning of particular concepts, principles, attitudes, and skills. Similarly, for one reason or another a student may or may not meet the requirements of a certain test and still may have learned what was intended. Finally, the word *outcome* indicates that our major concern is what the student will gain by completing the course.

The next step in developing a focus is selecting intended learning outcomes from the initial list of ideas and the course outline; you will add other ILOs later. The process of selecting important material to be learned is, in part, a process of "drawing a ring" around the course's learning objectives. This consists of deciding what the course will and will not be about. After you have reached this decision, the material can be further specified so that all the learnings important to the course are included.

Deciding on ILOs

The first step in the process of selecting intended learnings is to decide which items on the list of initial ideas and in the course outline represent intended learning outcomes. These ILOs may be facts, ideas, theories, or other types of information that the student is expected to learn as a result of the course. Ecosystems, food chains, the causes of World War II, and the characteristics of a good diet are examples of content to be learned. ILOs may also be skills, competencies, or values. Touch typing, math computation, clear speaking, and proper grammar are examples of skills to be learned. Intended learnings may also include values, such as respect for the environment, for honest advertising, and for the rights of others. Specific teaching strategies are not intended learning outcomes. Special materials, such as particular books, filmstrips, videotapes, or programmed instruction units, are not intended learning outcomes. We must also leave out field trips, group projects, and oral reports. Nevertheless, all these things must be examined carefully to ascertain what specific intended learnings they suggest. For example, if a field trip is on the list of initial ideas or in the course outline, consider why a field trip is important. What will you expect students to learn from the trip (for example, an ability to apply ecological concepts in a natural setting)?

An ILO comes into being because you think an item in your list of initial ideas or course outline is something to be learned. Use your judgment and imagination. Do not omit potentially important ILOs because an item "doesn't look like an ILO." Some ILOs are obvious and explicit; others, however, are implicit and require thinking if they are to be identified. It is better to have too many rather than too few ILOs. Later course planning steps will help you refine your ILOs.

EXERCISE 2.1*

The lists below represent possible lists of initial ideas. Identify obvious and explicit ILOs in the lists with a check mark.

1. *Creative Cooking*
    types of kitchen tools
    the student knows what a frying pan is for
    Rombauer and Becker's *Joy of Cooking*
    ability to test cake to see if done
    trip to local restaurant
    how to bake bread
    cooking not a specifically female task
    desserts
    knowledge of menu planning
    manual cooking skills: kneading, sautéing, flipping crepes, stir-frying
    how to plan before you cook
    meats

*Answers to exercises appear at the end of each chapter.

vegetable protein

each student prepares own dish—bring-a-dish meal

safe use of knives

2. *English Grammar and Composition*

complex and compound sentences

parts of speech (verb, noun, article, adjective, adverb, etc.)

correct punctuation

recognizes sentence fragments

choice of words

learns from reading

appreciates own good writing

uses commas with nonrestrictive relative clauses

avoids run-on sentences

doesn't use dialectical forms in formal writing

use of exercises as teaching device

assign compositions every week

short stories

spelling tests weekly

3. *Social Studies*

small-group discussions

knowledge of what constitutes an institution

institutions are self-perpetuating

enlightened self-interest in relationship to society

essay on democratic vs. autocratic institutions

cooperatives

media as used by social forces

recognizes institutional interests

extensive use of library sources

films

types of institutions: social, religious, commercial

how institutions change

4. *American History—The Post-Revolutionary Period*

knows significance of the dates: 1776, 1803, 1812

Jefferson, Adams, Madison

debates

understands the causes of the War of 1812

can describe the attack against Tripoli

can describe why Hamilton accepted a duel with Burr

film: *The Burr Conspiracy*

the U.S. Constitution

economic trends

America takes her place among the nations of the world

the situation with Britain and France at the time

projects

the Embargo Act of 1807

description of the burning of Washington

knows the origin of the national anthem

EXERCISE 2.2

In Exercise 2.1 you selected the ILOs already apparent in the lists. For this exercise, go back to the lists and develop possible ILOs that are implicit or suggested rather than explicit.

Course Planning Step 2.4   All ILOs, either explicit or implicit, in your list of initial ideas and your course outline should now be written on a separate list, "the list of ILOs." (See the appendixes for additional examples.)

Categorizing ILOs

Categorization is useful because different types of learning require different types of instruction, different considerations when sequencing and organizing the course, and different types of evaluation. At this point in the planning process, ILOs are grouped into two categories: skills and understandings. Generally speaking, understandings comprise the information and beliefs with which we think. Understandings can be thought of as "knowing that" (including "knowing" in a deep sense, not just memorizing). Ideas, concepts, facts, principles, theories, and generalizations are some of the things that can be known. Skills can be thought of as "knowing how." Skills are things students are able to do at the end of a course. Skills include mental abilities, such as problem solving, reading, arithmetic computation, interpretation, analysis, application; and physical abilities, such as bicycling and ball throwing.

For most courses, some balance between skills and understandings is desirable. A course stressing only skills is more characteristic of training than of education. Such a course aims at having students learn how to do things but not at learning the principles behind what they are doing. For example, a good physical education course teaches the rules of the game and the basis for good sportsmanship. On the other hand, a course stressing only understandings may equip students with a set of ideas but may leave them without any competencies. A course of this type may not provide students with the ability to use what they have learned. A good English literature course, for example, teaches the skills of literary criticism.

Course Planning Step 2.5   Categorize your ILOs into skills and understandings. This is the first time in the planning process that items are categorized under specific headings (skills/understandings), but you will be called on to perform this type of operation again. This is a part of the process of giving your course direction and assists you in planning and determining things such as completeness and balance. This categorization is not just an exercise, but an instrumental step in the planning process.

FORMULATING CENTRAL QUESTIONS*

Initial ideas, a course outline, and a list of tentative ILOs describe the scope of your course. Central questions, questions that are fundamental to the course and that identify the focus of the course, help to give these elements coherence. In order to develop central questions, formulate the most important questions addressed in the course. Different courses have different focal points and, therefore, different types of appropriate central questions. In some cases, the central questions can be answered correctly by a student successfully completing the course. In other cases, such as those in philosophy or literature, the questions may be open-ended, and the student who completes the course should be able to deal with these questions independently, rather than be able to answer them correctly. Courses range from those emphasizing understanding and appreciation, to those emphasizing problems or decisions, to those emphasizing skill acquisition and personal growth.

Inquiry Orientation

In general, an inquiry orientation aims at understanding. In some inquiry-oriented courses, the teacher and students explore topics in a search for underlying reasons for, meanings of, or implications of events. Inquiry-oriented courses might also investigate the structure or function of living things, objects, systems, or social organizations. Or they might study the meaning of particular concepts, such as humanity, reality, truth, or equality. Inquiry-oriented courses would be summarized best by questions such as the following:

> What is X?
> What are (or were) the causes of X?
> What are the implications of X?
> What is the structure (or function) of X?
> What does X mean (what is its nature or essence)?
> When does (did) X occur?
> How does (did) X happen?

These general questions are intended only to suggest the form some central questions might take, rather than to limit you in formulating central questions for your course.

Appreciation Orientation

Appreciation-oriented courses help the student develop taste, whether that taste is in literature, music, fine arts, dance, or theater. In such courses, students typically experience art through reading, viewing, listening to, or participating in the creation of an art product. While doing so, students develop personal preferences and also

*We are indebted to the work of Gowin (1970) for this idea, although he used the term *telling questions*.

learn the criteria that experts use in critiquing a piece of art. Central questions for such courses are of the sort, "What do I like, and why do I like it?"

Problem Orientation

Some courses focus on developing the students' ability to solve problems. For example, philosophers of science have described the training of physicists as instruction in how to categorize physical phenomena (such as pulleys) as a type of problem (an equilibrium-of-forces problem), and how to solve a variety of these problem types. Mathematics (for example, elementary algebra) can be similarly characterized, though being problem oriented does not mean that a course cannot also be inquiry oriented. The range of courses that focus on problems is very broad. Business courses focusing on management problems, interdisciplinary courses focusing on environmental problems, psychology courses focusing on coping with personal problems, and courses aimed at teaching general problem-solving methods represent only a sample of possibilities. In problem-oriented courses, the central questions would be of the type, "How does one solve problems X, Y, and Z?" A listing of the major problems or problem types is probably the best central question format for these courses.

Decision Orientation

Decision-oriented courses provide the student with information or frameworks on which to base decisions, and sometimes even with a step-by-step method for arriving at a decision. Decisions such as what career to pursue, what types of energy conservation measures to take, and what kind of used car to buy are typical. Included here would also be courses aimed at helping individuals with moral decisions. Some courses allow the decisions to be open-ended, whereas other courses assume a pre-specified decision. A course in car buying may or may not be biased toward fuel-efficient cars, but a drug education course is very likely to be biased toward a decision not to use (or, at least, not to abuse) drugs. Decision-oriented courses are best represented by central questions that simply list the decisions.

Skill Orientation

Still other courses are most appropriately described as skill oriented. A skill orientation emphasizes improving performance in carrying out physical tasks. Skill-oriented courses emphasize "how to do it, " whether "it" is driving a car, typing, or playing ice hockey. Central questions for such courses will typically be of the type, "How does one (or what is the proper way to) do X?" Often such questions include qualifiers for X such as "safely," "efficiently," "critically," and "with good sportsmanship."

Personal Growth Orientation

Though not entirely distinguishable from some other orientations, a personal growth orientation attempts to help the student define a personal goal (typically a psychological state, such as "self-actualization") and then to develop ways to work toward that goal. Such courses are usually grounded in theories of psychological counseling.

Appropriate central questions are of the sort, "What are my goals and how do I work toward them?"

It should be obvious that any real course is unlikely to represent only one of these types. Some courses might even be oriented toward inquiry, appreciation, problems, decisions, skills, and personal growth all at once. The important point is that your central questions should reflect the central concerns of *your* course. How many and what kinds of central questions naturally depend on the course. The following course titles accompanied by central questions serve as illustrations:

1. *Driver Education*
    What is the proper way to drive an automobile safely?

2. *American History 1700–1800*
    What political, social, and economic forces shaped America during this period?
    What was "revolutionary" about the United States?

3. *Environmental Science*
    How should I, as an individual, interact with my environment in a mutually beneficial way?
    What elements make up an ecosystem, and what is the nature of their interaction?

4. *Philosophy*
    What is the nature of reality?
    How do I give meaning to my life?

5. *Social Studies* (from *Man: A Course of Study*)
    What is human about human beings?
    How did they get that way?
    How can they be made more so?

Central questions do not include all the interesting or important questions for a particular course, but they should concern what is most fundamental to it. Central questions represent the "heart" of a course and are sometimes referred to as "essential" questions (Wiggins, undated). They are the questions that, once discovered by a student, serve as the focus for study. That is, a student who discovers a course's central questions might remark, "Aha! Now I see what this course is about. Now I see what the purpose is."

Obviously, the more central questions you specify, the less focused your course will appear. If you have a large number of central questions (more than five), you might attempt to organize them into major questions, each with associated subquestions. Such a procedure will maintain the scope of your course, while forcing you to examine its coherence.

One way to generate central questions is to imagine that you are developing a final examination for your course consisting of fewer than six essay questions. What would these questions be? This might be a good time to write out your ideal answers to these questions.

Course Planning Step 2.6   Examine your list of initial ideas, ILOs, and tentative course outline and write down the central questions that give coherence to your course. Now reconsider and expand your ILOs in light of these questions.

Thinking about central questions at this stage of course planning should help you identify the central or unifying theme of your course. You may find that your course will need revision in order to achieve a focus. In general, thinking about central questions is another way to evaluate and continue to develop your course. These questions are only one of several tools you will be taught for thinking about your course.

QUESTIONS FOR DISCUSSION: CENTRAL QUESTIONS

1. What do your central questions tell you about the focus of your course?

2. Are one or two of your questions the *real* focus of your course and the others secondary or subquestions? From your list of central questions, which ones truly represent the "heart" of your course?

3. What would be unacceptable answers to some of your central questions?

4. What kinds of questions are you asking? Are you more interested in "where" and "when" or in "why" and "how"?

   a. If you are more interested in "where" and "when" questions, what does that suggest about your course?

   b. If you are more interested in "why" and "how" questions, what does that suggest about your course?

5. What are some of the evaluative words you have used in your questions (*good, bad, useful, beneficial, harmful, efficient, growth, interest*)? What does this suggest about your course?

6. Are there some central questions that might appear relevant to your course, but which you would reject? Explain why you would reject them.

7. To what extent do these questions take the *student* into consideration? The *society* in which the student lives? The *subject matter*?

8. Show your questions to an expert in the field. Does the expert agree with your focus? How do you account for any discrepancies?

Although central questions, lists of ILOs, and course outlines are useful tools for thinking about the scope and coherence of your course, they are not sufficient. More schematic tools such as charts are needed. Two schematic tools will be discussed in this chapter: conceptual maps and flowcharts. Conceptual maps are appropriate for representing understanding; flowcharts are most useful for analyzing skills.

CONCEPTUAL MAPS

The technique you will learn in this section is called *conceptual mapping*. You already know about maps as diagrammatic representations of geographical regions. Maps of this type show where you are in relation to other geographical points. For example, road maps help you to "get your bearings and to proceed to your destination" (Anderson, 1979, p. 17). Conceptual maps are like road maps, but they are concerned with relationships among ideas, rather than places. Conceptual maps also help you to "get your bearings" in designing a course—to clarify the kinds of ideas you want taught—so that you can proceed toward your destination of real student learning.

This is the first stage of conceptual mapping. Here we will focus on identifying key ideas and arranging them in a reasonable pattern. In Chapter 4 we will elaborate on this technique further, identifying and representing specific relationships among ideas. You may want to continue with the discussion of maps in Chapter 4, temporarily skipping Chapter 3.

In a conceptual map, ideas are depicted as related to one another. These ideas include concepts, theories, facts, rules, propositions, principles, and generalizations. Maps may depict relationships among ideas as simple or complex, clear or indefinite.

Figure 2.5 is a simple map. It is definite and clear but gives us only limited information. The first thing the chart indicates is that each labeled node represents a subcategory under the category "cooking with heat." Reading down from the top of the chart shows us that there are two major subcategories for "cooking with heat," using the stove top and using the oven. If the oven is used, two methods can be employed: indirect heat and direct heat. This is a hierarchical map. It specifies only two things, but it does this definitely and exhaustively: subcategory identification and

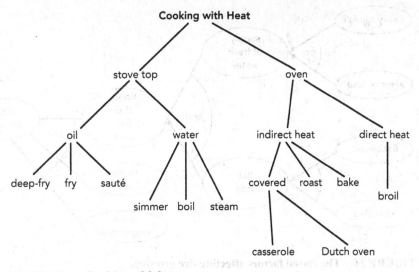

FIGURE 2.5   Cooking with heat.

membership. For example, simmer, boil, and steam are all members of the subcategory water. Likewise, oil and water are members of the subcategory stove top. This method of mapping is simple, definite, and complete. It specifies precisely every relationship it sets out to show. Nevertheless, it is important to note that many other relationships are not specified. For example, the relationship between bake and roast is seen here only as membership in the same subcategory. Likewise, the similarity of boil to deep-fry is not shown in the diagram. This simple hierarchical diagram simply does not have the capacity for showing these relationships. A hierarchical diagram is a graphic presentation of conceptual structure in terms of the relationship of classes to constituency.

But maps do not have to be hierarchical diagrams. Ideas may be related in ways other than class membership. One idea (a) may *cause* another (increased inflation is one *consequence* of government spending), (b) may be *compared* with another with regard to magnitude (the amount of solar radiation the earth absorbs *equals* the amount it radiates), and (c) may be a *property* of another (hurricanes *have* high winds and torrential rains). These are only examples of the many possible relationships among ideas.

For example, Figure 2.6 is a conceptual map for a social studies unit on rice growing. Instead of a hierarchical arrangement, causal relations seem more appropriate for this content. According to this map, four factors affect rice growing: fresh water, a flat area, fertile soil, and warm temperature. Other concepts could be added through more detailed analysis. For example, irrigation could be added between "river or lake," and "supply of fresh water." Collins (1977) discusses in detail how such a map could guide the teaching of a student using Socratic questioning.

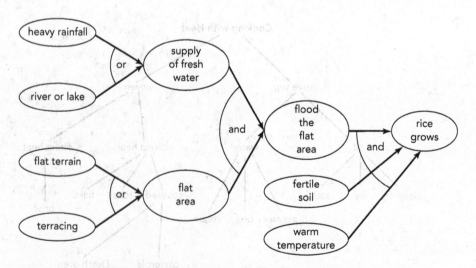

FIGURE 2.6   The causal factors affecting rice growing.
Source: Adapted from Collins, 1977.

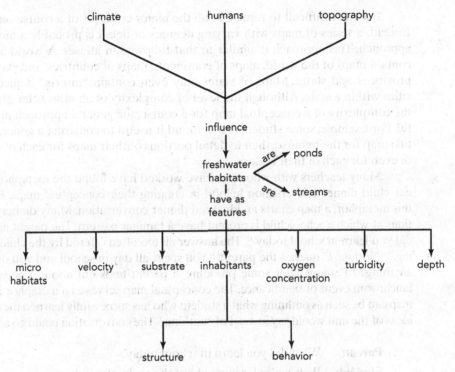

FIGURE 2.7   A conceptual map for a course on freshwater habitats.

When you construct a conceptual map you do not have to choose which one of the many possible relationships your map will feature. A map may employ several kinds of relationships. For example, Figure 2.7 illustrates three factors that *influence* freshwater habitats, and two *aspects* of the adaptation of freshwater inhabitants to their habitats.

Obviously, the kinds of relationships featured in your conceptual map will depend primarily on the subject matter and the relationships within that subject matter that concern you as a planner. Accompanying a map with a brief explanation is one way to clarify or highlight a map's relationships. Making those relationships more specific and explicit will be one of the topics treated in Chapter 4.

One issue that almost always surfaces when constructing maps concerns the appropriate level of detail. Using our earlier comparison of conceptual maps with geographical maps, we might think of a map as a "view" of the "conceptual terrain" in a course. In a sense, there is a trade-off between the level of detail (the "resolution") and the scope (the "field of vision") of information included in a particular view of the terrain. The broader the field of vision we wish for our view, the less resolution we can provide. Similarly, the higher the resolution of our view (the "finer grained"), the more restricted our field will be.

It is very difficult to represent all the major concepts of a course on one map. Instead, a series of maps with varying degrees of detail is probably a more fruitful approach. This approach is similar to that followed in atlases. A world atlas might contain maps of the world, maps of continents, maps of countries, and even maps of provinces and states. Maps of states may even contain "inserts" depicting major cities within a state. Although the level of complexity of an atlas is far greater than the complexity of a conceptual map for a course, the general approach may be useful. For example, some students have found it useful to construct a general conceptual map for their course, then to detail portions of their maps for each of their units or even for each of their lessons.

Many teachers with whom we have worked have found the metaphor of a parent–child dinner conversation helpful in creating their conceptual maps. Employing this metaphor, a map charts an idealized dinner conversation. Many dinner conversations at which a schoolchild is present have a familiar pattern. The parent asks, "What did you learn in school today?" The answer all too often offered by the child is, "Nothing." "Nothing?" queries the parent. "You spent all day in school and you didn't learn anything?" Perhaps after some prodding, a parent finds out about a playground or lunchroom event of significance. The conceptual map serves as a metaphor in that the map can be seen as outlining what a student who has successfully learned the important ideas of the unit would say instead of "nothing." The conversation could go as follows:

Parent: What did you learn in school today?

Student: Well, we're learning about the rocky shore ecosystem.

Parent: Really? Tell me about it.

Student: I know a lot about it. What do you want to know?

Parent: Well, I don't know anything. Better start at the beginning.

Student: Living things must adapt to their physical environment to survive. The rocky shore presents real physical challenges for living things....

In a more concrete sense, the map with an accompanying explanation is the kind of information that a teacher could send home to help parents focus a conversation on ideas being covered in school. (See Figure 2.8 for example.) Rather than ask a general question about what was learned in school, parents could ask questions like the following: "What are you learning about the plants and animals of the rocky shore?" "How do living things adapt to this environment?" "What are the important characteristics of the environment?"

Teachers sometimes mistakenly think that the ideas included on a conceptual map are to be taught directly. For elementary teachers this sometimes creates an image of heavy-handed instruction. The fact is, one teaches ideas through engaging and appropriate use of specific content. The story or theme is what ties the specifics together. Teachers need to refer to the theme or story to lend coherence to the material being taught. In creating a conceptual map, many teachers have been helped by thinking of it as a device that lays out the story line. This has helped them keep the specific content to a minimum and instead to focus on the unit's major underlying ideas.

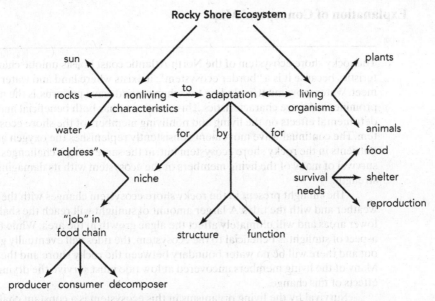

FIGURE 2.8   A conceptual map for a unit on the rocky shore ecosystem.

The Rocky Shore map, Figure 2.8, and accompanying explanation were designed for a sixth-grade science unit. The map shows that the ideas central to understanding an ecosystem include knowing the physical characteristics of that environment and knowing what lives there. The map also shows that it is the adaptive relationship between organism and environment that is the key to understanding the ecosystem. Below "adaptation" are concepts that will help students think about and understand the ways in which living things adapt to their environment. It is worth noting that this basic conceptual structure could be used to study any ecosystem, not just that of the rocky shore. The details would change, but the fundamental ideas and their relationship would stay the same. There is often a fine line between enough and too much specific detail on a conceptual map.

Maps are not supposed to be course outlines in two dimensions. The Rocky Shore map could include some specifics about this particular ecosystem. Waves and tides, for example, are crucial features of the physical environment of the rocky shore. Organisms of this ecosystem with some distinct adaptations that relate directly to physical conditions could be mentioned. By helping us see the underlying relationships among ideas, a map frees us from the constraints of specific content and thus enables us to convey the ideas more effectively. The Rocky Shore unit began with a slide show that contrasted successful and unsuccessful adaptation. A field teeming with dandelions was followed by the image of a bristlecone pine that has not had an offspring in over 1,000 years. A herd of caribou on the tundra was followed by hatching Galapagos turtles being picked off by predators on their way to the water. The show continued, its point being to set the stage for the specific story of the rocky shore.

Explanation of Conceptual Map

The rocky shore ecosystem of the North Atlantic coast boasts unique characteristics because it is a "border ecosystem"; it exists where land and water meet. Water movement, including tide changes and wave patterns, is the most prominent of these characteristics. This movement has both beneficial and detrimental effects on the living and nonliving members of the shore ecosystem. The continual wave movement consistently replenishes the oxygen and nutrients in the rocky shore ecosystem but, at the same time, it challenges the survival of many of the living members of the ecosystem with its damaging strength.

The sunlight present in the rocky shore ecosystem changes with the weather and with the tides. A larger amount of sunlight will reach the shallower areas and will ultimately affect the algae growth in the area. While this aspect of sunlight is beneficial to the ecosystem, the tides will eventually go out and there will be no water boundary between the rocky shore and the sun. Many of the living members uncovered at low tide must survive the drying effects of this change.

Survival by the living organisms in this ecosystem is a constant challenge. The ease with which an organism adapts to this environment determines its ability to obtain its survival needs: food, shelter, and reproduction. By adapting in both structure and function, an organism can take from this environment what it needs and, simultaneously, defend itself from the negative aspects of the environment. Organisms have various ways in which they meet their survival needs and, in doing so, they find a unique niche in the ecosystem.

This niche determines the activity that the organism performs in the food chain of the ecosystem. The food chain is the primary method by which all organisms divide the available resources of the environment. All the organisms in an ecosystem depend on one another for this distribution of resources; they are thus dependent on one another for the conditions of life. The niche also defines the place in which the organism spends its adult life. In the rocky shore ecosystem, the "addresses" of various organisms are clearly determined by the tidal divisions. The subtidal region is the area of the rocky shore that, except at the lowest tides, is completely submerged in water. The intertidal zone is the shore that is constantly wet by wave movement and is covered by water twice each day during high tide.

The teacher using this unit can and should use this conceptual map as a general outline for an ecosystem. Maintaining a consistent conceptual framework for all ecosystems will enable students to compare and contrast characteristics of other ecosystems studied. This map should also serve as an anchor upon which other more complex additions can be made.

The highest priority relationships (intended cognitions) represented by this conceptual map are the following:

- Ecosystems consist of the living organisms and the nonliving characteristics present.
- The nonliving characteristics determine that to which the living organisms must adapt.
- Living organisms adapt by structure and function in order to find a niche and meet survival needs (food, shelter, reproduction).
- The living organisms must divide the available resources and are dependent on one another to do so.
- The food chain is the primary way in which living organisms divide these resources.

Course Planning Step 2.7   Analyze the important terminology contained in your skill and understanding ILOs and course outline, and list all terms you feel are representative of the major ideas you want your students to understand.

The following list of words might represent the major ideas in one teacher's physics course on mechanics:

Mechanics	Motion	Acceleration
Body	Rest	Particle
Mass	Dynamics	Force
Kinetics	Direction	

Course Planning Step 2.8   Arrange the list of words in your course signifying ideas and add interconnecting lines until you have a diagram or set of diagrams illustrating the interrelationships among the ideas particular to the course. Add any ideas that you feel are needed to make your map(s) meaningful and complete.

Figure 2.9 on page 58 shows the arrangement of terms produced by one university faculty member. Other "correct" arrangements are possible.

Course Planning Step 2.9   Evaluate your map(s). Have you depicted major relationships clearly? Can the map(s) be simplified and still effectively communicate the relationships you consider most important?

Conceptual maps are useful for thinking about your course. In fact, mapping is an important step toward acquiring a clear conception of what you want learned. Understandings are, in many ways, more adequately expressed as a map than as a set of ILO statements (to be discussed further in Chapter 4). Knowledge has meaning in context and part of context is how ideas are interrelated. These interrelationships can be, at least partially, expressed by a map.

Maps can illuminate many important issues at this stage of planning. (See Novak & Gowin, 1984; West, Farmer, & Wolff, 1991.) For example, a map that includes only discrete and specific facts may indicate a need for more inclusive ideas. On the other hand, a map may show only inclusive and abstract ideas without the

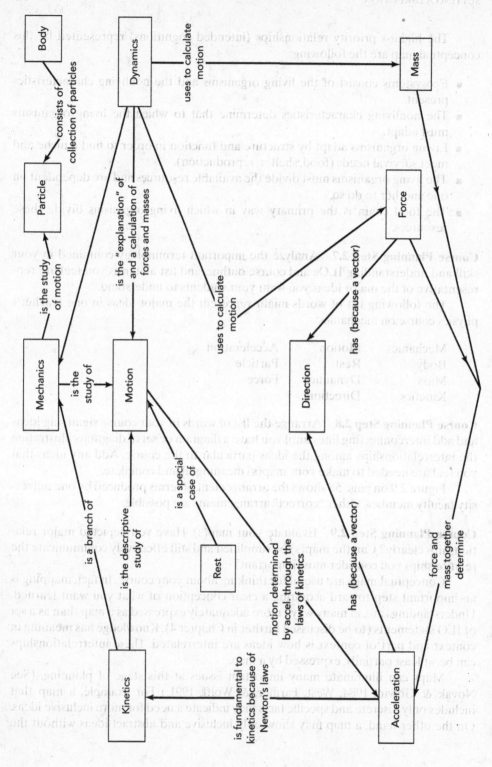

FIGURE 2.9 One possible arrangement of physics terms. Note the advantage to the reader when the mapmaker labels the arrows.

Source: Adapted from Champagne et al., 1980.

applications and examples that make these ideas understandable and useful. Noticing that a map lacks relationships among certain ideas may point out the need for additional ideas to make those relationships possible. These are only a few examples of the kinds of information a conceptual map may provide during planning.

As a sort of shorthand representation of a teacher's conceptual ILOs, maps often prove useful during instruction. Knowing how ideas relate should help teachers to respond to questions and comments in a more focused way. Remarks made by students can be seen as instances of a concept, and the teacher can try to help students understand the desired relationships. A teacher's cueing, questioning, and supplying of new information is apt to be more targeted when accompanied by a clear notion of the ideas and relationships the teacher wants learned. (See Collins, 1977, for several useful examples.)

The mapping process is flexible and a map for any given set of concepts can take many forms. Too often teachers worry about the "correctness" of their maps. Correctness is a secondary concern here. You, the teacher, will be teaching the course, and you undoubtedly have some view of the relationships among the course's ideas. Whatever framework you possess is likely to affect your teaching. Mapping allows you to make this framework explicit, revise it, and generally, be more conscious of it. Therefore, in constructing a conceptual map, your initial attempts should be made with the goal of getting this framework on paper and with the expectation that the framework will require revision. Relating all the important ideas in a course in two dimensions is a difficult task. However, mapping is usually worth the effort and will prove useful in thinking about and planning your course.

Course Planning Step 2.10   Create a conceptual map for your course, revising from Steps 2.8 and 2.9 as necessary.

QUESTIONS FOR DISCUSSION: MAPPING

1. If your map has lines connecting terms, do the lines mean different things? What do they mean?

2. Compare terms that are connected to many other terms with terms that are connected to just one other term. Does this comparison help you identify the important or central ideas in your course?

3. Was your map instrumental in finding any new ILOs?

4. Do you feel your course lent itself well to mapping, or did you find mapping inappropriate? How do you account for this?

5. Would your map help students find their way through your course? If so, you might want to use it as a handout, a kind of two-dimensional course outline.

6. Show your map to an expert in the field. Does the expert understand and agree with you regarding your map? Are any changes in order?

NARRATIVES

Developing and being clear about ideas and their relationships is a crucial component in designing effective courses. Using as many powerful intellectual tools as possible for achieving this goal makes good sense. Conceptual mapping is one such tool, developing a course "story" is another. A course "story" is a narrative expression about the course's main ideas and their relationship. Story or narrative is a useful tool for several reasons. One reason is that not all content is well suited to conceptual mapping. Some content is not well structured or has relationships among ideas that are so complex that links, even labeled links, do not fully convey the intended meaning. This is often the case in history, literature, and other social science and humanities disciplines. Another reason is that not all course planners think in ways that make mapping as powerful a tool as it otherwise might be. Narrative or story is a much more "natural" approach to expressing relationships among ideas.

The use of story or narrative to make meaning, to order and organize concepts, and to discover central themes is well established in literature related to teaching and learning. Egan (1986, 1997) writes of "teaching as storytelling" as a way of applying the structural features of stories to planning curriculum and instruction. Rosen (1986) contends that narrative has an importance much deeper and broader than the purely literary values we customarily give to it and that it is a "primary and irreducible form of human comprehension . . ." (p. 230).

Deal and Peterson (1999, p. 96) note "one of the highest forms of culture-shaping communication is the story. A well-chosen story provides a powerful image that addresses a question without compromising its complexity. Stories ground complicated ideas in concrete terms, personifying them in flesh and blood. Stories carry values and connect abstract ideas with sentiment, emotions, and events." Bruner (1986) reminds us that the narrative mode, the telling of stories, is how human beings express their understandings about the world. There is no doubt that stories provide a potent and readily grasped approach to expressing meaning and relationships.

The type of story sought here for planning purposes is one that expresses the underlying theme of the course. It need not, in fact it should not, be a narrative that includes specific content. As was true with conceptual maps, one story could serve to describe ideas and their interrelationships for a wide variety of content. Instructing planners in just how to write a story is a daunting task because it is such a familiar means of expression. The following examples are meant to instruct by way of illustration.

Inquiry Story

The first illustration is a story that was developed collaboratively by teachers and researchers working on a kindergarten through middle school curriculum development project. The development effort focused on a curriculum for teaching scientific inquiry. The teachers found the "steps" of the so-called scientific method too procedural and inadequate for expressing what it means to understand scientific inquiry. At the same time, the exhortations to teach using inquiry and children's authentic questions were too vague to be useful.

How do we know what we know?

Some of what we know we discover for ourselves. Some we learn from books, teachers, parents, friends, television, movies . . . there are many sources for what we know. Everything that there is to know had to be discovered or created by someone. In many instances, the process of creating knowledge is called inquiry.

Whenever we encounter something new or something about which we do not know everything and this encounter leads us to think, wonder, or ask questions, we are engaged in inquiry.

Sometimes we have an idea that answers our question immediately. Sometimes we have to think for a while about possible answers. Sometimes we observe more carefully or get more information before we answer our question.

Careful inquirers know that the initial answer to their question is really just a guess (hunch, conjecture, hypothesis, theory). Inquiry does not stop here. These hunches must be put to a test. We must seek evidence that will help us determine if our hunch is on the right track. Good evidence will help us refine our hunches and ask better questions.

This is precisely what scientists do. They know that their hunches (guesses, hypotheses, theories) must be tested. Scientists understand that only when there is strong evidence to support their ideas can they claim to know something. In order to have confidence that their inquiry produces strong evidence, scientists have devised procedures (methods) and rules for research.

Scientists know that their theories are never proven. There is always the chance that new evidence will create some doubts about what they know. Scientists are open-minded about this possibility and constantly seek new evidence. They know that the more they learn from their investigations, the more questions they will have. The inquiry process really does not end. As we learn about new and different aspects of our world, we develop new questions and continue to inquire.

Etheredge, Rudnitsky, and Freeman (1999)

Symmetry from the Eye of a Mathematician

This is a story written for a middle school unit on symmetry.

The symmetry that exists around us is both aesthetically pleasing and mathematically rigorous. Mathematically speaking, symmetry can take the form of horizontal translations, vertical mirror translations, glide reflections, mirror reflections, rotations, and/or any combination of the above. While we can identify millions of examples of symmetries in both natural and man-made forms, there are only a finite number of ways that the elements of a symmetric group may be combined. Mathematicians use the language of abstract algebra to articulate rigorous definitions and theorems of symmetry.

Susan D'Agostino (1998)

Sylvia Plath

This is a story written for a high school English unit on the work of Sylvia Plath. Note that Plath is never mentioned in the story. This is a very good illustration of a story highlighting underlying themes rather than specific content.

Literature is about the human experience. When we read the "classics" in school, it is easy to forget that people, like ourselves, created the characters in famous works. Therefore, the joys and the troubles that fictional characters are faced with throughout their literary lives often reflect the personal experiences of the author. Since we all have certain hopes, fears, and concerns in common, we find ourselves "drawn into" the lives of fictional characters.

Good literature features characters we can understand and with whom we can empathize. When we feel a "connection" to a particular character, it is often because we can relate to an emotion the character is "feeling," or a situation that a character finds himself or herself in. Great writers and great literature help us see and understand ourselves in new ways. Because of this, literature can be used as a tool for self-discovery and growth. Sometimes, when we think about decisions a character has to make, or the way a character's choices affect his or her life, we pause to reflect upon our own lives, and our own ideas and concerns for the future. Who has not read a book and reflected upon what they might have done if they were in a particular character's situation, or thought of a time when they felt the same way a character felt?

Finally, literature can give us a new perspective on the society in which we live and how it may influence our lives, including the goals we set for ourselves, and the way we perceive others. When we are reading a literary work, we have to take into account the way a character's society influences the choices he or she makes. This should encourage us to think about the influence that our society has over our own lives. To conclude, when readers come to care about the joys, trials, and tribulations of a fictional character, it is often because the author has done an exceptional job of infusing these characters with basic, fundamental human emotions.

Alyssa Krawczyk (1998)

Essay Writing Story

This is a story written for a high school English unit on essay writing. It illustrates the use of story in a more skill-oriented unit. Note that the author of this story includes argument for the importance of writing well. This could be included in the rationale for the course or unit instead of in the story.

Writing evolved from oral traditions that were translated into linguistic codes, symbols, and characters. The ability to record information in written form defines one of the most important steps in the evolution of civilization. It revolutionized communication in more profound ways than printing presses, telephones, or computers.

The broadest division of writing forms is prose and poetry. The essay is a type of prose, though other types of writing, including poetry, may inform what essays are made of and how they work.

Today, what is the use of writing well? Good writing is a tool with which we gain the power to communicate our thoughts, express our feelings, and get what we want—especially when employing the essay format.

There are several kinds of essays—narrative, persuasive, and descriptive. To varying degrees, each kind of essay depends on a well-organized structure, good prose, and the author's familiarity with rhetorical devices and dialectical constructs. There are rules for good writing that provide the principles of quality prose, and there are definite steps we take to help us organize our writing.

Essays may require research. Demonstrating a point in any essay requires evidence. Employing expert sources is often critical. So strong library skills go hand in hand with writing good essays.

When writing essays, it is important to consider the reading audience. It is important to consider tone. It is important to consider point of view (first person or third) and to develop your own sense of style and voice. The development of your individual voice reflects the development of your rhetorical integrity as a writer, thinker, and learner. Writing can then evolve toward a self-directed, knowledge-transforming process.

Jeff Lydon (1998)

Modern Dance

This is a story written for a high school unit on the history of modern dance.

Dance in some form or another has been an important part of numerous human cultures for centuries. It is sometimes considered to be the oldest of all the art forms. The roles that dance has occupied within a given society are quite numerous and varied. In many cultures, dance has been used as a tool for healing or as a vehicle for religious worship. The traditional dances of some cultures have remained almost unchanged for centuries. In all these traditional or "classical" forms of dance a codified tradition has evolved, consisting of very specific steps and rules for combining those steps. Even in the history of classical ballet, a discipline which has evolved over the years, innovations are only made by combining existing steps in novel ways. The established "vocabulary" of the discipline has been preserved through the years.

Earlier this century, American culture gave birth to a unique form of dance, which has come to be called modern dance. Lacking a codified tradition of dance, populated by a heterogeneous group of people, and principled upon individual freedom, America offered dancers the opportunity to search for something new. Modern dance in America emerged as a tool for individual artistic creation and expression. Without a traditional vocabulary of steps, modern dance artists were free to create new ways of moving through space, ways that they felt more appropriately reflected the modern era. Unconstrained by entrenched religious or social pressures, artists were able to explore and express their own inner landscapes. As the legacy was passed down from one generation of dancers to the next, modern dance was reinterpreted and reshaped by the beliefs and intentions of the individual artist at work.

As the decades passed, the face of modern dance continued to change drastically. Today, "modern dance" is an umbrella term that refers to a widely disparate collection of styles and techniques. All these different forms of modern dance share one thing among them: a tradition of innovation and individuality. The pioneers and success stories of modern dance are the individuals who are able to re-envision the definition of modern dance, challenge what came before them, and create new forms within the genre. These dancers express their own philosophies of dance and life through personalized movement styles. The only thing that has remained constant throughout the history of modern dance has been the ever-present redefining of the genre by individual artists.

Marion Johnson (1998)

Geology

This is a story written for an upper elementary unit on geology.

Geology is the study of time, forces, and processes that have shaped our earth. These forces include friction, pressure, and movement. Forces are revealed through earthquakes, tsunamis, and volcanoes. These processes and forces build slowly and it is the release of the pent-up energy that results in these devastating effects. An example of this would be the energy released at the site of a fault during an earthquake. The record of what these forces have done over time is most often found by examining the surrounding rocks and minerals for magnetic records, fossil records, and changes that have occurred in the mineral structure. Putting this evidence together allows a geologist to create a record of the earth's evolution and make predictions of what will happen next. It is through the charting of this information that we gain an understanding of the pace of geologic change and a perspective of geologic age.

Megan Kennedy (1997)

Many teachers have found it useful to write, in addition to thematic stories, more specific content-oriented stories. For example, the unit on Plath included a story about the life and work of the author. Who the audience is for the story is a question that often arises as stories are developed. The story is a tool for the planner. Its intent is to help develop and clarify the course's underlying themes and relationships among important ideas. However, the story is also a very useful instructional and assessment tool. These uses of story will be addressed in subsequent chapters.

Course Planning Step 2.11 Write a story that represents, in narrative form, the theme and/or relationships among main ideas in the course.

FLOWCHARTS

Arithmetic computation, reading, writing paragraphs, editing films, and parking a car are all complex skills in the sense that they each require a set of subskills and understandings for their performance. If we want to teach any of these skills we must do so by teaching the necessary subskills and understandings. Therefore, it is important to identify the components of these complex skills. So long as important aspects of a desired skill remain unidentified and untaught, achievement of the skill will be impeded. Identification of subskills and understandings allows them to be specified as course ILOs and subsequently taught using appropriate teaching strategies.

One tool for identifying such subskills and understandings is a cognitive task analysis utilizing flowcharts. Let us look at an example.

$$3/5 + 1/5 = ?$$

Try to solve this problem and analyze your thinking process at the same time. That is, think the steps through aloud as you do each of them. Note what you are doing and compare it with the flowchart in Figure 2.10.

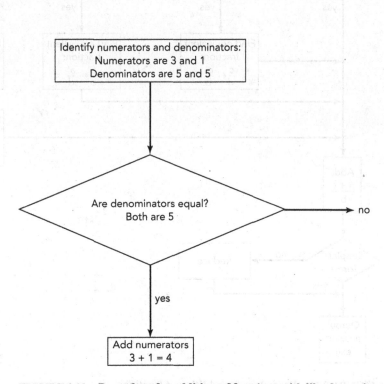

FIGURE 2.10   Procedure for addition of fractions with like denominators.

Now look at this more difficult problem.

$$3/5 + 2/15 = ?$$

Again, analyze your thinking process by verbalizing the steps you follow in solving it. A more general procedure for solving such problems is depicted in Figure 2.11. According to this more complex and generalized flowchart, these two problems require the addition of fractions that can be represented in a general form as:

$$a/b + c/d = ?$$

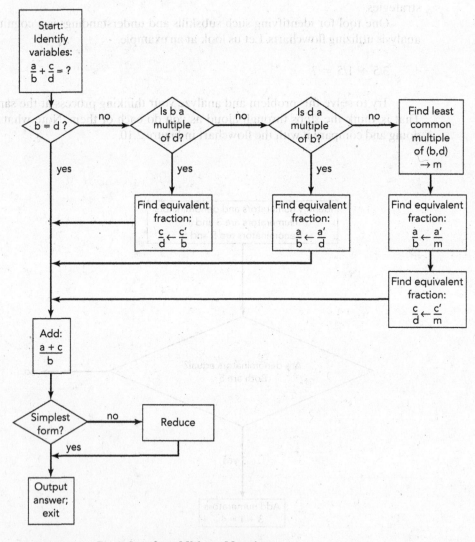

FIGURE 2.11   Procedure for addition of fractions.

Source: Adapted from Greeno, 1976.

In the first problem $b = d$ (both are 5) so we can add a and c (that is, $3 + 1$) and get 4/5 as an answer. Notice, however, that this flowchart begs the question of how we add 3 and 1. Do we count on our fingers, or in our heads, or do we just know the answer? Clearly, these analyses can be performed at different levels of depth.

In the second problem $b = d$, but d is a multiple of b (15 is 3 times 5). As in the first problem, each step in the procedure could be reanalyzed as a subskill for which we could identify additional and necessary subskills, facts, principles, and so on. The depth of our analysis will depend on what learning outcomes we can assume our students have already achieved.

In a similar way, we could analyze each of our skill ILOs by asking the question, "What process do I go through when I perform this skill, and, specifically, what skills and understandings does the ILO entail?" This analysis could be done at a general level for the whole course by analyzing the course's ILOs. For example, Figure 2.12 presents the skills and understandings entailed in playing a game of ice hockey.

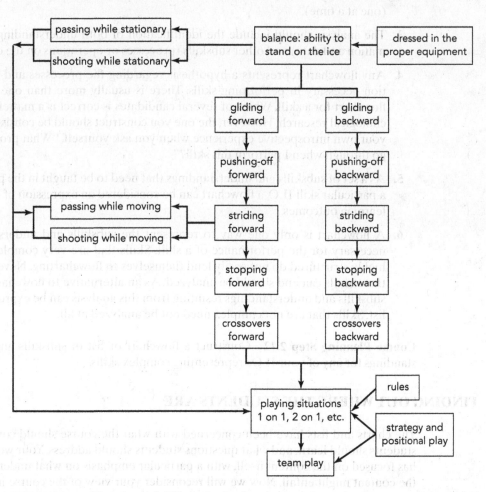

FIGURE 2.12 Flowchart of skills for ice hockey.

Then, at a more specific level, each of the skills in this general flowchart could be analyzed in greater detail.

In the analysis of most skills, the skills (or "tasks" as they are typically called) can best be described in terms of a series of internal and/or external actions performed on available information. Many cognitive psychologists distinguish between data or "information" and the operations or actions we perform on the data, termed "processes." These psychologists are concerned with how humans act on (process) data (information); thus, they use the term *information-processing analysis.*

There are several additional points to keep in mind as you construct flowcharts for your skill ILOs:

1. Many of the subskills you identify during the analysis may be internal thought processes rather than observable behaviors. This is to be expected.

2. It is usually best to think of the steps in the procedures as occurring serially (one at a time).

3. The analysis should include the identification of both understandings (information and data) and other subskills (processes or operations on the data).

4. Any flowchart represents a hypothesis regarding the processes and information necessary in performing skills. There is usually more than one possible flowchart for a skill. Which of several candidates is correct is a matter for psychological research. However, the one you construct should be consistent with your own introspective experience when you ask yourself, "What process do I go through when I perform this skill?"

5. As a set of subskills and understandings that need to be taught in the pursuit of a particular skill ILO, a flowchart can be considered an expression of intended learning outcomes.

6. A flowchart is only one way to represent the subskills and understandings necessary for the performance of a skill. Skills that are very complex or not highly structured do not easily lend themselves to flowcharting. Nevertheless, these skills can and should be analyzed. As an alternative to flowcharting, the subskills and understandings resulting from this analysis can be expressed as a list. Skills that are not complex need not be analyzed at all.

Course Planning Step 2.12   Construct a flowchart or list of subskills and understandings for any of your ILOs representing complex skills.

FINDING OUT WHERE THE STUDENTS ARE

The charts and lists have been concerned with what the course should cover, what students should learn, and what questions students should address. Your work so far has focused on the content itself, with a particular emphasis on what understanding the content might entail. Now we will reconsider your view of the course in light of the students' backgrounds, capabilities, and conceptions. Ball and Wilson (1996) talk about integrity in teaching. Integrity resides in teachers seeking a balance between honoring or respecting the content and honoring or respecting the students' thinking. This dilemma of balance seeking is sometimes expressed by teachers when they wonder whether their responsibility is to teach the material or teach the students. Achieving this balance is a challenge, one that teachers continually grapple with. The balance point is not the same for all students. Individual differences and the need and opportunity to differentiate curriculum and instruction are brought to center stage here. The direction you have been setting with conceptual maps, flowcharts, narratives, and statements are now reexamined with an eye toward student diversity.

Finding out what students know and can do is something teachers should accomplish well in advance of instruction. Otherwise the information is not likely to be helpful in planning. There may sometimes be reasons to begin a course or unit by asking students what they know about the topics or what they want to learn. But it seems wildly optimistic and also demeaning to the importance of planning to believe that teachers can learn about the students on day one of a course and then incorporate that into the course design by day two. (See Chapter 7 for more about when and how to find out what students know.)

Students with Diverse Backgrounds

In general, students from diverse backgrounds do not receive the same quality of educational experiences as students from so-called mainstream backgrounds. This is a situation that all educators are concerned about and need to make every effort to address. Teachers and planners should not subscribe to the belief that cultural differences among students are inconsequential. Knowledge of cultural differences can help teachers be more effective. This knowledge is not simple generalizations about a particular culture but specific knowledge about the lives and cultures of the individual students with whom the teacher is working. Kathryn Au (1993) describes two theories explaining why students from diverse backgrounds are less successful in school. One theory, cultural discontinuity, focuses on the mismatch between the culture of the home and the culture of the school. This leads to misunderstandings between teachers and students. Teachers need to help students cross the boundary from the home culture to that of the school. The second theory, structural inequality, focuses on larger political, economic, and social forces and sees the conditions in schools as resulting from these larger forces. In this view, schools function to maintain the status quo, in which the dominant culture has all the power. This theoretical point of view emphasizes the pervasive nature of discrimination and alerts educators to the fact that they may be acting in discriminatory ways even if they are not doing so intentionally. Cummins (1986) offers a framework highlighting four areas for addressing issues of diversity in educational practice. First, teachers should ensure that the students' language and culture are represented in the curriculum content. Second, teachers should make efforts to involve the larger community in the work of the school and classroom. Third, teachers should place less emphasis on the transmission model of instruction and more on a constructivist approach. And fourth, teachers should move away from legitimization-oriented assessment, which locates the cause of academic deficiencies within the student, and move toward advocacy-oriented assessment, which recognizes that by locating the problems of schooling in the social and educational context they are more readily addressed.

A multicultural approach to education encompasses all of these suggested practices and perspectives. A multicultural approach emphasizes reexamining your personal perspective as a teacher, considering the background of students and the communities from which they come, particularly in terms of their culture. We believe that a multicultural approach values as an educational goal the ability to see the world from alternative (cultural) perspectives. In the next chapter we will urge you to include these considerations in thinking about your course rationale. Modeling a multicultural perspective and using examples drawn from diverse cultures to teach content will have an impact on your subsequent instructional planning. Understanding the lives, contexts, and cultures of your students also matters at this stage of course planning—when you are setting your direction.

Course Planning Step 2.13   Consider the backgrounds of your students with particular attention to the broader, outside-of-school context of their lives and cultures. Consider also the students' ability to adopt a different cultural perspective in viewing the world. Are there concepts, skills, and attitudes that might support such perspective taking that fit the "story" of your course? Revise your ILOs in light of considerations about the contexts and cultures of students' lives.

Existing Knowledge

We would not want a course to cover the same ground as previous courses, except for review purposes. But the fact that students have or have not been exposed to certain ideas does not tell us what they do or do not understand. In fact, students' existing knowledge is not typically an all-or-nothing situation. Students do not come to any of a course's topics completely empty-headed. They may not know the terminology or have a precise understanding of the topic, but they usually have some ideas about it. Whether the course includes the study of how plants get their food, how to write an academic essay, the meaning of a fraction, the dangers of drug abuse, or how to "head" a soccer ball, students typically come to most courses with well-developed preconceptions.

Although much of the research on student preconceptions has been conducted in science education (see Driver, 1983; Eylon & Linn, 1988; Osborne & Freyberg, 1985; Resnick, 1983), there is enough research to suggest that students generally are not empty vessels into which we pour knowledge. Instead, they actively try to make sense of their experience (including classroom experience) based on what they already know or believe. When students' preconceptions are either incorrect or only partially true, instruction may become a task of changing people's ideas rather than instilling fresh knowledge.

Before we can adjust a course's ILOs and instructional method to the students, we must know in fairly specific terms what particular students know or believe about the topics we intend to teach. The best way to find out this crucial information is to talk with them in open-ended interviews and group discussion, asking them for their explanations or descriptions while listening to them very carefully. In these diagnostic settings, we can find out the extent to which their views are idiosyncratic or common to the other learners; whether their ideas derive from prior instruction, mass media, life experience, or their own "spontaneous reasoning" (Viennot, 1979, p. 205); and possibly how deeply held their beliefs are and, thus, how difficult they will be to change. The work of Nancie Atwell provides detailed accounts of how teachers can observe and listen to students to assess their present levels of understanding and their needs (see Atwell, 1987, 1991, 1998).

Without the opportunity to study students directly, the course planner has to settle for secondhand knowledge, for example, the observations of experienced, perceptive teachers. Although there are times when this type of information must suffice, firsthand knowledge of students gained from observations and discussions both inside and outside of the classroom is highly preferable.

It is important to find out what students know because then you, as the course planner, can determine not only which of their ideas the course needs to correct or extend, but also what resources students can bring to their understanding of the new material. The course can act as a bridge between what students already know and what you want them to understand. Analogies, metaphors, and examples are some of the instructional devices teachers use as bridges between familiar and unfamiliar ideas. We used the analogy between course design (unfamiliar) and building construction (familiar) in order to introduce this book in Chapter 1. Without knowing what students understand and what experiences they have had, teachers may use these potentially powerful strategies inappropriately and ineffectively.

One way to represent students' preconceptions is to construct a conceptual map describing which ideas and which relationships between ideas students seem to understand. In fact, you might try giving students a list of words representing the major ideas in the course after you complete Course Planning Step 2.7. You could then ask the students to try to complete Course Planning Step 2.8. While the students talk you through their maps by explaining the relationship between each pair of connected words, you develop a stronger sense of their understandings, misconceptions, and gaps in knowledge about the subject matter. As a result, you are in a better position to decide what aspects of the course need to be added, omitted, delayed, and/or emphasized.

Course Planning Step 2.14   Revise your course outline and ILOs in light of what you have learned about your students' existing knowledge.

MULTIPLE INTELLIGENCES

In his theory of multiple intelligences, Gardner (1983, 1993) maintains that people have (at least) eight different intelligences:

1. *Logical–mathematical:* Sensitivity to, and capacity to discern logical or numerical patterns; ability to handle long chains of reasoning.

2. *Linguistic:* Sensitivity to the sounds, meanings, and rhythms of words; sensitivity to the different functions of language.

3. *Musical:* Abilities to produce and appreciate rhythm, pitch, and timbre; appreciation of the forms of musical expressiveness.

4. *Spatial:* Capacity to perceive the visual–spatial world accurately and to perform transformations on one's initial perceptions.

5. *Bodily–kinesthetic:* Ability to control one's body movements and to handle objects skillfully.

6. *Interpersonal:* Capacities to discern and respond appropriately to the moods, temperaments, motivations, and desires of other people.

7. *Intrapersonal:* Access to one's own feelings and the ability to discriminate among them and draw on them to guide behavior; knowledge of one's own strengths, weaknesses, desires, and intelligence.

8. *Naturalist:* Abilities to recognize plants and animals, to make distinctions in the natural world, to understand systems and define categories.[2]

Another kind of intelligence, emotional intelligence, has been described by Goleman (1995). Emotional intelligence has to do with our relationships with others, how we understand and respond to our own and others' feelings and emotions. (Emotional intelligence can be thought of as some combination of Gardner's interpersonal and intrapersonal intelligences.) The notion of multiple intelligences has had considerable appeal for educators. Cuban (2004) has examined how the idea of multiple intelligences has affected classrooms. He finds that the major effect has been on educators' beliefs and talk, while very little impact has been felt in classroom practice. Implementation of multiple intelligences theory that has made its way into the classroom is frequently well-intended but misses the mark. Teachers often try to include something for every intelligence in everything they do. Gardner (1998) himself has expressed alarm at the way his theory has been implemented in practice. Among his chief concerns is that multiple intelligences and learning style are viewed and treated as the same thing. A manifestation of this is when teachers add music, or movement, or art activities to their instruction believing that this will ensure appeal to different types of learners, thus giving all students an opportunity to learn. Almost all of the implementation of multiple intelligences theory happens during instruction. If done well and not conflated with learning style, this can be valuable. However, at this point in the course design process it is curriculum and not instructional planning where multiple intelligences comes into play. We believe that having clear intentions for learning that go beyond the linguistic and logical–mathematical will help teachers meaningfully include instruction aimed at developing multiple intelligences. If, in fact, all students have the capacity for a variety of intelligence abilities, we should include learnings that will help develop these capacities. This allows learners who are inclined toward a particular kind of intelligence to thrive and, at the same time, provides opportunities for all children to become intelligent in diverse ways. In considering your intended learning outcomes, we believe

[2]From Gardner, H., & Hatch, T. (1989). "Multiple intelligences go to school." *Educational Researcher, 18*(8), 6.

that it is worthwhile to think about multiple intelligences and whether there are ILOs that will help students develop a range of intelligences. You need not add intended learnings for each and every type of intelligence. Instead, you should consider your course and think about whether there is an opportunity and a good fit for learnings that emphasize (any of) these intelligences. These ILOs will guide subsequent planning in ways that will ensure that various modes of thinking and acting are integral to what is at stake in the course or unit and are not just thrown into the instructional mix. For example:

- A unit on colonial history could include examples of early music; students might even learn to make and play Shaker instruments.
- Almost all units can employ tools and measurement devices that require skillful motor control.
- Many units can use visual art, both receptively and expressively, to expand on topics or ideas already included.

By explicitly including learnings that have to do with group processes and cooperation, students can increase their interpersonal, intrapersonal, and emotional abilities.

Course Planning Step 2.15   Consider your course in light of multiple intelligences theory. Revise your ILOs to include appropriate cognitions, affects, and/or cognitive skills that tap into a variety of intelligences.

Entry-Level Skills

Much of the previous discussion about preconceptions is also applicable to skills students bring to courses (their "entry-level" skills). Students base their approach to the learning of new skills on their current repertoire of skills. This fact suggests a view of students' current skills both as obstacles to learning (things to unlearn) and as foundations of new learning. Giving students tasks to perform and carefully observing their performance is the best means for diagnosing the skills they have, and thus for determining the starting point of the course. (See Barell, 1991; Eby, 1992; Kemp, 1985.)

The flowcharts developed in Course Planning Step 2.12 provide one basis for this diagnosis. You can use these flowcharts to identify which of the subskills students can and cannot perform, which ones need some polishing, and which ones are performed incorrectly. As in the case of preconceptions, this diagnosis provides an informed basis for reexamining the course outline and ILOs.

Course Planning Step 2.16   Revise your course outline and ILOs in light of what you have learned about your students' entry-level skills.

You now have a course outline, a list of ILOs, a set of central questions, one or more flowcharts, and one or more conceptual maps that, taken together, represent the skills and understandings to be acquired by students in your course. These lists and charts represent what you intend the students to learn and will be the foundation for a large part of subsequent course planning. They will influence the selection of materials, the design of teaching strategies, the development of evaluation techniques, and even the actual process of instruction. While there will be many opportunities to revise and edit them, it should now be clear how crucial they are to the process of course planning.

Course Planning 2.17   Look over your ILOs and think carefully about them. Review the process by which you developed them. Make any changes you think are appropriate at this time.

RELATED MATERIAL

This chapter completes the initial phase of selecting and clarifying statements of intended learning outcomes. The criterion of clarity for this phase is whether or not the ILO statement communicates clearly to you, the planner. The second phase of this process is the subject of Chapter 4, where a great deal more attention is given to the clarification of ILO statements. The criterion of clarity in Chapter 4 is whether or not the ILO statement communicates clearly to other planners, to teachers, and to students.

Chapter 8 shows how to translate each type of ILO into behavioral indicators that can be used to determine if the course's intended learning outcomes have actually been achieved. One criterion for an adequate behavioral indicator of an ILO is whether or not it is observable.

But before proceeding further with course planning on the basis of the ILOs you have produced so far, Chapter 3 asks you to give some thought to justifying these ILOs, thus giving your course an overall purpose.

ANSWERS TO EXERCISES

Answers to Exercise 2.1

1. *Creative Cooking*
   the student knows what a frying pan is for
   ability to test cake to see if done
   how to bake bread
   knowledge of menu planning
   manual cooking skills: kneading, sautéing, flipping crepes, stir-frying
   how to plan before you cook
   safe use of knives

2. *English Grammar and Composition*

    correct punctuation

    recognizes sentence fragments

    appreciates own good writing

    uses commas with nonrestrictive relative clauses

    avoids run-on sentences

    doesn't use dialectical forms in formal writing

3. *Social Studies*

    knowledge of what constitutes an institution

    enlightened self-interest in relationship to society

    recognizes institutional interests

4. *American History—The Post-Revolutionary Period*

    knows significance of the dates: 1776, 1803, 1812

    understands the causes of the War of 1812

    can describe the attack against Tripoli

    can describe why Hamilton accepted a duel with Burr

    knows the origin of the national anthem

Answers to Exercise 2.2

1. *Creative Cooking*

    recognizes and names types of kitchen tools

    believes that cooking is not a specifically female task

    knows how to prepare desserts

    knows how to prepare meats

    understands the importance of vegetable protein

2. *English Grammar and Composition*

    distinguishes between complex and compound sentences

    recognizes and names parts of speech in a sentence

    carefully chooses words when writing

3. *Social Studies*

    knows that institutions are self-perpetuating

    understands how cooperatives operate

    recognizes that media are used by social forces

    distinguishes among the types of institutions

    knows how institutions change

4. *American History—The Post-Revolutionary Period*

    understands the roles played by Jefferson, Adams, and Madison in shaping early America

    is familiar with the U.S. Constitution

    explains the economic trends occurring in early America

    understands America's relationship with Britain and France

    comprehends the impact of the Embargo Act of 1807 on trade

REFERENCES

Anderson, T. H. (1979). *Techniques for studying textbook materials in preparation for taking an examination.* Urbana: University of Illinois at Champaign-Urbana, Center for the Study of Reading.

Atwell, N. (1987). *In the middle: Writing, reading and learning with adolescents.* Portsmouth, NH: Heinemann.

Atwell, N. (1991). *Side by side: Essays on teaching to learn.* Portsmouth, NH: Heinemann.

Atwell, N. (1998). *In the middle: New understandings about writing, reading, and learning.* Portsmouth, NH: Boynton/Cook.

Au, Kathryn, H. (1993). *Literacy instruction in multicultural settings.* Fort Worth: Harcourt Brace.

Ball, D. L., & Wilson, S. M. (1996). Integrity in teaching: Recognizing the fusion of the moral and intellectual. *American Educational Research Journal, 33*(1), 155–192.

Barell, J. (1991). *Teaching for thoughtfulness: Classroom strategies to enhance intellectual development.* White Plains, NY: Longman.

Bruner, J. (1986). *Actual minds, possible worlds.* Cambridge, MA: Harvard University Press.

Champagne, A. B., Klopfer, L. E., Solomon, C. A., & Cahn, A. D. (1980). *Interactions of students' knowledge with their comprehension and design of science experiments* (LRDC Publication No. 1980-9). Pittsburgh: University of Pittsburgh, Learning Research and Development Center.

Collins, A. (1977). Processes in acquiring knowledge. In R. C. Anderson, R. J. Spiro, & W. E. Montague (Eds.), *Schooling and the acquisition of knowledge* (pp. 339–363). Hillsdale, NJ: Lawrence Erlbaum Associates.

Cuban, L. (2004). Assessing the 20-year impact of multiple intelligences on schooling. *Teachers College Record, 106*(1), 140–146.

Cummins, J. (1986). Empowering minority students: A framework for intervention. *Harvard Educational Review, 56*(1), 18–36.

Deal, T. E., & Peterson, K. D. (1999). *Shaping school culture: The heart of leadership.* San Francisco, CA: Jossey-Bass.

Driver, R. (1983). *The pupil as scientist?* Milton Keynes, U.K.: The Open University Press.

Eby, J. W. (1992). *Reflective planning, teaching, and evaluation for the elementary school.* New York: Macmillan.

Education Development Center. (1968). *Man: A course of study.* Cambridge, MA: Author.

Egan, K. (1986). *Teaching as story telling.* Chicago: University of Chicago Press.

Egan, K. (1997). *The educated mind: How cognitive tools shape our understanding.* Chicago: University of Chicago Press.

Etheredge, S., Rudnitsky, A., & Freeman, S. (1999). *Teacher's use of story: A cognitive tool for understanding, planning, and teaching.* Presented at annual meeting of the American Educational Research Association, Montreal, Canada.

Eylon, B., & Linn, M. C. (1988). Learning and instruction: An examination of four research perspectives in science education. *Review of Educational Research, 58*(3), 251–301.

Gagne, R. M., Briggs, L. J., & Wager, W. M. (1992). *Principles of instructional design* (4th ed.). Fort Worth, TX: Harcourt, Brace, Jovanovich.

Gardner, H. (1983). *Frames of mind: The theory of multiple intelligences.* New York: Basic Books.

Gardner, H. (1993). *Multiple intelligences: The theory in practice.* New York: Basic Books.

Gardner, H. (1998). Reflections on multiple intelligences: Myths and messages. In A. Woolfolk (Ed.), *Readings in educational psychology* (2nd ed.). Boston: Allyn & Bacon.

Goleman, D. (1995). *Emotional intelligence.* New York: Bantam.

Gowin, D. B. (1970). The structure of knowledge. *Educational Theory, 20*(4), 319–328.

Greeno, J. G. (1976). Cognitive objectives of instruction: Theory of knowledge for solving problems and answering questions. In D. Klahr (Ed.), *Cognition and instruction* (pp. 123–159). Hillsdale, NJ: Lawrence Erlbaum Associates.

Gronlund, N. E. (1970). *Stating behavioral objectives for classroom instruction.* New York: Macmillan.

Jones, B. F., Pierce, J., & Hunter, B. (1988/89). Teaching students to construct graphic representations. *Educational Leadership, 45*(4), 20–25.

Kemp, J. E. (1985). *The instructional design process.* New York: Harper & Row.

Mager, R. F. (1962). *Preparing instructional objectives.* Palo Alto, CA: Fearon.

Novak, J. D., & Gowin, D. B. (1984). *Learning how to learn.* Cambridge, U.K.: Cambridge University Press.

Osborne, R., & Freyberg, P. (1985). *Learning in science: The implications of children's science.* Portsmouth, NH: Heinemann.

Resnick, L. B. (1983). Mathematics and science learning: A new conception. *Science, 220,* 477–478.

Rosen, H. (1986, March). The importance of story. *Language Arts, 63,* 226–237.

Viennot, L. (1979). Spontaneous reasoning in elementary dynamics. *European Journal of Science Education, 1*(2), 205–222.

West, C. K., Farmer, J. A., & Wolff, P. M. (1991). *Instructional design: Implications from cognitive science.* Englewood Cliffs, NJ: Prentice Hall.

Wiggins, G. *Toward a more thought-provoking curriculum,* undated publication from the Coalition of Essential Schools, Brown University, Providence, RI.

Wiggins, G., & McTighe, J. (2001). *Understanding by design.* Upper Saddle River, NJ: Prentice-Hall.

DEVELOPING A COURSE RATIONALE

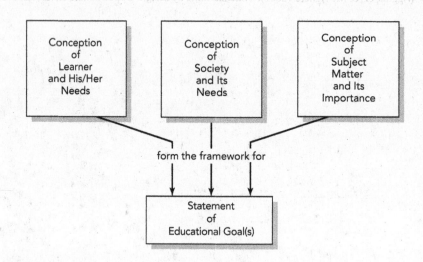

After completing this chapter, you should be able to:

1. Understand the relation between a rationale and a set of ILOs.
   a. Know that a rationale guides curriculum development by providing overall direction.
   b. Know that a rationale serves to justify a set of ILOs.
   c. Know why a particular rationale may justify many different sets of ILOs and a set of ILOs may be justified by many different rationales.

2. Know that a rationale incorporates a set of values within three frames of reference (that is, the learner, the society, and the subject matter), together with a statement of educational goals. This knowledge should include an understanding of how each frame of reference provides distinct bases for justifying the educational goals.

3. Construct a rationale for a given set of ILOs. This rationale should include all component parts.

4. Analyze a statement of the rationale for a course into its component parts, determine whether or not the goals are well stated, and identify the values and assumptions implicit in the statement.

"Why do we have to learn this stuff?" "What good is this going to do me?" "This is a waste of time, I'm never going to use this!" Such expressions, if not frequently voiced by students, are frequently thought by them. And answers all too often are not readily available or are unsatisfactory to both students and teachers. This lack of purpose and justification is also reflected in the conduct of a course. As a teacher, you should always be thoughtful about your work and able to articulate your goals and justify the time and resources spent striving for those goals. This chapter is about justification. It is not just an exercise in rationale writing but a framework for dealing with the "why" questions that could and should be asked about the course.

A course *rationale* is a statement that makes explicit the ideals, values, and educational goals underlying the course. Walker (2003) describes six broad areas of conviction or values that he refers to as ideals. These ideals include academic excellence, social relevance, social change, individual well-being, educational equity, and religious training. The rationale serves the purpose of justifying the learnings that students are to acquire during the course as well as justifying the methods and procedures employed in teaching the course. The rationale also serves the related purpose of guiding the planning of other course components. The values and educational goals expressed in a rationale reflect and underlie the way the course will be taught; they express the emphasis and tone that the teacher will give to the course. Last, the rationale serves as a check on the consistency of the various course components in terms of these values and goals. The values and goals expressed in a rationale are related; that is, goals are desirable only as they reflect certain values of the planner.

VALUES AND ASSUMPTIONS

As any parent of a preschooler knows, the answer to a "why" question can be followed by another "why" question *ad infinitum*. Although an educational goal answers the "why" question for a given set of ILOs, we can always ask the question, "Why these educational goals?" and follow the answer to that question with another "why" question. Our answers to successive "why" questions are framed in terms of more and more basic values and assumptions regarding education and, ultimately, life in general. Rarely do course planners examine these basic values and assumptions; nevertheless, they underlie the course's rationale.

The values and assumptions underlying the rationale concern the role of the individual in society, the societal role of education, the nature and purposes of society and human beings, the relation of the future to the present, the question of what knowledge is most useful, and the purpose for which it should be useful.

QUESTIONS FOR DISCUSSION: VALUES AND ASSUMPTIONS*

1. Individual–Society

   Is education an investment that should pay off to the society, or is its main purpose to increase self-realization? Are there other purposes that education fulfills?

   What is the individual's proper role in society—passive participant, rebel, agent for encouraging rationally directed change, middle-class conformist, rugged individualist, warrior, peaceable resister, employed person, parent, competitor, cooperator?

2. Societal Role of Educational Institutions

   Is it the job of educational institutions to perpetuate present society or to encourage a restructuring of society? If the latter, what direction should the restructuring take?

3. Societal Purposes

   What is it that makes a good society? Are free enterprise and capitalism as we now know them essential to democracy?

   What constitutes progress—technological advances, increased gross national product, improved social conditions, increased knowledge?

4. Present–Future Orientation

   Is education preparation for adulthood or should education help individuals live their present life to the fullest? Is the future predictable? Can it be used as a basis for planning?

5. Gratification of Needs

   Should needs be gratified when they arise or should gratification be delayed?

6. Termination–Recurrence of Education

   Should education terminate or should it recur throughout life as needs arise?

   Should education before adulthood be devoted to the pursuit of individual interests rather than the provision of basic skills? Can the individual afford to wait for these basic skills?

7. Utility of Subject Matter

   Is a subject matter useful if it enables the individual to solve a relatively narrow range of problems and perform a relatively narrow range of skills?

   Is a subject matter useful if it influences the way an individual experiences things, as the arts often do by enriching the individual's imagery?

   Is a subject matter useful if it enables an individual to interpret the world by providing concepts for use in processing information?

   Is a subject matter useful because it is helpful to adults in today's world? because it will probably be of use to the individual in the future? because it will be of use in further learning? because it can be applied in everyday practical situations?

   Which is of more utility—an exposure to and an understanding of popular culture or the classics?

8. General–Specialized Education

   Are liberal studies less or more useful to those secondary school students least likely to pursue them further in college?

   As the level of necessary training increases with an advancing technology, does the level of general education required to profit from training (and probable retraining) increase or decrease?

---

*Adapted from Grobman (1970, pp. 107–108).

These questions are obviously difficult for an individual to answer, let alone for a group of individuals to achieve consensus on. No wonder, then, that value differences and disputes about goals underlie much of the debate about what our educational institutions should teach (see Goodlad, 1984; Pai, 1990; Powell, Farrar, & Cohen, 1986). Although it would be overly ambitious to attempt a conclusive answer to these questions, a careful consideration of the purposes and significance of a particular course at this point in planning can contribute greatly to the coherence and validity of that course.

RATIONALE AND ENTRY POINT IN PLANNING

Logically, the rationale comes first in course planning. This is the often-cited position taken by Ralph Tyler (1950).[1] Nevertheless, other factors may influence what comes first in course planning. The "entry point" (that point at which the actual process of course planning begins) may be determined by any number of considerations. As we mentioned in Chapter 2, motivation to develop a course may come from a mandate or a philosophy. A grant, materials, the availability of an expert, or physical facilities such as a laboratory or special audiovisual equipment may suggest that the course planning process begin. State and national standards are playing an increasingly important role in course plainning. Planners need to consider, "Why these standards?"

In the absence of other compelling factors, the statement of the rationale fits best as a course planning step immediately after the initial thinking about ILOs and before the step in which ILOs are refined. This is true for several reasons. First, anyone planning a course has a notion, however vague or unarticulated, about the overall aims of the course. The task of clearly articulating this rationale is best accomplished after some thought has been given to the particulars of the course. Second, a well-articulated rationale provides a guide to the refining of course ILOs as well as to other steps in the planning process. This guide can serve to help keep the course components consistent and focused. In writing a rationale you will probably make decisions or confirm implied aims. Subtle or even major alterations in your viewpoint may make some ILOs no longer consistent with the rationale. In this case, it will be most appropriate to reconsider the ILOs. In any event, a carefully constructed rationale, one that accurately represents your overall purposes and shows how the ILOs express those purposes, is essential in helping you refine your ILOs.

COMPONENTS OF A COURSE RATIONALE

Every person holds values that express conceptions of people, practices, and institutions, as well as other aspects of that person's world. A course rationale, if it is to be useful and complete, should express a planner's values at least in terms of the learner, the society, and the subject matter. These valuative considerations, expressed in a

---

[1] But note that Tyler (1975) recognizes the need to be flexible with regard to entry point in planning.

rationale, are the "determinants" (Gwynn & Chase, 1969), "sources" (Tyler, 1950; Zais, 1976), "influences" (Tanner & Tanner, 1980), "data-sources" (Goodlad, 1966), "platform" (Walker, 1990), or "criterial sources" (Johnson, 1967, 1977) for the course. Historically, a major curriculum issue has been what values shall underlie the purposes of American education. Proponents for a society-centered, child-centered, or subject-matter-centered curriculum have at times opted for their value position to the exclusion of all others. Our view is that course planners must give careful consideration to all three of these value areas, although a completed rationale might emphasize only one or two of the areas.

The Problem

A rationale begins by presenting the problem or situation that the curriculum is intended to address. Curriculum development arises out of a desire to solve some practical problem. A practical problem (as contrasted with a theoretical problem) "arises when someone identifies conditions that they want to ease or eliminate" (Walker, 1990, p. 162). Formulating the problem that drives your curriculum, or as Vickers (1968) puts it, "appreciating the situation," is not a simple matter. As Walker has argued, "a completely adequate posing of a problem offers a model of the problem, which explains its symptoms, origins and causes, and an interpretation of the problem's significance, which explains why this problem deserves attention and cannot be lived with anymore" (Walker, 1990, p. 171). Clearly, your rationale will not be able to express a complete posing of the problem. However, the more completely and adequately you formulate the problem, the more likely your curriculum will address it.

The Learner

Values regarding the learner express conceptions of what individual learners are like and what they need. Smith, Stanley, and Shores (1957) identified two variations in conceptions of learners. The first one emphasizes education that prepares the individual for achieving maximum social and economic success. The second conception views individual needs and interests in terms of developing a well-balanced person. These two sets of values would probably underlie different sets of educational goals. The debate about "cultural literacy" highlights this issue (see Bloom, 1987; Hirsch, 1987; Ravitch & Finn, 1987).

Expressing a conception of the learner gives you the opportunity to deal with the issue of the individual learner's unique interests, abilities, learning style, and needs. It is important to specify the intended audience for the course and what you assume to be their unique needs and interests. The following examples illustrate conceptions of the learner as expressed in actual course rationales.

Literature, High School: Students may be seen as people working through life, looking for satisfaction, for pleasure, and for value. Every person needs to find beauty and meaning in the world. Beauty and meaning—these elements make the world more enjoyable in good times, more tolerable in bad. The worst situation is seeing life devoid of sense and without aesthetic pleasures. Many studies provide access to beauty and meaning (including science and religion, for example) but the study of literature, because it may be written about anything (including science or religion, for example), affords the student a direct and broad approach. Not every student may find interesting questions or tentative answers in literature, but if a literature course opens that form of art and knowledge (often depreciated in our technological society) to a few students, it is worthwhile. For young people trying to make sense of the world and themselves, reading works of literature may provide some insights. This means that students must have the opportunity to bring their own meanings to the text; a course that depends on the use of secondary sources and simply presents literature as others have read it will distance the works from the students.

Basic Math, Ninth Grade: Basic math is intended to help the individual gain self-confidence through success in math and take pride in the ability to meet or exceed societal standards for performance, including job-related uses. Most important, a knowledge of mathematics increases an individual's versatility in communicating with others, and in understanding the world through observations and through the media.

Views of learning are also a significant component of the course rationale. Issues related to learning include the following: Is the learner active or passive in the learning process? Do learners have preexisting ideas or skills before they begin the course, and what role do these ideas and skills play in the learning process? Do people learn best in competitive, cooperative, or individualistic settings? What is the basis for motivation? Is it curiosity, practical application, extrinsic rewards, or a sense of competence? What role do the learners' age and developmental stage play in the learning process? What your course assumes about learning and, therefore, how it answers these questions will have a profound effect on the rest of your curriculum development efforts.

The Society

The assignment of societal values might involve informed voting, environmental awareness, rapid social change, racial intolerance, uncontrolled technology, and so forth. Values with respect to the society concern conceptions of social responsibilities or societal constraints and ways that the course can help the individual meet these responsibilities or deal with these constraints. The attitudes, knowledge, and skills learned in a course are, from this perspective, those required for participation in the social group.

Societal values vary and may be directed toward socialization, preservation of the social order, or preparation for citizenship. Bilingual and multicultural education are two very important societal values having significant effects on the curriculum (see Ambert & Menendez, 1985; Banks, 1988). Occupational or vocational preparation is a societal value when implemented as a means to supply the workforce with the skilled people needed by society at any particular time. Conceptions of society also include those views that express the need for a restructured social order or the "destructuring" of present institutional arrangements. Whatever conception of society is implied by your course, it should be articulated in the course rationale. It should make clear your explanation as to why the course goals are of value to society. The following examples are illustrative of conceptions of society as expressed in actual course rationales.

Indian Music, High School: The United States is a young nation. Speed and practicality are its watchwords. There is no time for waiting. Instant tea, instant success, instant art, instant culture, instant salvation . . . these are the hallmarks of life here. The stress is more on "reaching outness," and "outgoingness" than on introspection or self-knowledge. A dash of orientalism through the music of India, if made available to the young, may inject a badly needed counterinfluence to the speed of life here.

English for Speakers of Nonstandard English, High School: If these symptoms (reading problems) do not have a pathological cause, perhaps the problem is social in nature. The job situation is one example that points to this possibility. Studies have demonstrated a high correlation between reading failure and supposed "speech irregularities," especially extraordinary slurring and deletion of consonants. And statistics indicate that candidates for employment who do not speak "standard English" (and, therefore, cannot read "standard English") are shunned by the nation's employers. Clearly, this is a social judgment, since many jobs do not entail reading or writing.

Although most courses serve both individual and societal needs, the distinction between the two is important and may reflect significantly different curricular emphases. For example, an occupational education course may view work or a career primarily as a means to self-sufficiency and self-fulfillment and thus respect individual purposes and lifestyles. However, another occupational education course may view as its primary purpose the supplying of society with workers in the proper number and with the proper qualifications. Such a course may attempt to produce an "organization man" and may derive its curriculum solely from labor data and task analyses. Some courses (for example, literature and art) may aim exclusively at self-fulfillment, with society receiving only the indirect benefits attributable to being populated by fulfilled individuals. Other courses (for example, social studies) may aim solely at "good citizenship," with the individual receiving only those benefits that all citizens gain from living in a stable or progressive society. Whatever the emphasis, the rationale should clearly indicate the planner's values with respect to the individual learner and to the society in which the learner lives.

The Subject Matter

The conception of the subject matter is the third area of values that needs explication in a course rationale. Values with respect to subject matter reflect the way you approach a particular subject and your conception of why that subject matter and that approach is significant enough to warrant a course. The rationale may stress the importance of a particular topic or discipline. Ancient history as the vehicle of our cultural heritage, mathematics as a necessary way of ordering the physical world, and literature as a storehouse of humanity's great thoughts are examples of the manner in which a rationale may treat subject matter. The balance of nature in science, the inquiry approach to history, and the Renaissance as the most magnificent period in art are examples of approaches to subject matter that might be justified in the rationale.

A rationale should express the value of the subject matter to its particular audience. Tyler (1950, p. 27) asks, "What can this subject contribute to the education of young people who are not specializing in it?" In part, your answer to this question will express the value of the subject matter.

The following examples illustrate conceptions of subject matter expressed in actual course rationales.

Poetry Unit, High School: Poetry is the speech of a man speaking to men, in the words of the poet William Wordsworth. In a sense, at its inception, language itself was poetry. The poet Karl Shapiro states, "Poems are what ideas feel like." And in this light, every word at its birth is a new flash of poetry by which an individual sees a thing in a new way. Thus, poetry has always been a method of discovery as well as a way of knowing. What we seek to know through poetry is the world and ourselves, perhaps mainly ourselves.

Filmmaking, High School: This course attempts to introduce the language of film in much the same way that a parent might introduce English to a child; the course focuses on the problem of getting the student to speak. Thus, the course is more interested in helping students *express* themselves adequately through film than it is, say, in filling their heads with notions of proper cinematic diction or syntax. Just as a parent might steer a child away from obviously incoherent phraseology, this course will attempt to steer the student away from the use of unintelligible images or image groups.

Thus the rationale should include a description of what the course is about. However, equally important is a description of what the course is *not* about.

Wildflowers Unit, Sixth Grade: This should *not* be considered a course in floral biology or botany. The children will be studying wildflowers as organisms—not the flower as the reproductive part of a plant. Therefore, parts of a flower, pollination, and seed formation are not covered in great detail. Rather, the emphasis is on ecological relationships and wildflowers. (If the other topics are to be covered, the course will have to be expanded considerably.)

As the conceptual map at the beginning of this chapter shows, conceptions of the learner, the society, and the subject matter form the framework for the course's educational goals.

The Educational Goal

Goals found in a course rationale should be educational goals. In considering what distinguishes educational goals from other types of goals, it is useful to consider the distinctions Zais (1976) makes among curriculum aims, goals, and objectives. Aims are described as "life outcomes, targets removed from the school situation to such an extent that their achievement is determinable only in that part of life well after the completion of school" (p. 306). Goals refer to "school outcomes," which are long-range and reflect schooling in general rather than specific levels of school. Objectives are viewed as specific outcomes of classroom instruction. Zais's description of goals and objectives corresponds closely to our notions of educational goals and ILOs, respectively. The goals expressed in a rationale should capsulize the intentions of the course and thus should be more general and inclusive than learning objectives (ILOs); yet they should remain school related, the cumulative effect or result of many learnings. Goals describe anticipated educational results. *Goals are attributes or characteristics of the well-educated person rather than the specific skills or knowledge that constitute that education.* Furthermore, the educational goal stated in the rationale must be consistent with the planner's conception of the learner, the society, and the subject matter.

The following guidelines should help you to state appropriate educational goals:[2]

1. Educational goals should describe the desired product. What units should be offered, what instructional procedures should be used, and what environmental conditions should be maintained to achieve those results should be determined later. This means that a statement of goals should not advocate the "opportunities" to practice this or experience that. It should describe the consequence of such practice and experiences, preferably in general terms of what the students should be like as a result of education.

2. Educational goals should be stated as desirable characteristics attributable to *learning*. Educational institutions may well be expected to achieve certain social goals, such as racial balance, reduction of dropout rate, and nutritional supplementation, but these are not *educational* goals because they are not achievable through learning.

3. If more than one goal is stated, priorities should be indicated. If all goals cannot be fully achieved, which goals should be given preference?

4. The goals should indicate what each *individual* should derive. Let society's benefit be indirect and implicit. Individuals with certain characteristics result

---

[2]Adapted from Johnson (1972, pp. 4–8).

from education. They, not the schools or colleges, will create the good society. Let not the "good citizen" be a stereotype; the properly educated *individual* is the best kind of citizen a democracy can have.

5. The scope of educational goals is an important consideration. Goals should not be so broad that they give purpose and justification to anything and everything and thus mean nothing. A statement such as "a person needs to be well educated" provides no guidance, purpose, or meaningful justification for any set of learnings. On the other hand, goals should not be as narrow as ILOs. A statement such as "a person should know the names of the major world capitals" is too restrictive to serve as a justification; it is more appropriately an ILO. Considering the proper scope for educational goals is a way to make sure that the rationale is more than educational rhetoric. Goodlad (1979, 1994) and Walker and Soltis (1997) provide excellent discussions of the issues involved in formulating goals as well as many examples.

A goal is an expression of educational purpose. As such, the educational goals for your course depend on your view of the problem or situation that your course is intended to address, the subject matter of the course, the intended learners and the learning process, and the relation between the school and society. For example, a view of the subject matter as objective facts contrasts sharply with a view of subject matter as a set of personally constructed meanings. Similarly, a view of learning that assumes information needs only a clear explanation in order for learners to acquire it contrasts with a view that learning is an interpretive process in which learners engage in the light of their preexisting ideas. In the same manner, a view that assumes a role for schools by which they prepare young people to fit into the social order contrasts with a view of schools as preparing young people to change the social order.

The following are examples of brief goal statements extracted from actual course rationales.

This course is designed for adults who are active in local voluntary organizations and is aimed at improving their confidence and skill in dealing with their local mass media.

Specifically, this course will provide good management and personnel for the parts function of the machinery business. Furthermore, this course will provide customers who are more knowledgeable as to what the parts function of a machinery dealership should be, so that they can make intelligent choices as to which dealerships to deal with.

The purpose of this course is not immediately to reject or regard as suspicious everything we read, but to learn how to understand the implications of what we read.

The curriculum hopes to provide parents with the necessary incentives to cultivate advantageous reading environments at home.

THE PLACE OF A RATIONALE IN COURSE DESIGN

Logically a rationale comes first in course design, but other considerations may put it in a different position in the actual planning procedure. In the absence of other compelling factors, the rationale should follow the initial thinking about ILOs (which it serves to justify) and should come before the refinement of ILOs (for which it acts as a background).

A rationale contains a general statement of educational goals. Conceptions of the learner, the society, and the subject matter form the framework within which the planner articulates these goals. The rationale serves as a guide and a check for all later steps in course planning.

A Sample Rationale

The following example is an actual course rationale developed by a teacher in training. It is not perfect, but it does illustrate one approach used in course rationales.

Writing from Experience, A One-Semester Course for College Freshmen

Individuals who know who they are in a deep and secure way will be able to lead lives that are meaningful to themselves and probably useful to other people. Education should encourage the growth of people in this direction of self-knowledge, self-confidence, and self-direction; it should not force people to grow in ways that are twisted or unnatural for them.

One place where many students are "twisted" is in traditional English classes. In reading literature, students are all too often forced to accept, without believing, a more mature and sophisticated interpretation of the work than they ever could have developed on their own, and which they find far-fetched. Their need to look into and explain their own responses to written work in any depth is usually ignored. Students are forced to write about things about which they know very little and sometimes care less; thus they develop the ability to hedge and a sense that writing—at least as far as they are concerned—is a matter of superficialities.

"Writing from Experience" is a course whose purpose is putting students in touch with their own thoughts, feelings, and experiences, and encouraging them to develop their sense of themselves, through writing and through reading other students' work.

Writing is a way of helping people think clearly. Almost all people who use writing regularly and seriously will say that writing helps them clarify their thoughts. Their descriptions of the process differ—some speak of fragmented thoughts on a topic coming together on paper; some of metaphors that suggest new possibilities; some of rough drafts whose ambiguities force writers to rethink what they want to say. In any case, good writers find a real connection between clear writing and clear thinking.

Similar processes take place when writers deal with their feelings as when they deal with their ideas. Since feelings cannot always be laid out as explicitly as ideas, a writer may have to work toward a kind of clarity that is not entirely verbal; he may have to establish a personal symbolism to deal with his feelings, for example, or he might find that he can best communicate by presenting a situation in a new and different form. However he writes about his experience, though, the writer uses writing to discover and develop himself in a way that goes below the surface.

This rationale is taken from a course design produced as a term project by Carol Lamm, Cornell University, 1974.

QUESTIONS FOR DISCUSSION: SAMPLE RATIONALE

1. Having read the rationale, discuss how it conceptualizes the learner, the subject matter, and the society.

2. Is equal emphasis placed on all three considerations? If not, which conception is emphasized?

3. What are the educational goals stated in this rationale? Does it seem to strike a balance between generality without being grandiose or elusive, on the one hand, and specificity without being trivial, on the other?

4. What kind of course does this rationale imply? See if you can describe the ILOs and the instructional plan that might follow from it. How would this course differ from other possible freshman writing courses?

5. What assumptions does the rationale make with respect to the role of the individual in society, the societal role of educational institutions, the nature and purposes of society and of human beings, the relation of the present to the future, the question of what knowledge is of most utility, and the purposes for which it should be useful? What would you like to ask the planner about her course in order to identify these assumptions?

EXERCISE 3.1

Below are four sets of statements, expressions, or words. Each set represents initial thinking about ILOs, and each set is for a different course. Read each list, then consider what a rationale for a course based on each list might include. Formulate for yourself (not necessarily in writing) conceptions of the individual, the society, and the subject matter, as well as goals that may be included in such a rationale. Last, try to justify these courses with another rationale that differs from the first and determine the ways in which the alternative rationale implies a different kind of course.

1. *Child Raising*

rewards	older/younger
discipline	family get-togethers
attention	privacy
sister/brother	fights

everything begins at home
good citizenship
fights between parents
protection from the cold world
overprotection
the spoiled child
permissiveness

imagination
stifling the child
home medical care
"shut up" and "you're really bad"
divorce
child abuse

2. *Team Games*

football
practice
good physical well-being
part of a health program
physical coordination
taught by games
a healthy body and a healthy mind
lacrosse
baseball

team games vs. individual sports
    such as swimming and running
praise/cheers
pride
injury
medical attention
teamwork
the need for play as part of growth

3. *Consumer Buying*

bargains
what is a bargain? (It's not a
    bargain unless you need it.)
buy in season
be sure to buy the sales
sensibly
quality vs. quantity
buying on time
guarantees

where can you haggle over the price
waste not—want not
making use of leftovers
our sometimes wasteful economy
returnable bottles
recycling
tools can be an investment
using the library

4. *The Environment*

pollution
food chain
ecology
balance of nature
cows
insects
role of predator
industrial waste
farming in India

the pond
life cycles
human beings in relationship to their
    environment
people should be aware of the consequences
    of their actions on the environment
field trip

RATIONALES FOR ELEMENTARY SCHOOL UNITS

Many people planning elementary units find a complete rationale for each unit unnecessary. The term *rationale* as explained in this chapter is more descriptive of the justification needed for a semester's or full year's worth of planning. For an elementary unit, we suggest that you consider including an "introduction." An introduction should contain the following: (1) educational goals for the unit; (2) explanation of where the unit fits into the overall curriculum, that is, what should precede or follow it and how it fits in with the rest of the year's work; (3) your view of the learners, what they should know going into the unit, and why this content is interesting and appropriate; and (4) comments or suggestions that convey the manner in which the unit should be taught. The introduction is your chance to tell others what you might say to them if they were going to teach your unit. You should certainly use this opportunity to think about your goals and values. You may want to write the introduction to your unit as a final course planning step.

Course Planning Step 3.1   Write a rationale for your course on the basis of your initial ideas and your thoughts about the course's focus. The rationale should clearly state the course's educational goals within the framework of the learner, the society, and the subject matter.

It is easy to get lost in the forest among the trees. One of the dangers in paying too much attention to the components of a rationale is that you will lose sight of the purpose served by a rationale. The components, after all, are mentioned in order to help you develop a clear, cogent, and compelling justification for your curriculum. The questions that follow will help you refocus on the forest now that you have noted all the trees.

QUESTIONS FOR DISCUSSION: COURSE RATIONALE

After reading another person's rationale, use the following questions as a basis for group discussion:

1. Are you convinced by the rationale's formulation of the problem that a curriculum change is worth the bother?

2. Do you have a clear enough idea of what makes this particular curriculum different from current practice?

3. Do you have a clear enough sense of what the curriculum based on this rationale will look like? Each person in the group could try to describe a curriculum based on this rationale. Did the rationale mislead in any significant ways? Do people have misconceptions that the rationale needs to address?

4. Are you convinced that the approach is reasonable? Are there any blind spots or flaws? Does the approach appear to get to the heart of the problem?

Course Planning Step 3.2   Revise your list of ILOs from Chapter 2 in view of your course rationale.

REFERENCES

Ambert, A., & Menendez, S. E. (1985). *Bilingual education: A sourcebook.* New York: Garland.

Banks, J. A. (1988). *Multiethnic education: Theory and practice* (2nd ed.). Boston: Allyn & Bacon.

Bloom, A. (1987). *The closing of the American mind.* New York: Simon & Schuster.

Goodlad, J. I. (1966). *School, curriculum and individual.* Waltham, MA: Blaisdell.

Goodlad, J. I. (1979). *What schools are for.* Phi Delta Kappan Educational Foundation.

Goodlad, J. I. (1984). *A place called school: Prospects for the future.* New York: McGraw-Hill.

Goodlad, J. I. (1994). *Educational renewal: Better teachers, better schools.* San Francisco, CA: Jossey-Bass.

Grobman, H. (1970). *Developmental curriculum projects: Decision points and processes.* Itasca, IL: F. E. Peacock.

Gwynn, J. M., & Chase, J. B. (1969). *Curriculum principles and social trends* (4th ed.). New York: Macmillan.

Hirsch, E. D., Jr. (1987). *Cultural literacy: What every American needs to know.* Boston: Houghton Mifflin.

Johnson, M. (1967). Definitions and models in curriculum theory. *Educational Theory, 17*(2), 127–139.

Johnson, M. (1972). *Stating educational goals: Some issues and a proposal.* (A background paper prepared for the New York State Commission on the Quality, Cost and Financing of Elementary and Secondary Education.) Albany, NY: State University of New York. Mimeographed.

Johnson, M. (1977). *Intentionality in education: A conceptual model of curricular and instructional planning and evaluation.* Albany, NY: Center for Curriculum Research and Services.

Lamm, C. (1974). *Writing from experience.* Unpublished design for a course produced as a term project. Cornell University, Ithaca, NY.

Pai, Y. (1990). *Cultural foundations of education.* Columbus, OH: Merrill.

Powell, A. G., Farrar, E., & Cohen, D. H. (1986). *The shopping mall high school: Winners and losers in the educational marketplace.* Boston: Houghton Mifflin.

Ravitch, D., & Finn, C. E., Jr. (1987). *What do our 17-year-olds know? A report on the first national assessment of history and literature.* New York: Harper & Row.

Smith, B. O., Stanley, W. O., & Shores J. H. (1957). *Fundamentals of curriculum development.* New York: Harcourt, Brace, Jovanovich.

Tanner, D., & Tanner, L. N. (1980). *Curriculum development: Theory into practice* (2nd ed.). New York: Macmillan.

Tyler, R. W. (1950). *Basic principles of curriculum and instruction.* Chicago: University of Chicago Press.

Tyler, R. W. (1975). Specific problems in curriculum development. In J. Schaffarzick and D. Hampson (Eds.), *Strategies for curriculum development* (pp. 17–34). Berkeley: McCutchan.

Vickers, G. (1968). *Value systems and social process.* New York: Basic Books.

Walker, D. (1990). *Fundamentals of curriculum.* New York: Harcourt, Brace, Jovanovich.

Walker, D. F. (2003). *Fundamentals of curriculum: Passion and professionalism.* Mahwah, NJ: Lawrence Erlbaum Associates.

Walker, D., & Soltis, J. F. (1997). *Curriculum and aims* (3rd ed.). New York: Teachers College Press.

Zais, R. S. (1976). *Curriculum: Principles and foundations.* New York: Harper & Row.

REFINING INTENDED LEARNING OUTCOMES

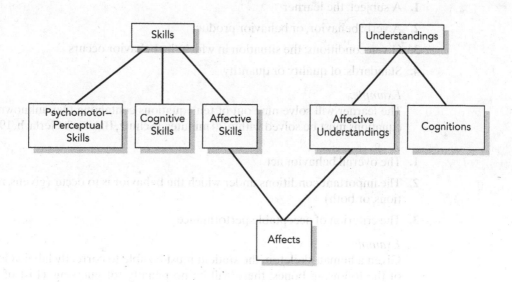

After completing this chapter, you should be able to:

1. Categorize ILOs into four classes: cognitions, cognitive skills, psychomotor–perceptual skills, and affects.

2. Write clear ILO statements for a course.

3. Check a set of categorized ILOs for balance.

4. Decide on the relative priority of each ILO in a set.

Chapter 2 helped you develop a set of intended learning outcomes initially categorized as skills and understandings, with little attention given to ILO format. This chapter presents guidelines for refining statements of ILOs based on your previous work. Your ILOs will become more useful for you, the course planner, and for others associated with the course. The result will be a set of clearly stated ILOs categorized according to the type of learning involved. This refined set of ILOs will be coherent, comprehensive, and consistent with the products of the preceding chapters. The ILOs will be important in later steps of course planning—in organizing the course into units, in selecting general teaching strategies, and in planning an evaluation strategy.

ILO STATEMENTS: FORM AND FUNCTION*

If you were to ask different groups of educators how ILOs should be stated, you would probably get several different answers. Educators with backgrounds in programmed instruction, educational measurement, or vocational education might list characteristics such as the following:

1. A subject: the learner
2. A verb: behavior, or behavior product
3. Given conditions: the situation in which the behavior occurs
4. Standards: of quality or quantity

Example:
The learner will solve nine out of ten equations containing two unknowns. The equations must be solved within 20 minutes. (Schutz, Baker, & Gerlach, 1971)

1. The overall behavior act
2. The important conditions under which the behavior is to occur (givens, restrictions, or both)
3. The criterion of acceptable performance

Example:
Given a human skeleton, the student must be able to correctly label at least 40 of the following bones; there will be no penalty for guessing. (List of bones inserted here.) (Mager, 1962)

1. The situation faced by the pupil
2. The learned capability
3. The object of the performance
4. An action verb
5. Tools and other constraints: how must the performance be carried out

*This discussion is based on Posner and Strike (1975).

Example:
Given instructions to interpret the meaning of Hamlet's soliloquy in simple terms, generate an alternative communication of the soliloquy by writing sentences of simple content. (Gagné & Briggs, 1979)

Differences among these writers are apparent both in terminology and in the precise number of elements considered important. But they agree on at least one point: A well-stated objective must specify the observable behavior that a student would exhibit if the objective was achieved. Because of this emphasis on behavior, we call objectives satisfying this requirement *behavioral objectives* (*performance objectives* is an equivalent phrase).

If, however, you were to present your question on stating ILOs to educators with a primary interest in the humanities, particularly in the arts, or with an allegiance to existentialism, phenomenology, and postmodernism, you might get a hostile response to the idea of using a set of predetermined intended learning outcomes as a basis for planning instruction (see Macdonald, 1965).

Viewed in the context of this broad range of positions, much of the current debate on ILO statements suffers from a fallacy of too few options. It is as though one must be an advocate of either behavioral objectives or antiobjectives. We hope to point the way to an approach that is more sound educationally than either of these two extremes and more consistent with prevailing value systems of teachers. The position we take is that ILOs can be invaluable in curriculum development, so long as we allow the form of ILO statements to fit the subject matter and the specific function we wish the statements to serve.

There appear to be three primary functions that ILOs should serve: (1) they should guide instruction and instructional planning; (2) they should communicate to others (for example, students and the public) what we are using precious time, money, and facilities for; and (3) they should serve as a basis for developing indicators or evidence of success.

Instruction and Instructional Planning

Many educators claim (and we tend to agree) that instructional planning should be based primarily, though not exclusively, on what we want students to learn. They say other criteria, such as interest and personal involvement, are important, but if our teaching is not designed to lead to desirable learning outcomes, we are wasting our students' time and the valuable resources of the community. What do you think about this claim? What would constitute an argument against this claim? Clearly, the view of curriculum would have to be different from the one presented in Chapter 1. (See, for example, Frankena, 1977; Peters, 1977; Schwab, 1978; and Walker, 1990, for discussions about whether or not there is a need for educational goals and objectives.) If you want instructional planning to be based on what students should learn, ILO statements should clearly specify the kind of learning outcomes involved so that appropriate instructional strategies can be designed to accomplish them. In addition, teachers should think about this during instruction, thus influencing their actions and responses in the classroom. As you will see in Chapter 7, the type of learning intended for students influences the kinds of instructional strategies that are preferred.

Communication

It is reasonable to claim that students and other interested parties have a right to know what we hope to achieve when we ask them to cooperate with us and commit themselves to a presumably valuable educational program. It is even likely that if students understand a program's direction, they will learn more easily. Another reason to discuss intended learnings with students is that it will help them develop a language of learning. Students need such a language so that they can think about distinctions between types of learning, such as skills, understandings, and factual knowledge. Helping students acquire a language of learning will enable them to set their own goals and move toward becoming intentional learners (Bereiter & Scardamalia, 1989). To serve this function of communication, ILO statements should express the planner's intentions as unambiguously as possible. Further, these statements should express these intentions clearly to someone who is not already knowledgeable in your subject matter. As you will see later in this chapter, clarity is no simple matter. Clarity usually turns out to be more an ideal than an attainable goal. In many cases, what is perfectly clear to one person is not to someone else.

Planning Evaluation

It is not enough for us to want students to learn important ideas and skills; we must also find out whether or not they are achieving these desirable learning outcomes. If we find a discrepancy between what we intend and what students achieve, then we have a basis for course revision. But we do not want the evaluation tail to wag the educational dog. We do not want to teach in a way that atomizes and perhaps trivializes our ILOs by requiring them to indicate not only what we want learned, but also what sample behaviors we will accept as evidence that we have been successful. In order to help us plan an evaluation, an ILO must be stated only with enough clarity for us to generate from each ILO a set of observable behavioral indicators. Each behavioral indicator points to a piece of evidence that can be used to determine whether an ILO is, or is not, being achieved.

However, there is a serious danger in establishing a set of behavioral indicators of learning. Research indicates that students take seriously work for which they will be held accountable. Some teachers who use behavioral objectives claim to be seeking understanding or other significant outcomes but need indicators in order to determine whether or not the students are "getting it." The problem here is that students quickly discern what teachers are looking for, that is, what "counts." Then the students merely adopt an approach to learning that enables them to perform as expected without attempting to achieve understanding of the subject matter. Students will not strive to understand unless teachers are prepared to hold students accountable for understanding. Perhaps you recall doing well on a test even though you did not really understand the material covered. Moreover, research indicates (Bereiter & Scardamalia, 1989; Doyle, 1983) that teachers all too readily abandon understanding goals for learning goals that are narrower, more behavioral, less abstract, and easier to teach and test for. Understanding and other high-level outcomes can get lost in this shuffle.

ILOs versus Behavioral Objectives

Any behavioral indicator is only evidence of learning (and tentative evidence at that) and should not be confused with the ILO to which it corresponds. In contrast to advocates of behavioral objectives, we believe that an ILO typically need not, and probably should not, be stated in terms of observable behaviors because many ILOs are understandings or unobservable skills. Here we are distinguishing between ILO statements and statements derived from ILOs for data collection. (See Figure 4.1.) These latter statements are more properly termed behavioral evidence or indicators, and their function is to guide our observations. These statements, in contrast to ILOs, must be stated in terms of observable behavior. Therefore, a "behavioral objective" represents a lumping together of two distinct concepts in a curriculum: ILOs or learning objectives (that is, what we want learned) and behavioral evidence (that is, how we will tell if the desired learning has occurred).[1]

From this discussion it should be obvious that there are no hard-and-fast rules for stating ILOs irrespective of audience, subject matter, and the particular approach to the subject matter. What can be claimed is that, by indicating the kind of learning involved and by using words that are not ambiguous, an ILO statement should be expressed clearly. Clarity does not typically require stating ILOs in observable, highly specific terms. If you restrict your options in stating ILOs, for example, by insisting that verbs must all describe observable behaviors, these restrictions will have a serious impact on your curriculum. You may well limit the kinds of ILOs that you will be able to express, thereby narrowing your curriculum or, worse yet, emphasizing trivial aspects of the subject matter while avoiding profound matters. You will also likely need large numbers of ILOs to express your intents.

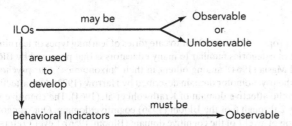

FIGURE 4.1   The relationship between ILOs and behavioral indicators.

[1]As noted in Chapter 1, this represents a major point of departure in the planning approach developed here and that of Wiggins and McTighe (2001).

Remember, course planning is not a strictly linear process but consists of constant revisions and improvements of earlier ideas as your thinking progresses. A final set of clear ILO statements cannot be written once and for all by simply working through this chapter. Instead, you will find that your course ILOs will be improved by a series of successive approximations. Chapter 2 resulted in your first approximation of ILO statements. This chapter should help you through a second and better approximation. Subsequent chapters dealing with instructional and evaluation planning will result in yet more revision. When and if your course is ever taught, still further revision will be required. A cyclical process of course planning is the one most likely to lead to an educationally sound course design.

With this rationale for our approach in mind, let us proceed to refining the ILOs you developed in Chapter 2.

CATEGORIZING ILOS

The first step in refining ILOs is categorizing them further according to the kind of learning involved. This additional categorization will have a significant impact on general teaching strategies (Chapter 7) and evaluation (Chapter 8) because each category entails special considerations for instructional planning and evaluation. Moreover, by classifying ILOs into these categories, gaps and redundancies will become evident, and revising, deleting, and generating new ILOs will become necessary. These are all aspects of the refinement process.

Categorization is an instrumental step in course planning. You may not always categorize ILOs when you plan a course. But the categories we use in this chapter will compel you to think more clearly about what you want learned in your course. It is these conceptual tools that we hope you will take from this chapter.

For the purposes of course planning, four categories of ILOs appear useful;[2] they represent a refinement of the understanding skill categories discussed in Chapter 2. The "skill" category is subdivided into "psychomotor–perceptual skills" (roughly speaking, physical skills), "cognitive skills" (mental skills), and "affective skills." Similarly, the "understanding" category is subdivided into "cognitions" (conceptual knowl-

---

[2] The categorization scheme proposed here is similar to categories of learning types or learning outcomes proposed by others. One set of categories familiar to many educators is that proposed by Bloom (1956), and Krathwohl, Bloom, and Masia (1964), among others, in their "taxonomies." Our psychomotor–perceptual category resembles the psychomotor domain described by Harrow (1972). Our affective category very roughly corresponds to the affective domain of Krathwohl et al. (1964). The cognitive skills in our scheme correspond to levels 2 through 6 of the Bloom (1956) cognitive domain. Our category of cognitions is a substantial expansion of level 1 of the cognitive domain (Bloom, 1956). Level 1 refers to memory of information, while our cognitions encompass the entire range of knowledge acquisition from memory to "deeper" levels of understanding. Gagné (1977) also describes categories of learning types. His "attitudes," "motor skills," "intellectual skills," and "verbal information" roughly correspond to our "affects," "psychomotor–perceptual skills," "cognitive skills," and "cognitions." Gagné's "cognitive strategies" represent a blend of our "cognitions and cognitive skills."

edge) and "affective understandings." Affective understandings and affective skills are then grouped together under the umbrella term "affects." The conceptual map at the beginning of this chapter provides a graphic summary of the relationship between this four-category system and the two-category system used in Chapter 2.

Categorizing Understandings

The ILOs classified as understandings in Chapter 2 are now further categorized as either cognitions or affects.

An important kind of learning in most schools and colleges consists of the ideas (that is, facts, concepts, generalizations) that teachers hope students will learn as a result of schooling. We label this type of knowledge or understanding *cognition*. Cognitions, in contrast to skills, have no directly observable referent. (Nevertheless, as you will see in Chapter 8, observable behaviors such as explaining, listing, comparing, naming, discussing, and the like will have to be used as indirect indicators that cognitions have been achieved.)

Remember that your categorization should include all possible cognitions. Cognitions may be in the form of statements, lists of terms, or conceptual maps like those in Chapter 2.

The following are examples of cognitions:[3]

1. The student should realize that almost all written and oral language affects individual bias to some degree.

2. The student should know that proper timing can affect media coverage and attention.

3. The student should understand that a proper diet is one that contains all the essential nutrients.

4. Set theory.

5. Associative property of addition.

6. Bill of Rights.

7. Minimalist art.

Affect is an umbrella term that could cover a wide range of outcomes. Here we will take a narrow view and treat affects in a manner appropriate for course ILOs. It is likely that underlying most affects is understanding or knowledge, and thus, one

---

[3]A word about examples. Throughout this chapter you will find exercises and examples consisting of ILO statements. These ILOs are meant to elaborate the points made in the discussion. At this point in *Course Design*, the ILOs with which you are working are those you developed in Chapter 2. These ILO statements are rough and were formulated without a great deal of concern as to their wording. For this reason, many of the ILOs used in the examples are worded so that they are similar to the kinds of ILOs with which you will be working. These ILOs, therefore, are not necessarily exemplars of clearly stated ILOs.

major subtype of affective ILO is affective understanding. Affective understandings are distinct from cognitions largely in the knowledge or content area with which they deal. Affective content focuses on the self or the interaction of self with others. ILOs of this type may be expressed with verbs such as *understand, know that,* or others commonly used to indicate cognitions. Whenever the *object* of these verbs reflects self-knowledge, however, they are more appropriately categorized as affects rather than as cognitions. ILOs embodying self as content include developing aspects of a positive self-concept, understanding how behaviors are self-serving, awareness of feelings and attitudes, and knowledge that one is a capable learner. ILOs embodying the interaction of self with others include knowledge or understanding of the factors motivating others' behavior, knowledge that questioning a teacher's authority often leads to conflict, and understanding of how to interact with others to achieve certain goals.

The other major subtype of affective ILO is *affective skill.* Affective skill involves being able to behave in ways that reflect certain attitudes. Counselors have to be able to listen and respond with empathy. Teachers and parents must act with patience when working with children. Members of a school committee must listen tolerantly to complaints by citizens. There are many situations when we must behave in a manner that can be characterized by an affective skill. These skills can often be taught and may, therefore, form a portion of the ILOs for a course.

Some people include aspects of personality as affective ILOs. We disagree. We believe that aspects of personality refer to those traits or attributes that describe the kind of person someone should become, not what the person should learn. Attributes are distinguished from affective skill and understanding in that they are *general* characterizations of people, rather than specific, teachable skills that can be applied at the student's discretion or specific, teachable knowledge of some affective content. For example, being honest in an interview situation is more specific and more teachable than being an honest person. The same could be said about being able to listen empathetically as opposed to being a sensitive person. In these two examples, the first items could be considered affective skills and the second might be viewed as attributes.

There are several reasons for not including attributes as ILOs. First, as we already pointed out, attributes can be modeled by a teacher, but they cannot be taught directly in the same sense that other ILOs can. Instead, students become more studious, honest, empathic, and the like as they develop intellectually and emotionally. Intellectual and emotional development involves both physiological maturation and the personal integration of things learned from teachers, parents, siblings, peers, and others. Even if we ignore the feasibility problems in teaching attributes, there may be serious ethical reasons for not considering attributes as ILOs.

We recommend that any attributes important to the course be incorporated into the rationale as educational goals. In this way their relationship to planning and teaching is more clearly defined. In addition, ethical and value issues are explicitly discussed in a rationale. While this approach doesn't eliminate the issues involved in teaching attributes, it does confront these issues more openly and directly, as a justification for these goals will be stated and thus will be readily available to debate.

The categorization of an ILO as affective has important implications because planning for affects raises issues and presents problems unique to this domain of learning.

The following are examples of affective ILOs:

1. The student should realize that commercial messages affect perceptions and judgments.

2. The student should be able to listen to others and respond with empathy without altering the content of the message.

3. The student should be able to avoid ethnic and racial stereotyping.

4. The student should be able to convey enthusiasm when talking.

5. The student should be able to treat children firmly and with warmth.

Notice that many of these ILOs can be achieved, in part, through cognitive learning. For example, "realizing that commercial messages affect perceptions" can be taught by showing students a variety of real-life situations in which their perceptions have been shaped by commercial messages.

Affective and cognitive ILOs may be conceptually distinct but, frequently, teaching one type of ILO also entails teaching other types. This interrelatedness of cognitive and affective (and, we might add, psychomotor–perceptual) aspects of learning is not surprising when we remember that education involves teaching wholly integrated individuals whose thoughts and feelings accompany almost everything they do.

Categorizing Skills

The ILOs classified as skills in Chapter 2 are now further categorized as either cognitive skills or psychomotor–perceptual skills.[4]

Cognitive skills demonstrate the ability to use or apply cognitions. Learning ideas without acquiring corresponding competencies does not necessarily enable the student to *use* the ideas. That is, cognitions may be prerequisites for performing cognitive skills, but they are not always sufficient. Often it is also necessary to teach students how to *apply* their ideas when analyzing a situation, creating a communication, predicting the occurrence of an event, solving a problem, constructing a logical argument, or comparing similar ideas.

The following are examples of cognitive skill ILOs:

1. The student should be able to recognize the outward signs of presupposition in English.

---

[4]For the sake of simplicity, our previous discussion assumed that *all* your affective ILOs were originally categorized as understandings. We then showed how these ILOs consist of affective understanding and/or affective skill ILOs. We will not discuss affective skill ILOs any further in this section, although, strictly speaking, they are skills.

2. The student should be able to analyze the decisions made by editors in terms of the factors that influence those decisions.

3. The student should be able to develop a logical argument.

4. The student should be able to distinguish descriptive from judgmental statements.

5. The student should be able to analyze and solve work problems involving the use of algebra.

6. The student should be able to evaluate a potential apiary site.

As you will recall, the flowcharts you created in Chapter 2 include either cognitive skills or psychomotor–perceptual skills. *Psychomotor–perceptual skills* encompass skills, abilities, and/or movements that are more observable than any of the other categories. The following kinds of learning are usually included in this category: fundamental and reflexive movements (for example, running, jumping, balance, and posture), perception and perceptual discrimination (for example, physical orientation, bodily awareness, visual tracking, and sound differentiation), physical qualities (for example, endurance, speed, strength, and agility), and complex skilled movements (for example, typing, sawing wood, playing golf, and performing trampoline stunts).

The following are examples of psychomotor–perceptual ILOs:

1. The student should be able to dodge a moving ball.

2. The student should be able to measure the volume of water using a 100-milliliter burette within a tolerance of 1 milliliter.

3. The student should be able to bisect a line with a compass and a straight edge.

4. The student should be able to move across the floor with grace.

5. The student should be able to adjust a carburetor's needle valve.

6. The student should be able to discriminate aurally among the calls of common local bird species.

7. The student should be able to correctly pronounce the *r* in French.

Blends of ILO Categories

Categorization will be useful in later planning steps. Nevertheless, you should not consider learning outcomes as belonging to only one of four discrete categories. More often than not, an ILO represents a "blend" of several categories, rather than belonging to a "pure" category. In fact, it is probably more useful to think of the categories as continuous rather than discrete.

It is difficult to think about a psychomotor–perceptual skill without a cognitive component. The sort of knitting one can do while watching TV comes close to being purely physical, since it requires little, if any, conscious thought. However, dismantling a carburetor or operating a 35-mm camera both have significant cognitive components and thus represent a blend of psychomotor and cognitive skills. Plotting a graph for equations of the type $y = 1/x$ is largely a cognitive skill but with the psychomotor–perceptual component of actually doing the plotting.

It is also difficult to think about a cognitive skill existing without accompanying knowledge (that is, an accompanying cognition). A person can rehearse and memorize information, and thus acquire the cognitive skill of being able to recall the information without knowing or understanding the information in any real sense. However, a cognitive skill, such as recall, is usually accompanied by some degree of comprehension. Being able to solve long-division problems involves knowing some procedure for doing it. Being able to analyze a novel requires substantial knowledge of the genre and literature in general. Cognitive skill ILOs almost always must be accompanied by cognitions to be meaningful. Cognitions can also be taught in a rather "pure" state. A person can be taught to know or understand something without also being taught to use the knowledge in the performance of some skill. While it is likely that once a person knows or understands something, this knowledge will be used in a variety of ways, the point is that none of these uses was intentionally taught.

Our purpose in having you categorize ILOs is not to force every ILO into a "pigeonhole" but to help you consider the kind of learning you are trying to accomplish in your course. Therefore, while you should try to decide if an ILO is properly categorized as a psychomotor–perceptual skill, cognitive skill, cognition, or affect, you need not base your decision on a criterion of "pure" membership. Since our categories are not mutually exclusive but instead continuous, you may want to categorize and label ILOs as being blends or mixtures of more than one category.

Course Planning Step 4.1   Review the ILOs you have categorized as either skills or understandings. Understandings should now be categorized as cognitions or affective understandings. Skills should be categorized as psychomotor–perceptual skills, cognitive skills, or affective skills. If an ILO does not fit neatly into a category, do not hesitate to create an appropriate blend. If a psychomotor skill requires an accompanying cognitive component, write this component in. Similarly, if a cognitive skill requires an accompanying cognition, supply it. Remember, by categorizing ILOs you are making an important decision regarding the kind of learning you want your ILO statements to communicate.

GUIDELINES FOR CLARIFYING ILOs

You should be careful not to go overboard when stating ILOs. It is better to teach a few things well than to compile a long list of ILOs that may detract from a coherent course focus. It is likely that your conceptual map and accompanying statement, and your outline of the course content, taken together, provide an elegant and clear statement of cognitions. It may be superfluous to include a separate statement for each cognition. Similarly, a well-developed flowchart succinctly expresses a set of skills. In general, consider the overall goals of clarity, communication, and usefulness in working through the remainder of this chapter.

In the following guidelines for clarifying ILO statements, each category is discussed separately.

Expressing Cognitions

Congitions—the stuff of understanding—as we have said before, is among the most compex and elusive of ideas. Cognitions involve the incorporation or storage of information in the brain.[5] Describing the precise nature of this information storage—how information is acquired, remembered, and used—is a major task of the interdiscipline of "cognitive science." Most cognitive science descriptions of acquired information stress the interrelatedness, structure, and context of knowledge elements. Knowledge elements themselves vary and can include data about people (for example, their ages, occupations, traits), objects (for example, their size, color, shape), and events (for example, their sequence, time of occurrence), and a variety of more abstract information (for example, context and causes of events, purposes and lifestyles of people). Thus, acquired information varies in its structure and the quality and quantity of component knowledge elements. (See the discussion of conceptual mapping in Chapter 2.) Numerous terms are used to characterize the structure and context of acquired knowledge elements. Examples include *concepts, facts, principles, propositions, generalizations,* and *theories.* Because these terms have no consistent and accepted usage, we will refer to these and similar cognitions by the everyday expression "ideas."

Ideas enable us to reduce the complexity of our environment through the use of abstractions. Abstractions make possible the grouping of objects, people, or events and thus enable us to respond to classes of things rather than to each and every thing that enters our awareness (Bruner, Goodnow, & Austin, 1956). When we acquire knowledge, we learn to make sense of our world, in contrast to the newborn child who perceives only "bloomin' buzzin' confusion" (Bruner, 1960). Ideas constitute our technical vocabulary and are our tools of thought; they are the units with which we think. The more fundamental and generative our ideas, the more potential we have for understanding basic processes (Bruner, 1960; 1966).

Acquiring knowledge enables us to analyze situations, solve problems, and discover relationships among events. While the acquisition of an idea may be necessary for the performance of such tasks, it is rarely sufficient. In addition to acquiring knowledge, we need to learn to use it; for the purposes of this book, such additional

---

[5]Bereiter (2002) finds the mental object approach to understanding problematic. He opts for viewing understanding as an attribute of a person's relationship with the thing to be understood. When the thing to be understood is an idea or set of ideas, it is treated as a "real" thing, what Bereiter calls "conceptual artifacts." We think Bereiter's treatment of understanding is excellent. We also think that the suggestions we offer for expressing cognitions go a long way toward clarifying the "it" (as Bereiter puts it, p. 126) that students are supposed to understand. Understanding is more than a mental representation; the representation is itself a conceptual tool useful for thinking about understanding.

learning is considered cognitive skill rather than cognition. If acquiring an idea is supposed to result in certain capabilities, then those capabilities should also be made explicit as ILOs categorized as cognitive skills.

Ideas can be linked to form other ideas. For example, ideas about investment, ownership, and free market economy may be related to form an idea of capitalism. The space shuttle may become part of a person's idea of aircraft. Sometimes relationships between two or more ideas form statements of ideas that assert something. For example, the ideas of force (simply stated as a push or a pull) and acceleration (the rate of change in an object's velocity) can be combined to form an idea expressed as the following *assertion:* The acceleration of an object is directly related to the force exerted on it. Or the idea of bachelor may be used with the idea of singleness in the following two ideas that are assertions: All bachelors are single. All single persons are bachelors.

Note that the first statement is true and the second statement is false. Ideas that are assertions can be either true or false depending on the veracity of the relationships. This is not the case with all ideas. Many ideas such as aircraft, capitalism, and acceleration may be useful or useless, but they cannot be considered true or false.

Just as ideas differ in their structure, complexity, and truth value, they also frequently differ in the ways in which they are best taught. Some ideas are best taught through typical examples, through definitions (note the definitions of force and acceleration given above), and by showing the relationships between ideas (as in a map). Other ideas (particularly those that are assertions) are taught through argumentation, experimentation, or, more generally, through convincing presentations of reasonable evidence (as in a geometric proof or a set of empirically derived data).

Learning the meaning of an idea that is an assertion also entails learning the ideas inherent in it. For example, learning that force equals mass times acceleration consists of learning what force, mass, and acceleration mean and learning the ideas of mathematical equality and multiplication. A teacher cannot reasonably expect students to learn the meaning of an assertion if the students do not know the component ideas.

Just as assertions can be considered as the relation of one set of ideas to another, assertions can also be linked, making the structure of the acquired information increasingly interrelated. At some level, this information begins to characterize our general thought in a certain area. We refer to ideas structured in this way as a *conception.* The origin of species can be considered from either an evolutionist or a creationist conception. In either case, a conception will influence how new information is interpreted and what new information is important. A pond observed by a biologist and by an elementary school child could lead to very different interpretations and even different observations. A child may have a conception of a pond as a place where frogs and other interesting creatures live. An artist may see a pond in terms of the interplay of light and shadow in the subtle shadings of reflection and shoreline vegetation. A biologist's conception could be dominated by energy transfer and ecological ideas. As a result, the biologist may observe the particular network of related organisms in a pond environment, the artist may observe a perspective and location for a landscape, and the child may observe the hiding place of a large bullfrog.

Any set of terms for describing acquired knowledge is actually a set of rough labels referring to the depth, structure, extent, and complexity of the acquired knowledge. Expressing cognitions clearly is difficult; we recommend several ways of expressing cognitions in order to achieve clarity. One way is to construct a conceptual map for the entire course, as well as for each unit. The maps should contain all the major ideas to be learned in the course. Relationships among ideas that correspond to assertions can be numbered. For an excellent and comprehensive treatment of conceptual maps and their construction, see Novak (1998). A fine example of the use of conceptual maps to express big ideas and their interrelationships can be found in the *Atlas of Scientific Literacy* (AAAS, 2000). Two examples of the use of conceptual maps with lists of numbered assertions follow.

Our Federal Government, Sixth-Grade Unit

1. The purpose of the federal government is to serve and protect its citizens.
2. The Constitution of the United States describes the rights of citizens and the structure and functions of the government.
3. The government has three branches—executive, legislative, and judicial.
4. The legislative branch enacts laws, the executive branch enforces laws, and the judicial branch interprets the Constitution.
5. The three branches are balanced; each checks the others' power, so that no single branch becomes too powerful.
6. Citizens influence government by electing representatives to the legislature and by participating in the election of the president (executive).

(See Figure 4.2.)

Energy, Eighth-Grade Unit

DEFINITIONS

Energy The capacity to do work; the property of a system that diminishes when work is done to another system.

Work A transference of energy equal to the product of force times the distance through which the force acts.

Fossil fuel Combustible matter composed of organic compounds from the remains of living organisms, usually plants.

Solar power Technology that uses the sun's energy directly to do work.

ASSERTIONS

1. The earth's energy comes from two major sources—either from substances on earth (nuclear energy) or from the sun.
2. The sun's energy is used by plants directly. Others use the sun's energy indirectly by using plants or a plant product as fuel.
3. Living things use energy for growth and the maintenance of life. People use energy to do work.

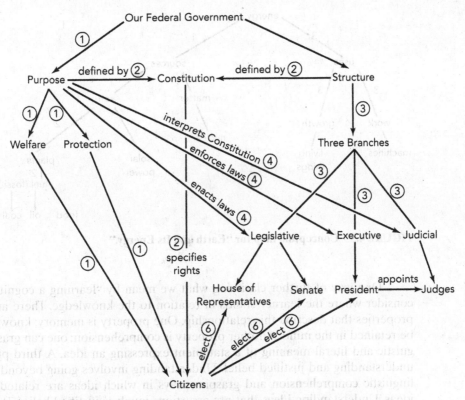

FIGURE 4.2   Conceptual map for "Our Federal Government."

Figure 4.3 on page 108 is a map of a junior high school science unit about how and from where earth derives its energy, and how this energy is used. (The map is incomplete.) Each term that signifies an important idea is listed and accompanied by a careful, clear, and concise definition. (If formal definition is not possible, the meanings of the terms can be explored using examples to help clarify them.) Ideas that are assertions desired as course ILOs are also represented on the conceptual map. Other examples can be found in the sample course designs presented in Appendixes A, B, C, and D.

A *conception,* as stated earlier, is more than the sum of the ideas that compose it. A conception constitutes a way of looking at the world. It roughly corresponds to a person's theory or belief system regarding some set of phenomena (for example, a conservationist's view of offshore oil exploration). Entire conceptual maps, or, in some cases, major aspects of the maps, will serve as representations of conceptions. Characterization of one's thinking by a conception is, in part, a result of acquiring considerable knowledge. If such a conception is a desired result of the course, it should be reflected in the map. In addition, the conception might be described in the rationale as an educational goal.

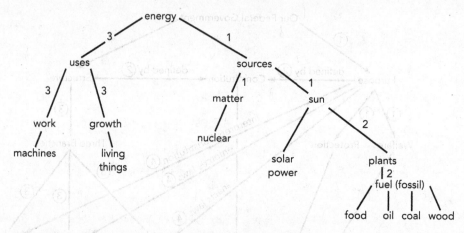

FIGURE 4.3   Conceptual map for "Earth and Its Energy."

One way of further clarifying what we mean by "learning a cognition" is to consider where the learner stands in relation to the knowledge. There are several properties that describe this relationship. One property is memory; knowledge can be retained in the mind. Another property is comprehension; one can grasp the linguistic and literal meaning of a statement expressing an idea. A third property is understanding and justified belief. Understanding involves going beyond literal or linguistic comprehension and grasping ways in which ideas are related to other ideas. Understanding ideas that are assertions involves justified belief. By justified belief we mean acceptance of an assertion as true based on good reasons. Each of these properties implies a different kind of learning and suggests a distinct instructional strategy and evaluation technique. Any particular cognition might embody one or more of these three properties. Note that being able to use knowledge to solve problems, interpret data or situations, generate questions, and critique a work of art are cognitive skill ILOs. Notice too that such ILOs are good illustrations of cognitive skills that must be accompanied by cognitions.

It is often wise to supplement a course's cognitions with explanations of their meaning, stipulating which of the three properties applies to each cognition. It is crucial for the planner not to shy away from ILOs just because clarity is difficult to achieve. Such a tendency can only harm the course by limiting its scope and perhaps rendering it trivial.

Finally, the use of the course or unit story, developed in Chapter 2, is an additional means of clarifying the course's cognitions. It is possible that the story as written will serve this purpose. However, it is a good idea to revisit and revise the story in light of subsequent planning that has taken place. Sometimes aspects of the story need elaboration. Some planners have found it useful to supplement the broad course story with several more specific stories. It is possible, likely even, that the story and the conceptual map and explanation are all really "saying the same thing." This is fine. At the same time, some content is better suited to and some planners are more facile with the narrative approach to expressing their course's cognitions. Whether the story needs revision or not, it should play a prominent role in clarifying what you want learned.

Course Planning Step 4.2   Using stories, maps, a list of definitions of major terms, a list of assertions, and statements with supplementary explanations (when needed), express your course's cognitions.

Expressing Affects

Expressing affects in a manner that clearly communicates their meaning to others is not a simple matter. In part, the difficulty arises from the fact that many verbs used in stating affects (particularly verbs for affective understanding, such as *realize, be aware of,* and *appreciate*) have broad and overlapping meanings. Furthermore, the referent for the verb in a particular affective ILO (for example, "the opinions of others") may be clear in your mind even though there are many different ways to use that referent in a clearly stated affective ILO. For example, "to listen tolerantly to the expression of others' opinions that differ from the student's own," "to be able to evaluate one's ability to attend to views that differ from one's own," and "to be able to seek out the opinions of others as a means of personal growth and development" are all different ILOs that have essentially the same referent (the opinion of others). Therefore, the key ingredients of a clearly expressed affective ILO are (a) a carefully chosen verb describing the affect, (b) the identification of the referent (or object) of the verb, and (c) a thorough description of the specific context for the affect. Your rationale or introduction is an ideal place to set the context so that affective ILOs communicate clearly.

How might you improve the clarity of the following ILO by incorporating each of the three ingredients mentioned above?

The students should appreciate others' opinions.

One interpretation of this rather ambiguous ILO is as follows:

The student listens attentively (the verb) to views of others that are different from his or her own (the referent or object of the verb), particularly during discussions on controversial issues (the specific context).

The following illustrate other clearly expressed affective ILOs:

1. The student should understand how he or she responds to a literary work— what in the work and what in himself or herself leads to that response.

2. The student should be able to criticize another student's fiction writing objectively and constructively.

3. The student should view the claims made in TV advertisements with skepticism.

4. The student should know what he or she likes in commercial architecture and why.

Course Planning Step 4.3   Using the guidelines discussed above, review your affective ILOs. Rewrite any affects that need clarification.

Expressing Cognitive Skills

Cognitive skills can often be expressed clearly in a single sentence. The range of verbs that can communicate the kind of behavior intended in a cognitive skill ILO is broad. The following verbs are useful in describing the behavioral aspect of cognitive skills: *define, acquire, identify, recognize, translate, give in own words, illustrate, prepare, represent, interpret, reorder, differentiate, distinguish, draw, explain, demonstrate, estimate, infer, conclude, predict, determine, extend, interpolate, extrapolate, fill in, apply, generalize, relate, choose, separate, organize, use, employ, transfer, restructure, classify, distinguish, detect, identify, clarify, discriminate, assert, categorize, deduce, analyze, simplify, devise, write, tell, produce, constitute, transmit, originate, modify, document, propose, plan, design, specify, develop, combine, organize, synthesize, compute, formulate, judge, argue, validate, assess, decide, compare, contrast, standardize, appraise.*[6]

Some verbs represent "higher order" or more complex cognitive skills than others (see Bloom, 1956). For example, "the ability *to distinguish* a valid from a faulty research design" is not as complex a cognitive skill as "the ability *to design* a valid research study for a particular problem." Likewise, "the ability *to organize* ideas and write an effective piece of expository prose" is a more complex cognitive skill than "the ability *to explain* a piece of expository prose in your own words." It is important in stating cognitive skill ILOs to write them at a level of complexity appropriate for the situation.

Earlier in this chapter we noted that cognitive skills are often complex blends of cognition and skill. In Chapter 2 we discussed cognitive task analysis of skills that results in a flowchart of subskills and component understandings (that is, cognitions). Just as conceptual maps form an important part of clearly stated cognitions, flowcharts form an important part of clearly stated cognitive skills. Statements of "higher order" or complex cognitive skills should be accompanied by a flowchart or list that represents major components of the skill. Keep in mind that you must determine the depth or level of detail that best serves to clearly state your cognitive skill ILO. The following examples illustrate complex cognitive skills stated with the help of a list or flowchart.

---

[6]The guidelines for stating cognitive skills and psychomotor–perceptual skills list some verbs that are descriptive of behaviors often sought in these types of ILOs. You might want to use a thesaurus when searching for a verb that accurately communicates your intention. The appropriateness of any verb used in an ILO depends on that particular ILO. There is nothing inherently "good" about a particular verb.

LIST

1. **The student should be able to design a simple experiment given a hypothesis.**
   a. Identify the variables of the hypothesis.
      (1). Determine which variables are presumed causes (independent) and which are effects (dependent).
   b. Operationalize the variables in measurable terms.
   c. Understand the idea of control and the need to vary variables one at a time (in a way that each variable's influence can be independently determined—thus one at a time or orthogonally).
   d. Form the set of all possible combinations of variables.
   e. Analyze the measured effect of independent variables on dependent variables in order to reach a decision about the hypothesis.

FLOWCHART

2. **The student is able to write a well-constructed narrative. (See Figure 4.4.)**

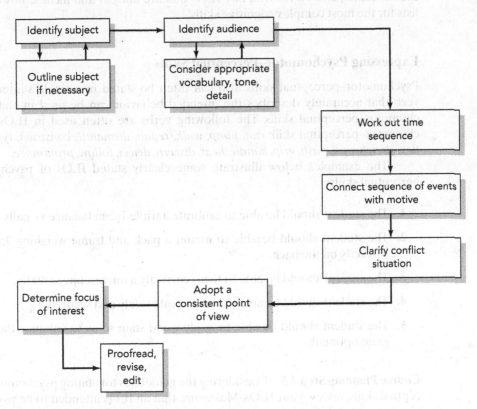

FIGURE 4.4   Procedure for writing a narrative.

Although the cognitive skill ILOs given in the following example consist of subskills and understandings, they are clear enough to guide further planning and thus do not have to be accompanied by a flowchart or list:

1. The student should be able to specify the information needed to calculate the trajectory of an object.

2. The student should be able to draw a Venn diagram illustrating a simple problem of set membership.

3. The student should be able to classify common foods into their appropriate nutritional groups.

4. The student should be able to detect underlying racism or sexism present in commercial messages and advertisements.

Course Planning Step 4.4   Considering the guidelines for stating cognitive skills, review your ILOs. Make sure that all ILOs intended as cognitive skills communicate their meaning clearly. Rewrite any ILOs that are unclear and include flowcharts or lists for the most complex cognitive skills.

Expressing Psychomotor–Perceptual Skills

Psychomotor–perceptual skills also can often be stated in a single sentence. Any verb that accurately describes the intended behavior can be used in stating psychomotor–perceptual skills. The following verbs are often used in ILOs of psychomotor–perceptual skill: *run, jump, walk, repair, dismantle, construct, type, write, flex, stretch, pull, push, grip, handle, hear, discern, detect, follow, pronounce.*

The examples below illustrate some clearly stated ILOs of psychomotor–perceptual skills:

1. The student should be able to calibrate a triple-beam balance visually.

2. The student should be able to mount a pack and frame weighing 75 pounds correctly on the back.

3. The student should be able to focus correctly a microscope at 400×.

4. The student should be able to band a crate safely and securely.

5. The student should be able to apply wood stain so as to enhance the wood's grain optimally.

Course Planning Step 4.5   Considering the guidelines for stating psychomotor–perceptual skills, review your ILOs. Make sure that all ILOs intended to be psychomotor–perceptual skills communicate their meaning clearly. Rewrite any ILOs that are unclear. Add flowcharts as necessary.

PRIORITY OF ILOs

Your list of ILOs may be short (5–10) or lengthy (more than 50). The list may include ILO statements with supplementary explanations (when needed), lists of concepts and assertions, and flowcharts or lists for skills. The list may be a conglomerate of crucial learnings and relatively trivial learnings. If the list is long, it may be wise to eliminate some less important items. Not everything can be taught. Often we accomplish more (in depth) by attempting to cover less (in breadth). Now is the time to consider priorities.

By indicating ILOs of highest priority, the set of ILOs as a whole communicates its meaning more clearly. Guidance for later phases of course planning (instructional planning and evaluation) is provided by specifying which ILOs are of greatest importance to the course and thus should receive greatest emphasis. Priority should be assigned in terms of the course as a whole rather than on the basis of each category of ILO. Your course may be balanced in terms of category or have a cognitive, affective, or psychomotor emphasis. Whatever the emphasis, high-priority ILOs are those cognitions, affects, cognitive skills, and psychomotor–perceptual skills that a student cannot leave the course without learning.

The following guidelines should assist in selecting the ILOs of highest priority in your course:

1. The basic question to consider in selecting high-priority ILOs is: If only a limited number of ILOs can be achieved by the students in your course, which would they be? ILOs thus identified are high-priority ILOs.

2. Consider the goals expressed by your course rationale. Which learnings are absolutely essential to achieving those goals?

3. Consider your ILOs in light of your central question(s). Which ILOs must be achieved to enable a student to answer or deal with the central question(s)?

4. Consider your ILOs in light of your conceptual map and flowchart. What ideas occupy central or high positions on your map? What relationships among which ideas are crucial to understanding the content?

5. Are some ILOs prerequisites for a number of other ILOs, so that they must be mastered early in the course?

6. What would a learner have to achieve for you to consider that learner as having successfully completed your course?

Course Planning Step 4.6 Identify ILOs in your course that are of highest priority based on a reexamination of (a) your course rationale, (b) your central questions, (c) your conceptual map, and (d) your flowchart(s). Place an asterisk next to each high-priority ILO on your list of categorized ILOs. Leave unmarked those ILOs that are important but not of *highest* priority. Now eliminate from your list any ILOs that you consider trivial.

OVERALL BALANCE OF ILOs

The final step in refining ILOs is to examine them in their entirety, focusing on their balance as a whole. Each ILO should be clearly stated by this point.

Balance entails completeness of ILOs as well as consistency with the course rationale. The following questions may be helpful when considering course balance:

1. Do the ILOs fit the rationale? Reread the course rationale and examine the set of ILOs. Are learnings in conflict with the rationale? Are additional learnings necessary to make the course fit the rationale more closely? Does the rationale now need revision?

2. Are there redundancies? This requires looking for ILOs that are essentially restatements of other ILOs. These can be literal repeats or ILOs stated so that they encompass other ILOs.

3. Are there gaps? This requires looking for ILOs that are not included. This may occur in the form of content or behaviors that are omitted.

4. Is there a predominant category? This requires looking at the four categories of ILOs. Are one or more categories missing? Does one category seem overloaded? For example, if someone is to define, describe, explain, and identify something, aren't there also some ideas that person should grasp? If someone is to value a procedure, should the individual understand or be able to do it?

5. Are high-level cognitive skills supported by appropriate cognitions? Conversely, are cognitions accompanied by learnings that make use of the ideas?

You have great freedom in determining the balance of the course. There may be valid reasons for gaps, redundancies, or the predominance of a particular category of ILOs. *These considerations are intended only to assist you in creating the balance you desire.*

Course Planning Step 4.7   Examine your ILOs as a whole, looking for an overall balance. This requires eliminating redundancies and filling in gaps. Check the rationale for consistency and make any necessary revisions.

SUMMARY

The combination of proper category, indication of relative priority, clear description of behavior and content, and supplementary explanation or elaboration when needed should give you a set of ILOs that is clear, coherent, and comprehensive. A person reading your intended learning outcomes should have little difficulty understanding what is supposed to be learned in your course. These ILOs will be used in instructional planning, which, among other things, consists of designing the units of your course. The ILOs should be appropriate to serve this function. That is, each ILO should be teachable and learnable rather than a goal that can be achieved only indirectly (that is, through other learnings). This chapter ends for the time being the curricular aspects of course planning. You have now clearly formulated the "what" and "why" of your course. What remains are instructional considerations (the "how") and evaluation ("Was it successful?"). Naturally, you will return to your ILOs and rationale as further planning lends new insights to your previous work.

QUESTIONS FOR DISCUSSION: INTENDED LEARNING OUTCOMES

1. Are the ILOs clear enough for each of the following:

    a. *Instructional planning.* Are there too many or too few ILOs to be helpful to someone attempting to plan units and lessons for the curriculum? Do the ILOs provide sufficient direction for this planning?

    b. *Communication.* Do the ILOs communicate clearly the important skills and understandings learners are to acquire?

    c. *Evaluation planning.* Do the ILOs provide enough direction for someone wishing to evaluate the curriculum? Remember, your ILOs need not suggest specific evaluation techniques. There may be many possible evaluation approaches appropriate for a particular ILO. The danger in worrying too much about evaluation at this point is that you might not try to teach something that is difficult to evaluate.

2. Are the ILOs consistent with the *rationale*? If not, which element (i.e., the rationale or the ILOs) needs to be adjusted?

3. Critique the ILOs on the basis of their *validity, importance,* and *feasibility.*

    a. A good test of validity is to give your ILOs to subject matter experts to determine if they agree that each ILO represents something that is true, up to date, and/or consistent with accepted practice. For example, you might ask if the facts you are proposing to teach are true, whether the theories are the most current ones available, and whether the skills are accepted by experts as the state of the art.

    b. A good test of importance is to ask experts if they think that you are proposing to teach any trivial ILOs, whether the high-priority ILOs are the most important for people to learn, and whether there are any significant ILOs that you have omitted.

    c. A good test of feasibility is to ask teachers if any of your ILOs are too ambitious or cannot be effectively taught to people at this particular age or with this particular background. Also, you might inquire about the length of time it is likely to take the learners to master each of the ILOs.

    Do not abandon your proposed ILOs just because someone has questioned their validity, importance, or feasibility. You might be able to show that the critic is wrong. But do consider the criticism.

REFERENCES

American Association for the Advancement of Science. (2000). *Atlas of scientific literacy.* Washington, DC: AAAS/Project 2061.

Bereiter, C. (2002). *Education and mind in the knowledge age.* Mahwah, NJ: Lawrence Erlbaum Associates.

Bereiter, C., & Scardamalia, M. (1989). Intentional learning. In L. B. Resnick (Ed.), *Knowing, learning and instruction: Essays in honor of Robert Glaser.* Hillsdale, NJ: Lawrence Erlbaum Associates.

Bloom, B. S. (Ed.) (1956). *Taxonomy of educational objectives, Handbook I: Cognitive domain.* New York: David McKay.

Bruner, J. S. (1960). *The process of education.* New York: Vintage.

Bruner, J. S. (1966). *Toward a theory of instruction.* Cambridge, MA: Harvard University Press.

Bruner, J. S., Goodnow, J. J., & Austin, G. A. (1956). *A study of thinking.* New York: John Wiley.

Doyle, W. (1983). Academic work. *Review of Educational Research, 53*(2), 159–199.

Frankena, W. K. (1977). Educational values and goals: Some dispositions to be fostered. In A. A. Bellack & H. M. Kliebard (Eds.), *Curriculum and evaluation.* Berkeley, CA: McCutchan.

Gagné, R. M. (1977). *The conditions of learning* (3rd ed.). New York: Holt, Rinehart, & Winston.

Gagné, R. M., & Briggs, L. J. (1979). *Principles of instructional design* (2nd ed.). New York: Holt, Rinehart, & Winston.

Harrow, A. J. A. (1972). *Taxonomy of the psychomotor domain: A guide for developing behavioral objectives.* New York: David McKay.

Krathwohl, D. R., Bloom, B. S., & Masia, B. B. (1964). *Taxonomy of educational objectives. Handbook II: Affective domain.* New York: David McKay.

Macdonald, J. B. (1965). Myths about instruction. *Educational Leadership, 22*(8), 613–614.

Mager, R. F. (1962). *Preparing instructional objectives.* Palo Alto, CA: Fearon.

Novak, J. D. (1998). *Learning, creating, and using knowledge: Concept maps as facilitative tools in schools and corporations.* Mahwah, NJ: Lawrence Erlbaum Associates.

Peters, R. (1977). Must an educator have an aim? In A. A. Bellack and H. M. Kliebard (Eds.), *Curriculum and evaluation.* Berkeley, CA: McCutchan.

Posner, G. J., & Strike, K. A. (1975). Ideology versus technology: The bias of behavioral objectives. *Educational technology, 15*(5), 28–34.

Schutz, R. E., Baker, R. L., & Gerlach, V. S. (1971). *Stating educational objectives.* New York: Van Nostrand Reinhold.

Schwab, J. J. (1978). The practical: A language for curriculum. In I. Westbury & N. J. Wilkof (Eds.), *Science, curriculum, and liberal education: Selected essays, Joseph Schwab.* Chicago: University of Chicago Press.

Walker, D. (1990). *Fundamentals of curriculum.* New York: Harcourt Brace Jovanovich.

Wiggins, G., & McTighe, J. (2001). *Understanding by design.* Upper Saddle River, NJ: Prentice-Hall.

CHAPTER FIVE

FORMING UNITS
OF THE COURSE

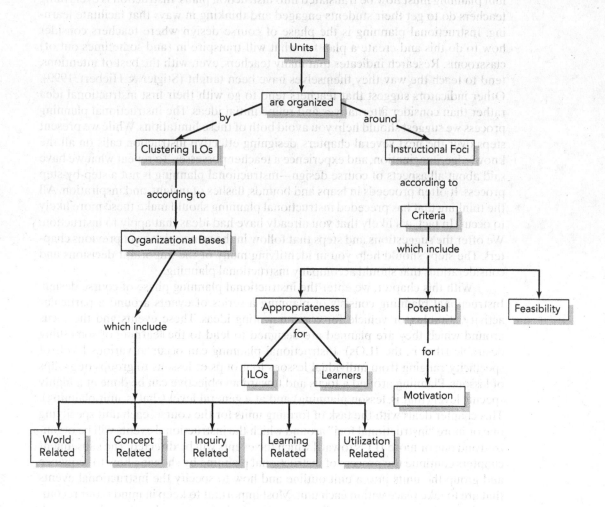

After completing this chapter, you should be able to:

1. Cluster a set of ILOs into coherent units after considering each of the five bases for clustering. This ability assumes an understanding of each of the five bases and how they can be used for clustering ILOs.

2. Design instructional foci for each of a course's units. This ability entails an understanding of four criteria: appropriateness for ILOs, appropriateness for learners' abilities, motivation, and feasibility.

To this point, we have been concerned with developing a set of refined and carefully expressed intended learning outcomes and with explicating educational goals in a course rationale. All the effort and thought that has gone into this curriculum planning must now be translated into instruction plans. Instruction is everything teachers do to get their students engaged and thinking in ways that facilitate learning. Instructional planning is the phase of course design where teachers consider how to do this and create a plan for what will transpire in (and sometimes out of) classrooms. Research indicates that many teachers, even with the best of intentions, tend to teach the way they themselves have been taught (Stigler & Hiebert, 1999). Other indicators suggest that teachers tend to go with their first instructional idea rather than consider alternatives and refine initial ideas. The instructional planning process we suggest should help you avoid both of these limitations. While we present steps over the next several chapters, designing effective instruction calls on all the knowledge, imagination, and experience a teacher possesses. To repeat what we have said about all aspects of course design—instructional planning is not a step-by-step process. It often proceeds in leaps and bounds, flashes of insight, and inspiration. All the thinking that has preceded instructional planning should make these more likely to occur. In fact, it's likely that you already have had ideas that apply to instruction. We offer the suggestions and steps that follow in the same spirit as in previous chapters. The steps should help you in identifying many of the important decisions and considerations that should accompany instructional planning.

With this chapter, we enter the instructional planning phase of course design. Instructional planning consists of planning a series of events around a particular activity, stimulus, or vehicle for communicating ideas. These events and the focus around which they are planned are designed to lead to the learning of something desirable (that is, the ILOs). Instructional planning can occur at various levels of specificity, ranging from individual lessons to groups of lessons to groups of groups of lessons. Planning around a focus and toward an objective can be done at a highly specific level (that is, lesson planning) and at a general level (that is, unit planning). This chapter deals with the task of forming units for the course, each unit specifying one or more "instructional foci" around which the instructional events will be organized and one or more ILOs toward which the events will be directed. The subsequent chapters continue the process of instructional planning by showing how to sequence and group the units into a unit outline and how to specify the instructional events that are to take place within each unit. Most important to keep in mind is our recommendation that elementary teachers organize and sequence what they plan to teach before engaging in daily lesson planning.

Forming the course's units can be approached in two distinct ways: We can cluster the ILOs into coherent groups, with each group then becoming a unit. Alternatively we can design units around an instructional activity (for example, a field trip), stimulus (for example, a case study), vehicle for communicating ideas (for example, a sonnet), or around groups of activities, stimuli, and vehicles for communicating such as themes and problems. Each activity, stimulus, or vehicle for communicating that serves as a means of learning a set of ILOs we will call an *instructional focus*. Whether we form units around clustered ILOs or instructional foci, we are breaking the course into "chunks"; each chunk represents a coherent portion of the course designed to achieve a specified set of ILOs. Since neither approach is appropriate for all courses, we present both approaches to forming units. Then you, as the course planner, can decide which approach (or combination of approaches) is most appropriate for your particular course.

Elementary teachers rarely plan courses. As we have said in Chapter 1, the *unit* is a more appropriate curriculum "chunk" for elementary planning. The next two chapters of *Course Design* deal with course organization and the arrangement of units in particular. If you are planning a unit instead of a course, you will have to make some adjustments so that the guidelines presented are appropriate for your level of planning.

If you are planning an interdisciplinary course or unit, you too will have to make some adjustments as you organize your course. Interdisciplinary courses are often organized around problems, issues, or themes. We believe that many of the course organization suggestions for elementary planning will be helpful for interdisciplinary planning. The principles of course organization will remain the same, but their application will have to be modified. We have incorporated suggestions for these changes at the end of this chapter. **Elementary teachers, those engaged in interdisciplinary planning, and any others planning units instead of courses should read through that section before doing further work.**

Forming internally coherent units is one major step in producing a coherent course design. This built-in coherence increases the likelihood that students will see the interrelationships of course elements and thus see how the elements fit together into a whole.

CLUSTERING ILOs INTO UNITS

The clustering of ILOs into units is a process of creating units from the list of ILOs previously developed. But before presenting guidelines for clustering ILOs, we must deal with some preliminary questions.

Units

How big is a unit? No precise answer, such as "between five and ten ILOs," can be given to this question. Nevertheless, considerations of coherence and scope may help you decide on the unit size for your course.

First, a unit should be a coherent whole. That is, the learnings composing the unit should make some sense together. Upon completion of a unit, the student should know or be able to do some things that are related to each other. Each unit should be given a title. This serves as one check of the coherence of each unit.

Second, each unit should be manageable in scope. Students should be able to view each unit as a coherent set of learnings that relate to one another. Each unit should not be so large as to inhibit discussing it as a whole. For example, a unit on the Civil War is probably more manageable than a unit on American History, 1850–1900. Similarly, a unit on Central Tendency in Statistics is more manageable than a unit on Descriptive Statistics.

Should ILOs from various categories be together in a unit? This is a difficult question to answer unequivocally. It probably makes sense to mix various categories of ILOs (that is, cognitions, cognitive skills, affects, psychomotor–perceptual skills) together in a unit. This is particularly true when the ILOs support one another. But a unit may, at times, consist of just one type of ILO. This can occur when basic ideas or skills need to be provided or a set of ideas or skills is so important that it must stand alone for emphasis.

Can a single ILO be included in more than one unit? Certainly, particularly high-priority ILOs. How many units should you have? As many as you need to cover or include all the ILOs, with repeated ILOs if necessary for emphasis.

As in earlier course planning steps, the guidelines presented here should assist you in making decisions but not make decisions for you. Which ILOs should be clustered to form a unit may sometimes appear obvious and at other times appear almost arbitrary. We recommend that you go through the guidelines and consider the options you have for clustering before deciding which ILOs will compose each of your units.

Bases for Clustering ILOs

There are five major organizational bases for ILOs. ILOs can be organized according to (1) the way the world is (*world-related*), (2) the way ideas are organized (*concept-related*), (3) the way knowledge is generated (*inquiry-related*), (4) the way pupils learn (*learning-related*), and (5) the way learnings are to be utilized in life (*utilization-related*). These five main bases for organizing ILOs are used in this chapter to help you think about clustering ILOs into units. These same bases are used again in the next chapter to help you organize the units into an appropriate sequence.

The world-related basis for clustering groups ILOs in a manner consistent with the temporal, spatial, and physical properties of things as they exist in the world. Some world-related dimensions include: chronology (should ILOs be grouped because they occur or occurred simultaneously or because they all represent causes or effects?); physical complexity (should ILOs be grouped because they deal with objects, processes, or entities alike in their physical characteristics?); and location (should ILOs be grouped because they entail content that is arranged together spatially in the world?). The world-related basis is particularly applicable for ILOs dealing with events, objects, or processes that have identifiable properties.

Following are two examples of ILOs clustered on a world-related basis:

UNIT: THE POND (LOCATION)

Identifies pond-dwelling insects.
Identifies pond-dwelling fish.
Compares types of plant life common in ponds.
Understands the contribution of various forms of pond life to ecological balance.

UNIT: LOW TIDE (CHRONOLOGY)

Understands the effect of the moon on tides.
Understands how some fish are trapped at low tide.
Remembers names of plant and animal life observable at low tide.

The concept-related basis for clustering is a consideration of the conceptual properties of ILOs. Some concept-related dimensions include: logical prerequisites (should ILOs be grouped because the ideas must be learned and understood before later ideas can be understood?) and conceptual similarity or relatedness (should ILOs be grouped because the ideas involved are related in some respect?). Note that the concept-related basis is particularly applicable to cognitions.

When considering clustering ILOs on a concept-related basis, the conceptual maps developed in Chapter 2 should prove helpful. Examination of the conceptual map should enable you to identify related or similar concepts. Some maps may also help you identify ideas that are logically prerequisite to other ideas.

Following are two examples of ILOs clustered on a concept-related basis:

UNIT: THE CIRCLE (PREREQUISITES)

Understands the notion of diameter.
Understands the notion of radius.
Understands the notion of circumference.
Remembers the value of pi.
Can relate the diameter to the circumference of a circle.
Can apply the formula for the area of a circle to various problems.

UNIT: RESPIRATORY SYSTEMS (CONCEPTUAL SIMILARITY)

Understands the mechanics of how people breathe.
Understands the process by which fish extract oxygen from water.
Understands respiration in reptiles.
Understands how seagoing mammals breathe.

The inquiry-related basis for clustering is a consideration of how knowledge is produced. Using this basis for grouping ILOs, the question to consider is: Should ILOs be grouped together because they represent similar phases of inquiry (that is, the process of generating, discovering, or verifying knowledge)?

Following is an example of ILOs clustered on an inquiry-related basis:

UNIT: FACTS ABOUT LIGHT THAT REQUIRE EXPLANATION

Knows that light travels in straight lines.
Knows that light can be reflected.
Knows that light can be absorbed.
Knows that light can be transformed into heat.
Knows that light can be diffracted.
Knows that light can be refracted.

The learning-related basis for clustering is a consideration of how students will learn the ILOs. Some learning-related dimensions include: familiarity (should ILOs be grouped because the learners are familiar with them or should familiarity vary within the clusters?); interest (should ILOs be grouped because they are of equal interest to the students or should relatively more interesting ILOs be grouped with relatively less interesting ones?); and difficulty (should ILOs be grouped because the ease or difficulty with which they can be learned is similar or should the groups have a mix of difficulty levels?). Another dimension of the learning-related basis is empirical prerequisites. An empirical prerequisite as used in reference to ILOs is something a student must learn to do before learning a subsequent ILO; that is to say, skill B cannot be learned unless the student has already mastered skill A. This dimension is particularly appropriate in the areas of psychomotor and cognitive skills. Your flowchart(s) will be particularly relevant here. In general, the learning-related basis is appropriate for any course because how students learn is an important consideration in planning.

Following are two examples of ILOs clustered on a learning-related basis:

UNIT: ENGLISH CLASSES (EASE OF IDENTIFICATION)

Can identify nouns.
Can identify the singular/plural distinction and formation.
Can identify irregular nouns.
Can identify verbs.
Can identify inflectional endings of verbs.
Can identify irregular verbs.

UNIT: BEGINNING SKATING (EMPIRICAL PREREQUISITE AND DIFFICULTY LEVEL)

Ability to start.
Ability to balance standing still and gliding.
Ability to stride.
Ability to stop.
Ability to regain one's feet.
Ability to push off.
Ability to maintain posture.

The utilization-related basis for clustering is a consideration of how the ILOs are to be used in the future by the learner. If there are skills that are part of a procedure and hence will be performed together in the future, you may want them to be grouped into a unit. Here again your flowcharts may be useful. Certain facts or theories may be expected to be used together in solving personal or societal problems, so this is a consideration for clustering. The utilization-related basis for clustering is probably most appropriate in occupational, recreational, or problem-oriented courses because the future use of the ILOs is specific and even predictable; and this future use of the learnings is probably a prime, if not the only, reason for the course.

Following is an example of ILOs clustered on a utilization-related basis:

UNIT: WATER POLLUTION (SOCIETAL PROBLEM)

Understands how industry contributes to pollution.
Understands how municipalities contribute to pollution.
Understands how private citizens contribute to pollution.

Clustering Guidelines

1. When clustering, do not hesitate to include a particular ILO in more than one unit. This may be necessary to emphasize a high-priority ILO or because more than one unit's topic suggests its inclusion.

2. Undoubtedly the five bases for clustering vary in their appropriateness for particular courses. There may be other bases for clustering ILOs. Moreover, any set of ILOs composing a course can be clustered in many ways. What is important here is flexibility; you should at least consider the many alternatives available to you.

3. Consider your course rationale in making clustering decisions: Think about what you have said about your approach to the subject matter, about your conception of the individual learner and the learning process, and about how you see that individual interacting with society. Course planning decisions are interdependent; what you decided about the course's approach should influence present decisions.

4. Keep in mind that any one consideration for clustering is probably inadequate and that the ILOs composing a unit are probably best clustered on several bases simultaneously. Don't hesitate to use a novel approach to unit organization.

Course Planning Step 5.1   Cluster the ILOs of your course into units. You may find it convenient to use code numbers from your list of ILOs so that you do not have to write them over (for example *CS1* refers to the first of your cognitive skills in your list from Chapter 4).

If you experience difficulty in completing Step 5.1 or if you find that the clustering of ILOs seems an inappropriate approach to forming units for your particular course, you may want to try forming units around instructional foci. This alternative approach to forming units is particularly appropriate for those courses in which nearly all the ILOs cut across all or most units. Naturally, if most ILOs apply to many units, clustering the ILOs into units presents serious problems. In such cases, some focal points other than ILOs would have to be designed to produce a set of coherent units. The section that follows presents such an approach. You should read this section whether or not you use this approach to forming units; eventually you will have to select instructional focal points in order to plan a teaching strategy for each of your units.

FORMING UNITS AROUND INSTRUCTIONAL FOCI

Clustering ILOs into units is a useful approach in constructing units for most courses. Nevertheless, many planners have difficulty thinking about units without first considering their teaching strategies.

Instead of forming units around clusters of ILOs, you can design units around themes and problems; around instructional activities such as projects, debates, field trips, papers, and experiments; around stimuli for thinking such as case studies and photographs; or around vehicles for communicating what we know or feel such as books or poems. Such themes, problems, activities, stimuli, and vehicles for communicating are *instructional foci;* they serve as focal points for learning and lend coherence to a set of ILOs.

Chapter 7 shows how an instructional focus forms the "heart" of a teaching strategy (that is, what teachers and students *do* with the instructional focus). But the point here is that instructional foci may be useful for you to think about as an approach to course organization.

Instructional Foci

The concept of an instructional focus for learning has been most clearly explicated by John Goodlad (1963). Notice that he uses the term *organizing center,* which we will consider equivalent to our term *instructional focus.*

> *The organizing center is a focal point for teaching and learning. It is instructional flesh on curricular bones. The organizing center for learning occupies a segment of time and of space, being intended for identifiable learners in a specific instructional setting. It may consist of a picture to look at, a book to read, an idea to contemplate, an issue to resolve, a place to visit. The organizing center may be useful for a few minutes, hours, days, or even weeks. It may be intended for one person or for hundreds. (p. 94)*

Instructional foci (or organizing centers) are not aims or ends in themselves but are instrumental in nature. For example, "understanding the wave properties of light" could not be considered an instructional focus, while "experiments with shallow, glass-bottomed tanks of water ('ripple tanks')" might well be an instructional focus through which the properties of waves might be observed and understood. In a similar manner, "appreciating the beauty of late Beethoven quartets" couldn't be an instructional focus, though it is a potential ILO; but "a series of performances by the local chamber orchestra" is a good candidate for an instructional focus.

Much attention has been given to "ends," in terms of specified ILOs. Now we turn to the "means" by which these ends are to be accomplished. One caution is appropriate here: It is sometimes difficult to distinguish clearly between means and ends. For example, if one activity in a course is to "type several original business letters," this could clearly be expressed as an ILO, "the student has the ability to type grammatical and correct original business letters" or as an instructional focus, "creating original business letters." It could even be seen as an evaluative device to determine whether or not the above ILO has been accomplished. The temptation in such a situation is to shrug and plead indifference. After all, as long as the student really does type several original business letters, does it matter what we call it? The answer to this is that it isn't just "what we call it," but how we see, understand, and plan the educational process.

Instructional foci (as the term implies) serve as focal points for course-related experiences; ILOs provide direction for those learning experiences. Together they give the structuring of learning experiences coherence and rationality. Thus, while it may not appear consequential to determine what is a means and what is an end, it is important to decide on means and ends and to consider the implications of these decisions for the course as a whole.

In his discussion, Goodlad (1963) specifies several criteria for good instructional foci. First, instructional foci should encourage students to practice the type of behavior desired. In our terms, this would suggest that the instructional focus should put the student in a position to use the psychomotor or perceptual skills to be taught, to use cognitive skills in making genuine choices, and to come to an understanding of content. Next, the instructional focus should encourage the practice of several behaviors simultaneously. This is not only for the sake of economy and efficiency but is also completely consistent with the formation of unit-sized course chunks. It is the function of the instructional focus to help students achieve a coherent set of ILOs within a particular unit.

Goodlad (1963) goes on to specify other criteria. The good instructional focus should support and complement learnings in different areas of instruction. It should be planned with both past and future learning outcomes in mind and should be designed so that all levels of student accomplishment, from the highest to the lowest, are reached and so that a variety of interest and learning styles are accommodated. A good instructional focus has an educational significance of its own. It has intrinsic merit and contributes to a worthwhile learning experience. Whenever possible, literature should be good literature, art and film of recognized worth, and texts of high quality. Finally, Goodlad suggests, a good instructional focus "leads beyond itself to other times, other places, other ideas" (p. 100). We believe that Goodlad's considerations continue to provide an excellent basis for thinking about instructional foci.

One example of an instructional focus that might be used for a course is a field trip to a local historical museum. This might have been chosen to accomplish ILOs such as the following:

The student has a sense of history about the community.

The student recognizes the change in lifestyle accompanying technological change.

The student recognizes certain artifacts as characteristic of the Revolutionary period.

Many of the same ILOs might be appropriate to several other instructional foci, a certain book, for example, or a film. The course would have many more ILOs, and not all would be accomplished by or even related to the field trip to the local historical museum. For example:

The student knows the major causes of the American Revolution.

The student can remember tactics in the major battles of the Revolution.

The student recalls the names of the major military leaders of the Revolution.

It is hard to see how a trip to a local historical museum could be instrumental in accomplishing the above outcomes.

In thinking about instructional foci like this field trip, we might think of unexpected but nonetheless valuable things that could be gained. Perhaps something unusual in the museum will catch the interest of a student strongly enough so that she does independent research on material related to the course. Such an unexpected spinoff is characteristic of good instructional foci. While these things cannot be written into the plan of a course (you certainly can't plan the unexpected!), no course should be so inflexibly formed that it can neither admit nor capitalize on surprises.

Another instructional focus might be a case study of prejudice in a suburb. Discussions of the case study might relate to ILOs concerned with the student respecting his or her own opinions, valuing the opinions of others, and having a high regard for logical and accurate discussion. An instructional focus of this sort, although addressed directly to a body of content (bias, justice, tolerance of others, equality under the law, etc.), can be an indirect means for accomplishing affective understandings.

Selecting Potential Instructional Foci

Which instructional foci you select for each of your units and how you use them will be crucial for your course. Therefore, this step in course planning should receive a great deal of serious thought. First you will be asked to develop a set of potential instructional foci that are interesting, appropriate for your audience, and appropriate for your ILOs. If you already have formed units by clustering ILOs, then the discussion should be placed in the context of selecting instructional foci for units with specified ILOs. If you are still in the process of forming units, then you should consider this discussion in the context of the course as a whole.

In order to stimulate your thinking on instructional foci, the following general considerations may be useful:

1. **a.** How do you want your audience to perceive the unit or units?
   b. What instructional foci will provide for interaction with students that will be exciting? fun? challenging? comfortable?

2. **a.** What emotional climate is desired?
   b. What instructional foci will contribute to group cooperation? competition? self-fulfillment?

3. What energy levels should be developed?
   a. Do you want to provide for variety by shifting from an intense to a more relaxed setting?
   b. Should the pace be fast or slow, or should it vary?
   c. When during the course do you need an interest "grabber"? For example, energy typically drops about two-thirds of the way through a course. Is that the time to try to provide an "engaging experience"? How about something special in the beginning to get the students into the course and again at the end to leave them on an "up" tempo?

In addition to the considerations mentioned above, this is a critical juncture in the planning process at which to consider issues of diversity, learning style, and other factors related to the characteristics of the students. Choice of instructional foci should take into account and, whenever possible, include examples that come from varied cultural, language, ethnic, racial, and gender backgrounds. This is more than a matter of sensitivity. It is directly related to the potential effectiveness of the instructional foci both from the standpoint of the students for whom content is now being "included" and students who get to experience content exhibiting greater diversity. James Banks (1994, 1997) notes that multicultural education goes beyond integrating perspectives, histories, accomplishments, and concerns of non-European people. Banks sees this sort of content integration as only one facet of multicultural education. Others include helping students understand how knowledge is influenced by beliefs, reducing prejudice, creating social structures in schools that support learning for all students, and using teaching methods that reach all students. Clearly, you cannot address all of these considerations by way of instructional foci. To be effective, these elements must make their way into all aspects of the educational process. Including these as part of the considerations that go into the creation and choice of instructional foci will make this goal more attainable.

Course Planning Step 5.2 With these general considerations, together with your ILOs, jot down a list of potential foci for each of your units (if you already have formed units) or for your course as a whole (if you are presently in the process of forming units around instructional foci).

The process of sorting through your *potential* instructional foci and selecting the ones *most appropriate* for each unit is best done by considering your ILOs. Some instructional foci increase the probability for instructional events that foster the achievement of key ILOs. Others do not make such events probable but do make them possible. Still other instructional foci, however interesting, make such events improbable and perhaps impossible.

Selecting the Most Appropriate Foci

In deciding which instructional foci are most appropriate for your units, you should consider four major criteria: appropriateness for the ILOs, appropriateness for the learners' abilities, potential for motivation, and feasibility. The appropriateness for the ILOs will depend on the degree to which an instructional focus provides an opportunity for learners to practice the intended learnings (for ILOs that are skills) or for learners to engage with good examples of the ideas to be learned (for ILOs that are understandings). The appropriateness for the learners' abilities will concern the background understandings and skills necessary for competent use of an instructional focus. The capacity an instructional focus has for motivation will depend on how well it challenges the learners and stimulates their interests. The feasibility of an instructional focus will depend on the availability of resources, their ease of use, and the cost involved.

We cannot prescribe how to make your decisions about what instructional foci to select. Nevertheless, we suggest that you consider your ILOs and then rate each potential instructional focus as 1, 2, or 3 (high to low) on each criterion.

Several examples that illustrate the selection of the most appropriate instructional foci follow. Each of these examples illustrates a different design problem through an actual student-developed project. The first three illustrate the process of selecting instructional foci for as-yet-unformed units. Examples 5.4 and 5.5 illustrate the process of selecting instructional foci for units already formed. As such, these examples should be examined carefully by all planners after they have formed their units by whatever approach has proved most useful.

Example 5.1 In a course entitled "German, Level III,"[1] the ILOs could not be clustered into units. Instead, the planner decided to organize units around themes. Each theme would serve as a vehicle for learning most of the course ILOs. Each unit in turn could be taught through a number of more specific instructional foci. The themes can be considered instructional foci (or categories of specific instructional foci) because they serve as focal points for teaching a set of ILOs. They introduce content into the course that is not represented in ILOs but is used only as a device for accomplishing ILOs. In other words, each theme represents a category of *instrumental content* (that is, content used as a vehicle for learning) rather than a category of *curricular content* (that is, content that is to be learned). For convenience we will call this sort of design element a *thematic instructional focus*.

Within each unit, methods and materials must be selected. Within-unit instructional foci are still necessary. Because Examples 5.4 and 5.5 illustrate the process of selecting instructional foci for units already formed, we will discuss here only the process of selecting thematic instructional foci (that is, units) for this course.

[1]We are indebted for this material to Raquel Thomison, Cornell University, 1977.

TABLE 5.1   Chart for German, Level III

Total Score	Possible Unit Title	ILOs	Ability	Motivation	Feasibility	Comments
			CRITERIA FOR UNIT TOPICS			
6	Politics	1	2	2	3	Complicated subject matter
4**	Religion	1	1	1	2	Important unit on Christmas; appropriate materials might be difficult
6	Industry	1	2	2	2	Stimulating articles difficult to find
4**	Family	1	1	2	1	Partial repetition from Level II
3**	Women	1	1	1	1	Timely topic
3**	Youth	1	1	1	1	Excellent for motivation
3**	School	1	1	1	1	Good opportunity to compare school experience
5	University	2	2	2	1	Less appropriate than topic on school
6	Science	3	1	2	2	Survey in German, Level II
4**	Occupations	1	1	2	1	Good materials available
6	Modern History	2	1	1	2	Too broad
6	German/Austrian Cooking	2	2	1	3	Difficult to find materials; topic included in other units
3**	Free Time	1	1	1	1	Opportunities for cultural comparison
3**	Social Life	1	1	1	1	Opportunities for cultural comparison
4**	Sprache	1	1	2	1	Unifies topics
5	Description of German/Austrian Cities	3	1	1	2	Highlights covered in Level II: is a detailed approach warranted?

*Scale: 1 = Good, 2 = Fair, 3 = Poor
**Indicates a thematic instructional focus rated high enough to be used as a unit.

After some research, the planner was able to list potential themes for her course. See the results in Table 5.1.

Example 5.2   In forming units around instructional foci (IF) the important decision is often not which foci to use (if they are all equally appropriate for the ILOs and learners' abilities, and are equally stimulating and feasible) but how to organize them into coherent units. This situation is typically faced when each focus requires only a brief amount of time.

For example, one planner[2] designed a course to make "readers aware of how authors consciously or unconsciously influence the readers' feelings, moral attitudes, and social values." This course attempted to help pupils "read with discrimination and care in order to understand just what it is a writer is portraying as 'good' or 'bad,' how those values relate to accepted societal values, and how the author's values affect the reader."

This planner decided on the following instructional foci:

Comic books	Magazine articles
Folk songs	Popular songs
Advertisements	Novels
Newspaper articles,	Religious songs
columns, and editorials	Protest poetry
Nursery rhymes	Plays
Fairy tales	Ethnic poetry
Short stories	English and American
Children's stories	"accepted" poetry

Then she organized these foci into the following units:

UNIT 1: OBVIOUS PROPAGANDA TECHNIQUES

IFs: advertisements

UNIT 2: NEWSPAPERS AND OTHER WRITTEN MEDIA

IFs: newspaper articles, columns, and editorials
IFs: magazine articles

UNIT 3: YOUNG PEOPLE'S LITERATURE

IFs: comic books
IFs: children's stories
IFs: nursery rhymes
IFs: fairy tales

UNIT 4: PROSE, FICTION

IFs: novels
IFs: short stories

UNIT 5: POETRY

IFs: popular songs
IFs: folk songs

[2]We are grateful to Margaret Berger for material from her project at Cornell University, 1974.

IFs: religious songs

IFs: ethnic poetry

IFs: protest poetry

IFs: English and American "accepted" poetry

UNIT 6: DRAMA

IFs: plays

Example 5.3 Often in designing units for a course, the decision we face is what *kind* of instructional focus will be the *primary* one around which to form our units. For example, one planner[3] developing a course on nineteenth-century British literature stated the following ILOs (among others):

1. Students will be able to recognize their own feelings, thoughts, and values as they encounter them in their reading of great works of fiction and nonfiction.

2. Students will be able to analyze and organize these familiar feelings, thoughts, and values as they encounter them in great works.

3. Students will be receptive to and will comprehend feelings, thoughts, and values that are unfamiliar to them as they encounter them in great works.

Clearly, this planner is attempting to bring together two sources of content, one from the literature and one from within the student. Since these ILOs could not be clustered into units, this planner considered various ways of forming units around instructional foci. For example, the planner could have organized units around themes such as the following:

The child in society	Class consciousness
Women in society	Humans and their thoughts
The individual in society	Writers and their art

Or the planner could have organized the units around genres:

Prose fiction: Dickens (*Oliver Twist*), Brontë (*Jane Eyre*), Carroll (*Alice in Wonderland*), Butler (*The Way of All Flesh*), Hardy (*Jude the Obscure*), Conrad (*The Secret Sharer*)

Poetry: The Romantics (Wordsworth, Byron, Keats), Tennyson, Browning

Nonfiction: Carlyle (portraits of his contemporaries), Arnold and Mills (essays), Keats (letters)

Secondary sources: texts, histories, biographies

[3]We are indebted for his ideas on this course to Chris Connelly, Cornell University, 1974.

Or units could have been organized around activities:

> Hypothetical problem situations
> Discussions
> Lectures
> Laboratory groups dramatizing passages
> Tutoring sessions

Instead of choosing only one of these three designs, the planner could combine all three designs. For example, the planner could organize units around themes, then around genres within each unit, and then employ the five activities whenever appropriate. This is only one of several possible solutions to the problem. Which solution is best depends on which aspect of the course (that is, themes, genres, activities) the planner wishes to emphasize.

These three examples show that there are many ways of forming units around instructional foci because there are many kinds of instructional foci. There is no single approach appropriate for all courses. All we can recommend is to consider as many alternatives as you can think of and analyze the strengths and weaknesses of each.

Examples 5.4 and 5.5 illustrate the selection of instructional foci for units already formed.

Example 5.4*

UNIT: ECOSYSTEMS

1. The student grasps the concept of an ecosystem and its four subdivisions. (Grasping the concept here involves knowledge of what constitutes an ecosystem and what does not, as well as a knowledge of what phenomena are explained by "ecosystem.")

2. The student understands the interrelationships of the component parts of ecosystem subdivisions. ("Understand" here includes the belief that these subdivisions are related, the knowledge of what counts as evidence for this belief, and an awareness that the subdivisions act as one system.)

3. The student is able to trace the flow of energy through a food chain.

4. The student is able to define habitat and niche and will know how each relates to the other. ("Know how" here involves recognition of what counts as evidence of the relationship between habitat and niche.)

POTENTIAL INSTRUCTIONAL FOCI

Basic Ecology, Buchsbaum
field trip to wetland and climax forest

*The inclusion of ILOs is intended to give you a better feel for the sample unit. The ILOs are not meant to represent a complete unit.

Table 5.2 Selecting Instructional Foci (IF): Ecosystems[*]

	CRITERIA[**]			
Potential IF	*ILOs*	*Ability*	*Motivation*	*Feasibility*
Basic Ecology	1 (high)	2	2	1
Field trip	1	2	1	3 (low)
Terraria	2	1	1	2
SRA film	2	2	2	2
Reading	2	1	3	1
Lecture	1	1	3	1

[*]Using this chart as an aid in evaluating potential instructional foci, the following instructional foci have been selected for this unit: *Basic Ecology* as text; terraria.

[**]Scale: 1 = Good, 2 = Fair, 3 = Poor

> terraria
> SRA film series
> outside reading, in-class reports
> lecture with visuals

These potential foci were then placed on a chart (see Table 5.2) and rated on the criteria.

Example 5.5

UNIT: MANIPULATIONS THROUGH LANGUAGE

1. The student will know that language is a powerful manipulative tool. ("Know that" in this ILO refers to the student believing in the power of language and understanding why language is powerful.)

2. The student will be able to recognize words and phrases that often convey misleading meanings.

3. The student will be able to identify what impression an author wants to make on a reader.

POTENTIAL INSTRUCTIONAL FOCI
> teacher presentation
> newspapers and magazines
> commercials (produced by students)
> commercials (TV)

These potential foci were then charted (see Table 5.3 on page 134) and rated on the criteria.

TABLE 5.3 Selecting Instructional Foci (IF): Language Manipulations*

	CRITERIA**			
Potential IF	ILOs	Ability	Motivation	Feasibility
Teacher presentation	2	2	3	1
Newspapers and magazines	2	1	2	1
Writing commercials	2	2	1–2	2
Viewing commercials	1	2	1–2	3

*Using this chart as an aid in evaluating potential instructional foci, the following instructional focus for this unit has been selected: newspapers and magazines.

**Scale: 1 = Good, 2 = Fair, 3 = Poor

Course Planning Step 5.3   From your list of potential instructional foci, select those that are (a) most appropriate for the ILOs, (b) most appropriate for the learners' abilities, (c) most likely to provide motivation, and (d) most feasible. When considering appropriateness for ILOs, pay particular attention to high-priority ILOs. If you are selecting instructional foci for units already formed, limit yourself to two foci per unit. If you are selecting instructional foci as an approach to forming units, then each instructional focus or coherent group of foci you choose will constitute a unit.

Course Planning Step 5.4   If you are designing each of your units around an instructional focus, list the ILOs appropriate for each unit. That is, key ILOs to each of your units based on what each instructional focus or group of foci (that is, unit) is supposed to accomplish.

TITLING THE UNITS

Providing the title for a unit is very similar to the elementary school exercise of choosing the best heading for a paragraph or title for a story. In the context of course design, titling a unit serves as a check of the coherence of a unit. If a group of ILOs together with a small group of instructional foci cannot be titled, it may be wise to examine them for coherence and make any necessary changes.

Course Planning Step 5.5   Title each of the units of your course.

ORGANIZATION AND SEQUENCE FOR ELEMENTARY UNIT PLANNING

One of the most important benefits of unit planning is that teachers have a "bigger picture" on which to base their decisions and actions. Unit plans form the bridge between the curriculum and daily lesson plans. Daily lesson plans need to be part of a long-term planning effort. Having thought about the unit as a whole, teachers can plan and teach with greater flexibility. Pace is more easily adjusted, "teachable moments" are more readily recognized and taken advantage of, misconceptions are more apparent, and enrichment can be better conceived. Perhaps most importantly, the themes, ideas, or stories underlying a unit can be appropriately emphasized in every lesson.

Most elementary teachers plan *units* rather than *courses*. These units have neither the length nor the scope to make clustering ILOs a useful approach to organization. Elementary instruction typically employs a wider variety of instructional foci and learning activities than secondary instruction does. Compared to secondary and postsecondary teachers, elementary teachers must deal with shorter student attention spans, students who cannot reason formally, and, often, students with fewer areas of common knowledge in their backgrounds. This usually necessitates a more active instructional mode with different foci of shorter duration.

The units are typically organized into subunits. Elementary teachers use a variety of formats to express subunits. (See Dick, Carey, & Carey, 2004, and Meyen, 1981, for examples.) Most include an introduction that briefly describes the emphasis or focus of the subunit and where it fits in the overall unit sequence. Following this section, many teachers list or refer to the intended learnings related to the particular subunit. Typically material or instructional foci are also listed. Last comes a brief description of the general teaching strategy. It is from this description that the specific daily lesson plans are derived. Lesson plans may include questions, discussion starters, all forms of grouping or other instructional arrangements, the specifics of assignments and homework, decisions about timing, and more. As is true of other unit plan components, the subunits are revised and supplemented as they are taught. This is the place for teachers to record what worked particularly well, what needs improvement or replacement, and so forth.

Several examples of subunit plans follow the discussions below of two units—Native Americans and World Geography. These plans include teaching strategies that you will read about in Chapter 7. They are included here to give you some ideas about the shape your plan may take.

The Native American unit has a subunit format quite different from the River unit in Chapter 7. The description and explanation of the sequence comes in a single introductory section. The ILOs for all the subunits are also listed before any instructional strategies are outlined. Excerpts from the introduction and the relevant ILOs are included. The instruction for this subunit consists largely of student research projects. Much of the teaching strategy outlines the skills and procedures that students will need to benefit from this project.

The World Geography unit is designed to carry through the entire fourth-grade year. At times the work on geography is the primary focus of the class's work in all content areas. At other times geography takes a "back burner" position to other aspects of the curriculum. After an introductory subunit, students are introduced to maps and taught some skills that they will use throughout the unit. Subunit I is the introduction to maps and consists of three distinct pieces: mapping the classroom, round earth versus flat maps, and types of maps. Each piece is worked out in considerable detail. In fact, this is a unit that has been taught once, and the teaching strategies presented here reflect the kinds of additions and revisions that come with experience.

Native American Culture

The close connection of the Native Americans' culture to their environment is the underlying concept in this unit. This concept will be built up gradually throughout the unit. The goal is to have a clear understanding of Indian cultural values with respect to nature so that the conflict between the white culture and the Indian cultures can be understood in part in terms of the differences in their cultural values. The beginning point to develop this concept is to understand the basic relationship to the environment that all cultures share. Students need to understand the concept of a culture in general along with understanding that a culture adapts to its environment. All cultures meet basic needs by using the resources of the environment, and so all people share a relationship to nature, since they must meet their basic needs.

The unit moves to a study of three cultural areas. Applying this framework of culture developed through the introductory activities, students study environments across North America and the ways that Indian cultures evolved to meet their needs in these environments. In this part of the unit, they will be learning specific information about the Native American cultural areas. In this way, students will be able to understand values shared by Native Americans while also learning about their diversity. Understanding the Native American attitude toward nature, students have a way of bringing together the information about the different Indian cultures. Without this conceptual background to pull together information, the study of Indian cultures would be only a catalogue of different shelters, clothing, food gathering techniques, and folk tales.

The last part of the unit is about the history of the contact between the Europeans and Indian tribes. The difference between the two cultures' views of man's relationship to nature will be contrasted. It is not the aim of this unit to include a thorough chronology of the history of European and U.S. interaction with the Native Americans. Instead historical events were selected to typify the issues central to the conflict between the Native Americans and European/U.S. settlers. This material uses storytelling and drama to present the conflict between the European and Indian cultures. Listening to stories read aloud is engaging to fourth graders and drama is highly motivating.

Europe and the United States developed increasingly sophisticated ways to control the environment. They were so successful at using natural resources for energy and for manufacturing that after a while they lost sight of their basic connection to nature. This difference and related developments are what accounts for much of the misunderstanding and conflict between the white and Indian cultures.

Activities that involve students experientially with the topic are important for creating a concrete understanding of what Native American cultures were like. The field trip led by a Native American woman at the Skan center in Shelburne, in the beautiful rural countryside, is a central activity for the unit. Students spend time in a small village and in teepees and have the opportunity to experience a little of what it would be like to live in this way. As a group, students discuss how the space would affect how people related to each other. They also listen to stories, sing songs, and handle Indian tools.

In order for students to appreciate the culture and values of Native Americans, they need learning activities that help them understand the Indian perspective. Literature about Native Americans allows students to "live" this perspective. Discussing the underlying themes in Native American myths and stories should be incorporated throughout the unit. There is a danger when studying another culture of having a "museum" perspective, viewing the information about Indian tribes as artifacts to be categorized. Although being able to classify information is a skill that is important for this unit, these activities should be balanced by activities that bring this information to life.

Arrangements will be made so that the art program corresponds to the social studies unit being taught in the classroom. For this reason, there are a few activities involving Indian crafts. These activities add interest and motivation to the unit.

A goal of a social studies unit in general is learning skills for getting information from nonfiction sources and organizing this information. At this age, taking notes is a relatively new experience. The act of writing is still fairly time-consuming and difficult for many students. Through the use of outline maps, or webbing, students will classify information around categories. The students will be reading short pieces and using sources of information such as photographs, speeches, stories, art objects, and slides. (There is an extensive source of Native American art at a local college art library.) It is important to have reading selections at different reading levels, if possible, or the selections could be taped for students to listen to while reading the text. The process of organizing information from a text will be modeled with the class.

The content outline includes a broader range of material than has been included in the unit plans. This information has been included in the outline to show the scope of the topic and other possible topics to include in this unit. For example, the unit could have focused more on ancient Indian cultures to show the evolution of cultures over a long period of time. Another alternative focus would be the Indian tribes of New England.

Although the final area of the unit—current issues for Native Americans—is not developed in this unit plan, it should be included for a thorough coverage of the topic and for closure.

ILOs FOR SUBUNIT 2: NATIVE AMERICAN CULTURAL AREAS

Know that a Native American cultural area is a geographical area in which the environment is fairly similar and the tribes within the area have similar cultures.

Be able to organize and classify information into an outline map.

Describe the environment and know the main tribe names of the cultural areas (Northeast, Southwest, and Plains).

Know information about the culture (food, shelter, clothing, art, and tools).

Know information concerning the lifestyle and community structure (government, decision making, organizations).

Know information about religion and ceremonies of Native American cultural areas.

Describe similarities and differences between the different cultural areas.

Describe the shared values and religious views of Native Americans regarding nature and the environment.

Be able to restate information and ideas in a text in the student's own language.

Be able to use the concept of a culture (i.e., aspects of a culture) to identify and to classify information from texts and other sources.

TEACHING STRATEGY FOR SUBUNIT 2: NATIVE AMERICAN CULTURAL AREAS

Introduce procedure for studying culture areas. Begin with the Northeast, as this is the first group to come in contact with the Europeans and it is the area the students live in.

As a class, study the Northeast cultural area together.

Model the procedure for organizing information into an outline map and displaying this information so it clearly communicates to others.

PROCEDURE

1. Introduce outline web.

   Review categories of a culture. Write each aspect and subcategories on cards. Explain the idea that we want to show how these ideas are related and fit together. Cards include: culture, Northeast, food, shelter, clothing, basic needs, community structure, religion, and so on. Discuss where to place the cards, starting with just a few. Introduce the idea that you can show ideas are related with connecting lines and by writing a phrase to show how they are connected. Students arrange the cards on poster paper and draw lines to show relationships.

   With some cultural aspects, like community structure, ask what these mean in their own words. How would you find out about this? What would you look for? For example, lifestyle would include whether a tribe was nomadic, settled, or warlike.

2. Introduce notetaking.

   Each student has a short section on the Northeast cultural area. The students understand that their purpose for reading is to add information about the Northeast Native American tribes to the class cultural area map. To introduce the notetaking procedure, the teacher reads aloud part of the passage and the students underline when they hear a part that gives information about the culture that they can add to the map. The steps for turning the information read into an outline map are (1) put information into own words; (2) determine what kind of information it is, or what category; (3) add the information to the map.

3. Discuss ways to illustrate the information and whether some information would be easier to understand with a picture, such as a shelter. In small groups, students illustrate information on the map using art materials and natural materials (leaves, grass, twigs) and add to the map.

In addition to reading texts for information, have other sources available—pictures, art objects, tools, slides, stories, and music. To learn about religion and values, use stories and statements by Indian leaders expressing these views. Make a listening center in the room for music, stories, and games using a small tent. Stories, music, and so on could be taped and students could have a text to look at while they are listening. The tent could be decorated by the class to resemble a Southwest *kiva* (used for ceremonies and meetings).

4. Practice reading the map by asking students to describe aspects of the culture and how aspects are related.

5. After this procedure is clear and the research and outline map of the Northeast cultural area is complete, the class is divided into pairs to work on one of two cultural areas, the Plains or the Southwest. The advantage of having many students working on the same information independently is that they can compare different ways to organize information.

The task is divided into steps that the teacher checks before the students go on: (1) Read overview and answer questions (questions to help focus students on the aspects of culture categories, suggesting ways information is related); (2) add information to their map from the section they read; (3) use further materials (pictures, tapes, maps, etc.); (4) find ways to illustrate items on map for final draft using pictures or collages.

Using information on their finished map, students make a diorama, or three-dimensional model, of their cultural area as a way of putting together information about the culture.

World Geography: Subunit I—An Introduction to Maps

The conventions, types, and sources of maps, as well as applications of map skills, will be explored in this introduction. Since this area of study involves a wide range of skills and information with a multitude of possibilities, it is divided into a number of sections or activities, each of which builds on the others. Since map skills and understandings are an integral part of a study of geography, it is appropriate to begin the unit with a fairly in-depth look at maps.

A. MAPPING THE CLASSROOM

This section of the introduction to maps introduces students to a number of essential terms and skills necessary for success in this course. Students will have the opportunity to create their own maps.

Intended Learning Outcomes: 2, 6a, 6c, 6d, 6h, 6j

Terms to Be Presented: directionality, perspective, grid, proportion, scale, cartographer, key

Instructional Foci: paper, pencils, grid (string and tape), chalkboard, fine-line markers, colored pencils

Teaching Strategy: The end product of this series of lessons will be a map of the classroom from a bird's-eye perspective that includes a key and is fairly in proportion. Before instructing students to create such a map, it will be necessary for the teacher to introduce or review a number of concepts and skills. To begin, students will be oriented to the concept of directionality (north, south, east, west). Directionality is discussed and signs with each of the directions are hung on the appropriate walls in the classroom for all students to see.

Next, the idea of a bird's-eye perspective is explored. The teacher will begin by asking if students have ever heard the term *bird's-eye view* and ask if they can explain what it means. The teacher will ask students to imagine themselves flying (northward, for example) above the playground and to explain what they would see. A diagram can be drawn on the chalkboard. The teacher can use the diagram as a teaching point to introduce the need for the depiction of correct proportions and the possibility of including a key. Here, too, the teacher should explain that it is from the bird's-eye perspective that most maps are drawn, and that accurate proportion and the representation of the objects or places seen below are problems with which mapmakers (cartographers) struggle. The teacher should assure students that these are ideas that will be explored in greater detail in the days to come.

The students will then be introduced to the idea of a grid and its purpose in facilitating location and proportion. The teacher can explain and provide examples that demonstrate the idea that grids can be used to create an accurately proportioned, shrunken or enlarged representation of a given picture or field. The teacher, using tape and string, will set up a grid on the classroom floor. Students will then be informed that they will be using this grid to draw a map of the classroom. The teacher will provide each student with a grid on a sheet of paper. This grid has the same number of squares as the grid on the classroom floor. The teacher should explain that this grid is drawn from a bird's-eye perspective as if looking down on the classroom from the ceiling. (The teacher may choose to allow students to draw their own grid, but it may require a considerable amount of time. Perhaps this would be a more appropriate task for older students.)

The teacher will then point out that the two grids are identical except in size. The concept of scale should be introduced here. Students will be asked to label north, south, east, and west on their own grids. (The teacher can model with a grid taped to the chalkboard.) Once this is completed, the teacher will involve the students in an activity. The teacher repeatedly stands in a box on the floor and asks students to point to the corresponding box on their own grids. Students are then asked to find the box in which they would find their own desk. The teacher should also develop, with the students, a procedure for naming a particular location (e.g., B3).

The teacher could then ask students to work in pairs to locate where various objects in the room (teacher's desk, bookshelf, sink, pencil sharpener, clock, etc.) would be found. Here, the teacher should point out the problem students might encounter when drawing the clock or other objects on the wall—they may be positioned above other objects. In addition, he or she should point out the difficulty students might have including the representation of all the desks and chairs. The teacher should emphasize that a key is the solution to these problems. The purpose and ways that keys work should be reviewed.

The teacher will then give instructions as to how the students should go about creating the map of the classroom and set specific expectations for the maps. For example:

1. From a bird's-eye perspective, in pencil and on the grid, students should draw a map that includes everything in the classroom. When this is complete, the map must be checked with the teacher before students move on.

2. Fine-line markers should be used to go over all lines except for the grid.

3. The grid should be erased.

4. Students should make a box for the key.

5. Colored pencils should be used for coloring the map.

6. Students should fill in the key.

7. The end product should be as simple as possible so as to be easily read, and it should be pleasing to the eye.

The teacher will then divide the class and send a pair of students into each box to draw the contents of that box on the grid provided. A predetermined signal will initiate a change in box. The teacher should assure students that details can be completed at a later time if necessary.

Suggested Time: Three to five lessons (45–60 minutes each)

B. ROUND EARTH VERSUS FLAT MAP

In this section of the introduction to maps, students will be exposed to the representation of a spherical earth on a flat field and the difficulties that arise from such a representation. Students will be introduced to a number of projections while the issue of distortion is explored.

Intended Learning Outcomes: 2, 6c, 6d, 6e, 6g, 6h, 6j

Terms to Be Presented: distortion, equator, tropic of Cancer, tropic of Capricorn, latitude, prime meridian, longitude, projection, degrees

Instructional Foci: a globe, a variety of projections (Mercator, Peter's, Interrupted, Robinson's, etc.), an orange

Teaching Strategy: The teacher will attempt to elicit from students observations about the spherical nature of the earth and that our everyday view of the earth can lead us to think it is flat. The teacher should initiate a discussion on the nature of a globe—that it is the same shape and proportion as the earth, only a different scale. The teacher should point out that a globe is the most realistic representation of the earth, but that globes are sometimes awkward to work with, going on to explain that this is the reason we have maps and that maps are really "flattened out" globes. In order to make this idea as concrete as possible, the teacher can peel an orange, without dividing the peel, and flatten the peel. This will also illustrate the distortion that is inherent in the flattening process.

The idea of a grid of the earth can be described through the introduction of the equator, tropics of Cancer and Capricorn, and lines of latitude as the horizontal lines of the grid, while the prime meridian and lines of longitude make up the vertical lines. It should be explained that these imaginary lines that are organized by degrees help us to locate points on the earth and show scale.

With the flattened orange peel in full view of all students, the teacher will display a variety of maps—Peter's projection, Interrupted projection, Mercator projection, and Robinson's projection. The teacher will introduce the term *projection* and discuss the fact that different maps have varying functions and political biases. The teacher will ask students to verbalize any differences they see in the maps displayed. If these are not brought up by the students, the teacher should initiate a discussion of distortion and point out that this is a problem of all maps. Students will be encouraged to find distortions. The teacher will expand on this disscussion, using the "problem" of Greenland as an illustration.

Suggested Time: One lesson (45–60 minutes)

C. TYPES OF MAPS

A study of maps would be incomplete without an examination of different types of maps, each with its own purpose. Although students will primarily be working with political maps throughout the year, other types of maps will be encountered as well. Students will be asked to recognize the different types introduced here and to be able to use the conventions to extract information from each.

Intended Learning Outcomes: 2, 6a, 6h, 6f

Terms to Be Presented: projection, political map, physical map, thematic map

Instructional Foci: chalkboard, overhead transparencies, teacher-made dittos, political map, physical map, thematic map, road map

Teaching Strategy: The teacher will hang four different types of maps on the chalkboard: a political map, a physical map, a thematic map, and a road map. If available, all four of the maps should represent the same geographical area.

Maps of the local region would be ideal, since students would already be familiar with the area.

Before introducing each type of map, the teacher will ask students to comment on some of the differences and/or similarities they notice among the maps. Students will be encouraged to go to the board and point out anything they see as relevant. A list of specific characteristics of each map will be generated and written on the board next to each. The purpose of each map should be explored in detail and the name of each type introduced. The teacher will need to instruct students on how to read the various maps and how to extract information from each. Overhead transparencies and/or dittos of each map type should be used to reinforce and test students' understanding.

The teacher should go on to explain that political maps will be the most widely used maps in this study of geography. Also, he or she should explain that physical and thematic maps will be encountered on a number of occasions, and students should be familiar with the conventions of each. Road maps, on the other hand, will not be used during the year and were used in this lesson only as a point of comparison.

Suggested Time: One lesson (45–60 minutes)

SUGGESTIONS FOR ELEMENTARY UNIT PLANNING

We suggest that elementary teachers proceed through Chapters 5, 6, and 7 as follows:

1. Review all the planning you have done so far. Return to your list of initial ideas. Gather and browse through any resources containing activities, materials, and other instructional ideas related to your unit. Compile *all* the instructional ideas that you find appealing. Instructional ideas include a great many things. Some examples are library research projects, teacher demonstrations, reading and discussing newspapers, debate, simulations, experimentation, teacher presentation, writing assignments, and building scale models. In short, any of the many tasks elementary students typically engage in qualify here.

2. ILOs should now be "keyed" to these instructional ideas. That is, decide which activities are likely to lead to which ILOs and indicate this.

3. Examine the list for coverage. Are all your high-priority ILOs included at least once? Add instructional ideas if necessary.

4. Eliminate some of the instructional ideas on your list. To do this, use the criteria suggested for selecting instructional foci. Decisions about appropriateness, feasibility, and motivation should, of course, consider the age and the development of the students. Priority of ILOs must be considered in making this selection; be sure to specify any time constraints with which you must work. You should now have a list of ideas that you intend to use in teaching your unit.

5. Chapter 6 discusses the sequence of course units. As we noted with secondary teachers, elementary teachers have more alternative instructional sequences than they usually realize. You should read Chapter 6 now and then make a sequence of the instructional ideas you have developed. Many suggestions in Chapter 6 should prove helpful; your instructional ideas will probably fall together into groups and these groups can then be put into a sequence.

6. Chapter 7 deals with the development of general teaching strategies. You should find the chapter's guidelines helpful. We suggest that you consider teaching strategies for each of your clusters of instructional ideas.

QUESTIONS FOR DISCUSSION: FORMING UNITS

1. Which do you feel are your best instructional foci? Why? What does this choice indicate about your own personal criteria for choosing foci?

2. What does your choice of approach in forming units indicate about your course?

3. Have you decided on the sequence of your units or is this decision still open?

4. What approach to forming units was followed in *Course Design*? What are the book's "units"?

5. Does any instructional focus predominate in this book?

REFERENCES

Banks, J. A. (1994). *Multiethnic education: Theory and practice.* Boston: Allyn & Bacon.
Banks, J. A. (1997). *Educating citizens in a multicultural society.* New York: Teachers College Press.
Dick, W. O., Carey, L., & Carey, J. O. (2004). *The systematic design of instruction.* Boston: Allyn & Bacon.
Goodlad, J. I. (1963). *Planning and organizing for teaching.* Washington, DC: National Education Association.
Meyen, E. L. (1981). *Developing instructional units* (3rd ed.). Dubuque, IA: Wm. C. Brown.
Stigler, J. W., & Hiebert, J. (1999). *The teaching gap.* New York: The Free Press.

CHAPTER SIX

ORGANIZING THE COURSE'S UNITS

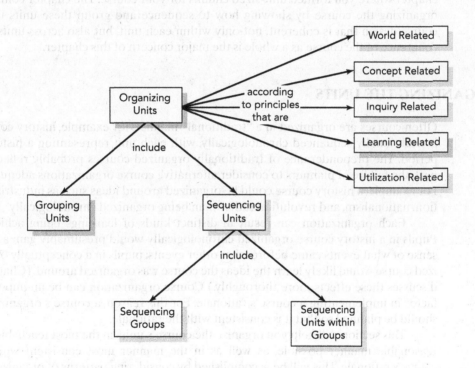

After completing this chapter, you should be able to:

1. **Know that there are alternative ways of sequencing content.**

2. **Think about alternatives when faced with the task of sequencing content.**

3. **Group and sequence a given set of units into a coherent outline.**

In part, instructional planning consists of organizing instructional content into a coherent, feasible design for teaching. The previous chapter dealt with one part of this process, that is, forming unit-sized chunks of content for the course. The overriding goal of this chapter is to have you think about course organization and sequence. *Course Design*'s fundamental premise is that planners need to be aware of points in planning when they have the opportunity to make decisions. Considering alternatives makes planning choices deliberate rather than occurring by default. How you have formed units or subunits will certainly influence, perhaps even dictate, your course structure. It is likely, however, that you have a great deal more flexibility and possible courses of action than you might think. Considering course organization at this level is worthwhile. Doing so may very well result in some changes in some of the work you have already done. This is exactly the way good course planning should proceed. This chapter builds on your work in the previous chapter where you formed unit-sized chunks for your course. The chapter continues organizing the course by showing how to sequence and group these units into a course design that is coherent, not only within each unit, but also across units. The coherence of the course as a whole is the major concern of this chapter.

ORGANIZING THE UNITS

Often courses are organized in a "traditional" manner; for example, history content is traditionally sequenced chronologically, with each unit representing a historical period. The preponderance of traditionally organized courses probably reflects, in part, the failure of planners to consider alternative course organizations adequately. For example, a history course could be organized around ideas such as industrialization, nationalism, and revolution rather than being organized chronologically.

Each organization can result in distinct kinds of learnings being achieved. Pupils in a history course organized chronologically would presumably gain a good sense of what events came before what other events; pupils in a conceptually organized course would likely learn the ideas the course was organized around. (Chapter 8 discusses these effects more thoroughly.) Course organization can be an important factor in implementing a course's rationale. For this reason, a course's organization should be planned so that it is consistent with the rationale.

This section will help you organize the course's units in the most teachable and reasonable manner possible, as well as in the manner most consistent with the course's rationale. This will be accomplished by considering patterns of organization.

Organized units are units in the order in which they will be presented to students taking the course. This organization is expressed in the form of a unit outline. There are three levels of unit organization: (1) the grouping of units, (2) the sequencing of groups, and (3) the sequencing of units within groups.

Grouping units consists of clustering units together in a meaningful fashion. This is analogous to clustering ILOs into units, except that it is done on a more macro level, that is, units themselves are clustered. Sequencing groups consists of ordering the grouped units in the way they will be taught. Sequencing units means ordering the units within a group in the way they will be taught. The lists that follow should help clarify what we mean by levels of grouping and sequencing of units. In these lists, the *ILOs* for a course in general math have been *clustered* into the following *units:*

> the set of whole numbers
> measurement
> the system of decimal fractions
> the metric system
> subtraction and division of whole numbers
> finite decimal operations
> addition and multiplication of whole numbers
> set theory
> whole numbers—bases other than ten
> the number line
> real numbers

These *units* could be *grouped* as follows:

MEASURING

> the metric system
> measurement

WHOLE NUMBERS

> subtraction and division of whole numbers
> the set of whole numbers
> addition and multiplication of whole numbers

DECIMALS

> finite decimal operations
> real numbers
> the system of decimal fractions

SETS

> set theory
> the number line
> whole numbers—bases other than ten

The *groups* could then be *sequenced* as follows:

> whole numbers
> sets
> decimals
> measuring

Within these *groups* the *unit sequence* may be as follows:

WHOLE NUMBERS

the set of whole numbers
addition and multiplication of whole numbers
subtraction and division of whole numbers

SETS

set theory
whole numbers—bases other than ten
the number line

DECIMALS

the system of decimal fractions
finite decimal operations
real numbers

MEASURING

measurement
the metric system

The example illustrates an organized course in which ILOs have been clustered into units, the units have been organized into groups, the groups are sequenced, and the units within each group are sequenced. There are really two major decisions to make: One is deciding at what levels you wish to organize your course; the other is the choice of actual organizational principles for those chosen levels. We will not attempt to prescribe which decision you should make first. For some planners, depending on the course, choosing levels of organization may be the appropriate first decision. In other instances, the planner must begin planning at one level, and wait to see if other organizational principles suggest themselves as the planning proceeds.

ALTERNATIVE ORGANIZATIONS: SOME EXAMPLES

To illustrate what is meant by alternative approaches to organization in the context of course design, let us examine some examples of unit outlines for various courses that have each been organized two different ways. You will probably receive maximum benefit from the discussion following the examples by closely examining each of the examples and then carefully comparing them.

Example 6.1

AMERICAN HISTORY I

1. Exploration of North America

2. Early Settlement of North America

3. Europe and the New World

4. British Dominance of Eastern North America

5. Colonial Life

6. Relationship between Colonies and Great Britain

7. American Revolution

8. Foundations of American Government

9. Westward Expansion of North America

AMERICAN HISTORY II

Settlement of North America

1. Exploration of North America

2. Early Settlement of North America

3. Westward Expansion of North America

Colonial Society

4. Colonial Life

5. Foundations of American Government

Issues in Colonial North America

6. Europe and the New World

7. British Dominance of Eastern North America

8. Relationship between Colonies and Great Britain

9. American Revolution

The nine units of American History I are organized in chronological sequence. That is, the events in Unit 1 temporally precede those in Unit 2, the events in Unit 2 precede those in Unit 3, and so on. American History II is an example of a conceptual organization. That is, the units are grouped around three historical ideas: settlement, society, and issues. The units within the groups can be considered chronologically sequenced. An American history course that has a goal of providing students with an appreciation or understanding of causal factors in history or a sense of the timing of various events would probably best be sequenced chronologically. Course emphasis, on the other hand, could be on underlying issues, major themes in history, or the ability to think about history in a conceptual way, in which case a conceptual sequence would be most suitable.

Example 6.2

GEOLOGY I

Observable Features of the Earth

1. Gross Features of the Earth
2. Rivers and Valleys
3. Atmosphere, Weather, Climate
4. Minerals and Rocks
5. Snow and Ice
6. Elements and Compounds

Forces Acting on the Earth's Form

7. Rock Weathering and Soil
8. Groundwater
9. Valley Glaciers
10. Continental Glaciers
11. Wind as an Agent of Gradation
12. Gradation by Mass Movement of Surface Materials

GEOLOGY II

Units of Earth's Geologic System

1. Elements and Compounds
2. Minerals and Rocks
3. Atmosphere, Weather, Climate
4. Snow and Ice

Forces Shaping the Earth

5. Rock Weathering and Soil
6. Valley Glaciers
7. Continental Glaciers
8. Wind as an Agent of Gradation
9. Gradation by Mass Movement of Surface Materials

Physical Features of the Earth

10. Gross Features of the Earth

11. Groundwater

12. Rivers and Valleys

Geology I contains units sequenced within groups according to the assumed familiarity of the content of the learners. The units progress roughly from those most familiar to the learner to those least familiar. Note that sequencing on the basis of familiarity requires information about the audience because different audiences may find different topics more or less familiar. The groups are formed on the basis of common properties: features and forces. Geology II contains units grouped in a conceptual organization. The units are formed around three geological ideas: basic units, forces, and physical features. The groups are, in turn, logically sequenced from raw materials, to forces acting on them, to the resulting geological features. The two sequences reflect very different though not incompatible concerns on the part of the course designer. Geology I is sequenced in a manner designed to facilitate learning based on the assumption that the content is difficult because of students' unfamiliarity with it. Geology II emphasizes a concern for the students being able to grasp geological ideas and to relate physical features to their shaping forces. The difference between Geology I and II is one of emphasis.

Example 6.3

THE MEDIA I

Media Functions

1. Role of the Media in Shaping Society

2. Current Activities of Broadcast and Print Media

3. Differences among Various Media

4. Advertising

Historical Context

5. Development of U.S. Media

6. International Media Systems

7. The Future of the Media

Influences on the Media

8. External Influences on the Media

9. Legal Constraints on the Media

Accessibility

10. Public Access to the Media

THE MEDIA II

1. Advertising
2. Public Access to the Media
3. Role of the Media in Shaping Society
4. Current Activities of Broadcast and Print Media
5. The Future of the Media
6. External Influences on the Media
7. International Media Systems
8. Differences among Various Media
9. Development of U.S. Media
10. Legal Constraints on the Media

The Media I and II represent part of a high school senior English course. The Media I has a conceptual organization of units. That is, the units are grouped around the concepts of function, historical context, influence, and accessibility. The units in The Media II are ordered on the basis of interest. That is, the sequence progresses from those units thought to be of greatest interest to the learner to those units thought to be of least interest. The Media II reflects a greater concern, on the part of the planner, with the motivation of learners. That is, an emphasis on understanding conceptual relations (stressed in The Media I) is sacrificed for an emphasis that is likely to get the students interested in the course.

EXERCISE 6.1

Now try suggesting alternative organizations. For each set of units below, decide on two possible types of organization that could be employed and organize the units in each of the two selected patterns. You will probably find that additional units must be added to effect your chosen patterns. Feel free to add these units. The units presented in the exercises are listed in random order. Your task is to create a sensible pattern or flow of units.

EXERCISE A: BASIC ECOLOGY

Biomes of the World
The Community
Ecological Succession
Periodic Changes in Communities
The Living Environment

What Is Ecology?
The Distribution of Plants and Animals
Climatic Gradients in Plants and Animals
The Physical Environment

EXERCISE B: INTRODUCTION TO SOCIOLOGY

Culture
Groups
Social Organization
Collective Behavior
Socialization
Social Stratification
Major Social Institutions
Urbanism and Industrialism

EXERCISE C: AMERICAN HISTORY I

The Jacksonian Era
The Road to Revolution
The Origin of the Thirteen Colonies
The Confederation and the Constitution
The War of 1812
The Winning of Independence
The Development of the Thirteen Colonies
People Moving West
Jefferson in Power

To this point the outlines presented have been examples of relatively pure types. A "pure" type refers to the use of just one basis or principle of organization at a particular level. Often it is impossible or undesirable to produce a pattern that represents a pure type of organization. For example, you might want your course organization to reflect the way the world is, the way people learn, and the way they will utilize learnings in life. In such cases, you attempt to produce a unit organization that reflects an optimal blend of principles. A "blend" refers to an organization of content that embodies more than one principle or basis.

Example 6.4

ECONOMICS AND HISTORY I

1. Basic Economic Concepts

2. The Depression (an in-depth view)

3. The New Deal (policies and politics)

4. The Development of the U.S. Economy

5. The Economy Today

6. Economic Futurism (the next 50 years)

ECONOMICS AND HISTORY II

1. The Economy Today

2. Basic Economic Concepts

3. The Development of the U.S. Economy

4. The Depression (an in-depth view)

5. The New Deal (policies and politics)

6. Economic Futurism (the next 50 years)

Economics and History is an advanced high school course. Economics and History I begins with basic ideas; takes a micro look at a period of economic upheaval in the United States; then takes a macro look at past, present, and future economic conditions. The organization of units represents a blend of logical prerequisites (that is, basic economic ideas), level of abstraction (since a "micro look" at the Depression is more concrete than a "macro look" at the New Deal), and chronology (that is, past, present, and future). Economics and History II begins with the present, moves to basic ideas, then to a macro-to-micro view, and finally ends with a look at the future. The organization of units represents a blend of learning theory (since the unit starts with something familiar, that is, the present), conceptual structure (that is, the basic ideas), and chronology (that is, past to future). The major difference between these two units is that Economics and History II is sequenced so as to interest and presumably motivate students. Economics and History I reflects the planner's concern for providing basic economic ideas at the very outset of the course.

Example 6.5

JUVENILE DELINQUENT BEHAVIOR I

1. The Prevalence of Juvenile Delinquency

2. Types of Juvenile Delinquent Acts

3. Types of Juvenile Delinquents

4. Primary Causes of Juvenile Delinquency

5. The Prediction of Delinquency

6. The Prevention of Delinquency

7. The Treatment of Delinquency

JUVENILE DELINQUENT BEHAVIOR II

1. Primary Causes of Juvenile Delinquency
2. The Prediction of Delinquency
3. Types of Juvenile Delinquents
4. Types of Juvenile Delinquent Acts
5. The Prevalence of Juvenile Delinquency
6. The Treatment of Delinquency
7. The Prevention of Delinquency

Juvenile Delinquent Behavior I begins with an overview describing the prevalence of delinquency. Ideas are then presented (that is, types of acts, types of delinquents, primary causes), and methods of prediction, prevention, and treatment are included. Thus, Juvenile Delinquent Behavior I represents a blending of learning-, concept-, and utilization-related bases. Juvenile Delinquent Behavior II intersperses methods of prevention, prediction, and treatment of delinquency with a logical development of ideas (that is, causes, types of delinquents, types of acts, prevalence). Thus, Juvenile Delinquent Behavior II represents a blend of utilization- and concept-related sequencing principles. These two organizations are similar in emphasis. Juvenile Delinquent Behavior II integrates theory and practice to a greater extent than Juvenile Delinquent Behavior I. Delinquency II is directed more toward people who might actually counsel youth, whereas Delinquency I emphasizes an understanding of theory and of treatment instead of an understanding of how theory and practice are related.

This discussion of blending should be viewed as a representative rather than a comprehensive cataloging of options. Once understood, these alternatives should serve merely as a basis for thinking about unit organization flexibly, not as a structure into which thinking must be forced.

EXERCISE 6.2

Organize the set of units below into a pattern that embodies two or more organizational principles or bases. Again, feel free to add any units you may need.

INTRODUCTORY BUSINESS MATH

Interest and Compound Interest
Stocks and Bonds
Fundamental Mathematical Processes
Payrolls and Taxes
Fractions: Decimal and Common
Financial Statements
Percentage in Business

The organizational alternatives in both pure and blended forms should provide you with a number of options when organizing units. You should keep in mind the goals of teachability, reasonability, and consistency with the course rationale.

Again, flexibility is of primary importance when organizing your units. Carefully consider the various alternatives available before deciding on an organization.

Also, try to approach course organization imaginatively. For example, one course planner used an approach that included "floating units," those units that can be inserted at any time in the course. A floating unit provides a breather at various times during a course, although course-related learnings are involved.

The makeup of each unit (that is, the particular cluster of ILOs) determines to some extent where that unit falls in a course. You may, at this time, want to reform some of your units in order to organize the course in a way that appears most appropriate to you.

Course Planning Step 6.1   Organize the units of your course into a unit outline. This step involves a combination of grouping and sequencing your units as explained by the various options. If in the process of organizing your units you find that the units themselves need to be reformed, don't hesitate to do this. Also, take another look at your rationale, making sure it is consistent with the unit outline. Now is a good time to revise your list of ILOs, adding new ones as needed or eliminating some if you find that they do not fit into any of your units.

Remember, course design is not a linear process. You will constantly need to go back to previous work, revising, adding, and deleting as you progress.

QUESTIONS FOR DISCUSSION: THE UNIT OUTLINE

1. Is your organization of the units consistent with the course rationale? What does the course rationale imply (if anything) about the organization of the course?

2. Is the curriculum coherent? Around what does it cohere? Content? ILOs? Projects? Problems? Media? Other foci?

3. What does the organization of the curriculum contribute to the curriculum as a whole? For example, does it highlight the conceptual nature of the subject matter (as in a history course organized around conceptual themes)? Does it emphasize the utility of the subject matter (as in a course guiding the learner toward the completion of some product, such as *Course Design* attempts to do)?

4. In the process of organizing your unit outline, were any new ILOs suggested? If so, specify them.

5. Suppose that considerations of time forced you to abbreviate your course by 20 percent. How would you do this? Would you shorten units, delete one or more units, combine units, or none of these?

6. Suppose you were able to add 20 percent more instructional time to your course. What would you do? Would you expand some units (which?), add new units, split some units into two, or would you do something else?

7. Is there a midpoint "break" in your course? Should you have a "review" unit at any place in your unit outline?

8. Sometimes a unit may serve more than one purpose. Could any of your units be retitled to indicate their other purpose? Which ones?

9. How are your high-priority ILOs distributed across your units? If they are distributed unevenly, does this accurately reflect the relative priority for each unit? Are any units crucial? Are any units trivial or of little consequence?

10. You may have rejected several alternative organizations. What grounds can you give for rejecting them?

SCOPE AND SEQUENCE CHARTS

Curriculum development teams typically do not work on courses or units in isolation. They work on a multigrade curriculum. In their work they may depict the curriculum as a matrix in which the themes, topics, or concepts are delineated on the horizontal axis and the grade-by-grade progression through the curriculum is delineated on the vertical axis. Matrices of this sort are termed *scope and sequence charts,* where the horizontal axis depicts the scope and the vertical axis depicts the sequence. Figure 6.1 on page 158 is an example of a scope and sequence chart.

In major curriculum development efforts, these charts merely summarize more detailed and extensive work on scope and sequence. In such cases, the document that describes this work is also called the "scope and sequence." Figure 6.2 on page 159 shows one page from an actual scope and sequence. In some school districts it is the scope and sequence that the school board must pass, before one can say that "the curriculum has been adopted by the school district." The scope and sequence, not as a brief chart, but in an elaborated form, is also typically the document that the state education department might send to the school district as the curriculum required by the state.

Since your project is not a multigrade curriculum, you will not have the opportunity here to develop a scope and sequence chart like the ones depicted in Figures 6.1 and 6.2. However, you can summarize the decisions you have made about the formation and organization of the course's units into a scope and sequence chart. By doing so, you will gain familiarity with the development of these useful charts and you will produce a document that will provide a valuable overview of your entire curriculum.

A scope and sequence chart, for our purposes, will list the sequence of the course's units along the vertical axis and the scope of the course along the horizontal axis. In order to produce such a chart, you will first decide how to represent the course's scope. Choices include the following:

The central questions
The major themes or concepts
The general ILOs
The educational goals

	Strand			
	1 **Physical Health,** **Nutrition, and**	**2** **Sociological**	**3** **Family Life and**	**4** **Environmental,** **Community, and**
Grade	**Disease Prevention**	**Health Problems**	**Emotional Health**	**Consumer Health**
K	Health Habits; Food Variety; Senses; Care of Teeth—Personal; Feelings—Well/Sick	Uniqueness of Self/ Choices; Safe and Unsafe Substances; Smoking Effects on Self; Kinds of Alcohol	Feeling Special/ Friends; Family Lifestyles; Living and Nonliving Things; Body Parts/Parent Communication; Privacy/Touch; Trusting Feelings/Saying No	Self/Environment; School Health and Safety Helpers; Personal Health Products and Services
1	Growth; 4 Basic Food Groups; Body Parts; Primary and Secondary Teeth; Cause and Spread of Disease	Variety of Feelings/ Decisions and Consequences; Proper Use of Drugs; Smoking Effects on Senses; Effects of Alcohol	Expressing Feelings/ Handicaps; Family Members; Functions of Living Things; Questions about Sexuality; Victim/Offender; Confusing Touch/Support Systems	Community Environment; Community Health and Safety Helpers; Factors that Influence Choices
2	Food, Sleep, and Exercise; Eating Habits; Functions of Body Parts; Care of Teeth—Professional; Communicable and Noncommunicable Diseases	Sharing and Accepting Feelings of Others; Harmful and Helpful Drugs; Smoking Addiction; Alcohol Abuse	Communication Skills/ Handicaps; Family Needs and Support Systems; Gestation/Birth/Dying; Facts and Feelings/Media Messages; Neglect and Abuse; Recognizing Problems/Reporting	Environmental Factors; Responsibilities of Community Health and Safety Professionals; Consumer/Media
3	Maintain Balance/ Intake-Exercise; Food Choices; Body Systems (5); Parts of a Tooth; Risk Factors	Risk-taking Behaviors; Media Influence; Decision Making/Peer Pressure	Decision Making/ Handicaps; Family Changes and Responsibilities; Reproductive Systems/Life Cycle; Sexual Problems and Decisions; Feelings and Rights Regarding Abuse; Effective Reporting	Improving School Environment; Responsibilities of Citizens/Training of Health Personnel; Advertising Techniques
4	Overweight/Underweight; Food—Past and Present; Body Systems (4); Tooth Decay; Prevention and Control of Diseases	Coping Skills; Prescription vs. Nonprescription Drugs; Social and Economic Factors; Alcohol Effects on Body Systems	Personality/Relationships/ Handicaps; Families—Past and Present; Puberty/Male and Female Roles; STDs/AIDS; Respect for Self and Others; Uncomfortable Situations/Terminology; Embarrassment/Confidentiality	Types of Pollution; Environmental Health Practices—Past and Present; Consumer Decision Making
5	Body Types; Diets; Interrelationships of Body Systems; Structure of the Mouth; Health Laws and Agencies	Assertive Implementation of Decisions; Effects on Body Systems; Smoking Effects on Body Systems; Laws and Agencies	Emotional Needs/ Stereotypes; Family Roles and Problem Solving; Physical, Emotional, and Social Changes During Puberty; Teenage Pregnancy/Family Communication; Manipulative Strategies of Offenders; Assertiveness/ Helping Friends	Society's Effects on the Environment; Environmental Health Laws; Emotional and Rational Buying

Figure 6.1   A scope and sequence chart for a kindergarten–fifth grade health curriculum.

Source: Adapted from the Ithaca City School District Curriculum.

Health Curriculum—Grade 4

STRAND I   PHYSICAL HEALTH, NUTRITION, AND DISEASE PREVENTION

I-A GOAL: To understand there are many factors that influence the state of a person's health.

Learner Outcome:
Student will:

- Review physical similarities and differences.
- Evaluate the interrelationships between body systems in maintenance of good health.
- Discuss the causes of being overweight or underweight.

I-B GOAL: To understand that certain daily food choices and eating habits are necessary to maintain total health and body growth.

Learner Outcome:
Student will:

- Identify essential nutrients that help promote one's health.
- Analyze school lunch program as to meeting daily nutritional requirements.
- Compare the way the early pioneer family met nutritional daily requirements with present lifestyle.

I-C GOAL: To understand how our senses and body systems help us function.

Learner Outcome:
Student will:

- Review body systems—muscular, skeletal, digestive, circulatory, respiratory.
- State functions and identify the parts of the nervous, reproductive, excretory, and endocrine systems.

I-D GOAL: To understand the importance of knowledge, skills, and attitudes appropriate to the promotion of dental health.

Learner Outcome:
Student will:

- Compare healthy tooth and decayed tooth.
- Discuss causes of tooth decay.
- Contrast past dental techniques and habits with today's practices.

I-E GOAL: To understand how behaviors and habits prevent noncommunicable diseases and the transmission of communicable diseases.

Learner Outcome:
Student will:

- Research the methods developed for the prevention and control of diseases.
- Describe the chain of infection and how to break it.
- Identify personnel responsible for maintaining good health.

Figure 6.2   One page of a kindergarten–fifth grade health education scope and sequence.

Source: Adapted from the Ithaca City School District Curriculum.

You are trying to identify a way to capture the scope of the course using a manageable set of items (e.g., three to ten). For example, the curriculum presented in Appendix D employs four central questions that adequately summarize the scope of the curriculum.

If there are a large number of ILOs (e.g., more than ten) with no way to group them into general ILOs, then they will be unmanageable as a tool for summarizing the course. In such a case, you will need to use some other way of representing the course's scope (e.g., educational goals, central questions, or major themes). In some courses you will have a choice, since two or more of these devices would feasibly represent the scope of the course. In such a case, you might want to experiment with each device in order to determine which one works best.

Course Planning Step 6.2   Develop the skeleton of a scope and sequence chart. To do this, first describe the scope of your course horizontally along the top of a sheet of paper, specifying themes, concepts, general ILOS, and educational goals on central questions. Then list the sequence of units vertically along the left side of the sheet.

Course Planning Step 6.3   Now it is time to add substance to the skeleton. Fill in all cells that signify that an item in the course's scope is covered in a particular unit. Each cell should contain an ILO showing specifically what students will learn in a particular unit that relates to a particular item in the course's scope. Once this is complete, you will have developed a scope and sequence chart.

ANSWERS TO EXERCISES

Answers to Exercise 6.1

The organizations or "answers" given here represent possible orderings of the units provided in the exercise. "Correctness" of your answer rests on whether or not your organization is justifiable as being both teachable and reasonable.

EXERCISE A: BASIC ECOLOGY

1. What Is Ecology?

2. The Physical Environment

3. The Living Environment

4. The Community

5. Periodic Changes in Communities

6. Ecological Succession

7. The Distribution of Plants and Animals

8. Climatic Gradients in Plants and Animals

9. Biomes of the World

The above is a concept-related sequence. Each chapter or unit is logically prerequisite to each succeeding chapter. The ideas presented in one unit are necessary to understand ideas presented in later units. Another possible ordering of units is illustrated below. This organization is also concept-related, but the units are grouped into categories.

EXERCISE A: (ALTERNATIVE)

Introduction

1. What Is Ecology?

Adaptation of Living Things

2. The Distribution of Plants and Animals

3. Climatic Gradients in Plants and Animals

4. Biomes of the World

An Ecosystem

5. The Physical Environment

6. The Living Environment

7. The Community

Changes in Ecosystems

8. Periodic Changes in Communities

9. Ecological Succession

EXERCISE B: INTRODUCTION TO SOCIOLOGY

1. Groups

2. Social Organization

3. Collective Behavior

4. Socialization

5. Social Stratification

6. Major Social Institutions

7. Urbanism and Industrialism

8. Culture

The above ordering of units is illustrative of a sequence based on conceptual sophistication. The units progress from least to most sophisticated.

EXERCISE C: AMERICAN HISTORY I

1. The Origin of the Thirteen Colonies

2. The Development of the Thirteen Colonies

3. The Road to Revolution

4. The Winning of Independence

5. The Confederation and the Constitution

6. Jefferson in Power

7. The War of 1812

8. The Jacksonian Era

9. People Moving West

The units of the above sequence are presented in chronological order.

Answers to Exercise 6.2

1. Fundamental Mathematical Processes

2. Fractions: Decimal and Common

3. Percentage in Business

4. Interest and Compound Interest

5. Payrolls and Taxes

6. Financial Statements

7. Stocks and Bonds

This sequence is a blend of two major types. Units 1, 2, and 3 are logically prerequisite to each other and logically prerequisite to the other units. That is, fundamental mathematical processes are needed in order to learn fractions. Likewise, the operations of the first three units are needed in order to calculate interest. Units 4 through 7 are sequenced on the basis of how frequently they are used. That is, problems and situations involving interest arise more frequently than problems or situations involving financial statements.

SUGGESTED READINGS

Ausubel, D. P. (1964). Some psychological aspects of the structure of knowledge. In S. Elam (Ed.), *Education and the structure of knowledge* (pp. 220–262). Chicago: Rand McNally.

Ausubel, D. P., Novak, J. D., & Hanesian, H. (1978). *Educational psychology: A cognitive view.* New York: Holt, Rinehart, & Winston.

Bruner, J. S., Goodnow, J. J., & Austin, G. A. (1956). *A study of thinking.* New York: John Wiley.

Dewey, J. (1916). *Democracy and education.* New York: Macmillan.

Elam S. (Ed.). (1964). *Education and the structure of knowledge.* Chicago: Rand McNally.

Ford, G. W., & Pugno, L. (Eds.). (1964). *The structure of knowledge and the curriculum.* Chicago: Rand McNally.

Gagné, R. M. (1970). *The conditions of learning* (2nd ed.). New York: Holt, Rinehart, & Winston.

Kliebard, H. M. (1965). Structure of the disciplines as an educational slogan. *Teachers College Record, 66,* 598–603.

Parker, J. C., & Rubin, L. J. (1966). *Process as content.* Chicago: Rand McNally.

Phenix, P. H. (1964). *Realms of meaning.* New York: McGraw-Hill.

Phillips, D. C., & Kelly, M. E. (1975). Hierarchical theories of development in education and psychology. *Harvard Educational Review, 45,* 351–375.

Posner, G. J., & Strike, K. A. (1976). A categorization scheme for principles of sequencing content. *Review of Educational Research, 46,* 665–690.

Schwab, J. J. (1962). The concept of the structure of a discipline. *Educational Record, 43,* 197–209.

Schwab, J. J. (1964). Structure of the disciplines: Meanings and significances. In G. W. Ford & L. Pugno (Eds.), *The structure of knowledge and the curriculum* (pp. 1–30). Chicago: Rand McNally.

Shulman, L. S. (1970). Psychology and mathematics education. In E. G. Begle (Ed.), *Mathematics education. The sixty-ninth yearbook of the National Society for the Study of Education.* Chicago: University of Chicago Press.

Sockett, H. (1992). The moral aspects of the curriculum. In P. H. Jackson (Ed.), *Handbook of research on curriculum* (pp. 543–569). New York: Macmillan.

Sullivan, E. V. (1967). *Piaget and the school curriculum:A critical appraisal* (Bulletin No. 2). Toronto: Ontario Institute for Studies in Education.

CHAPTER SEVEN

DEVELOPING GENERAL TEACHING STRATEGIES

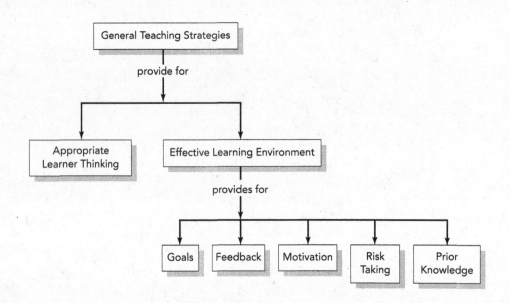

After completing this chapter, you should be able to:

Elaborate instructional foci into general teaching strategies for course units.

Instruction, in our framework, is made up of all the teacher's purposeful activities aimed at producing, stimulating, or facilitating learning by students. Instruction deals with how and what environments, methods, materials, strategies, tasks, and incentives can be employed to encourage learning. Instructional planning is a task carried out by teachers and may set the stage for learning. Once actual instruction begins, students occupy center stage.

Learning is an active process and, therefore, requires that students engage in some activity. As Walker (1990) succinctly states:

*The most important principle of classroom activity design is that **the students' actions determine what will be learned**. . . . The kernel of an educational activity, then, is what the student is to do. (pp. 366–367, emphasis original)*

What learners do need not be overt and physical; it can be listening, reading, and thinking. In fact, except perhaps for simple motor skills, it is mental activity that is the most important thing students do to learn. Teachers should try to design instructional tasks, activities, and environments that will engage learners in the appropriate kinds of processing, thinking, or mental activity. Appropriateness is gauged by the kind of learning being sought. Different kinds of thought are needed for different types of learning outcomes. Instruction is well planned to the extent that it succeeds in fostering appropriate thinking.

The rest of this chapter makes suggestions that we hope are helpful in designing the right tasks. As any teacher knows, this is more easily said than done. Translating learning goals into effective instruction is an incredibly challenging undertaking. Planning instruction, as was true of planning curriculum, cannot be accomplished by following a step-by-step recipe. We believe that a clear idea of what you want students to learn provides a sort of compass that can guide you in your instructional planning. The discussion and suggestions that follow are intended to help you think about your role in getting students engaged and thinking.

EFFECTIVE LEARNING ENVIRONMENTS

Effective instruction exists in many forms and varieties. A comprehensive treatment of instruction and instructional planning is beyond the scope of this book. However, there are many available guidelines for effective instructional design. For example, Yelon (1996) describes "ten powerful instructional principles":

1. *Meaningfulness.* Motivate students by helping them connect the topic to be learned to their past, present, and future.

2. *Prerequisites.* Assess students' level of knowledge and skill and adjust instruction carefully, so students are ready to learn the material at the next level.

3. *Open Communication.* Be sure students find out what they need to know so they can focus on what to learn.

4. *Organized Essential Ideas.* Help students focus on and structure the most important ideas, to be able to learn and recall those ideas.

5. *Learning Aids.* Help students use devices to learn quickly and easily.

6. *Novelty.* Vary the instructional stimuli to keep students' attention.

7. *Modeling.* Show students how to recall, think, act, and solve problems so that they are ready to practice.

8. *Active Appropriate Practice.* Provide practice in recalling, thinking, performing, and solving problems so that students apply and perfect their learning.

9. *Pleasant Conditions and Consequences.* Make learning pleasing, so students associate comfort with what is learned; and make learning satisfying, so that students keep learning and using what is learned.

10. *Consistency.* Make objectives, tests, practice, content, and explanation consistent, so that students will learn what they need and will use what they have learned outside of the instructional setting. (p. 3, italics in original)

We have already discussed several of these principles in the preceding chapters. For example, we have built Yelon's fourth principle, "organized essential ideas," into the entire process of curriculum design through the focus on identifying the most important understandings and skills and through the use of conceptual maps and flowcharts to structure those ILOs. Similarly, we have built Yelon's tenth principle, "consistency," into the entire process by insisting on consistency among various course elements, including ILOs, rationale, and unit organization. We continue this theme of consistency in this chapter by giving guidelines for teaching skills, cognitions, and affects and emphasizing the importance of designing teaching strategies that are consistent with the ILOs specified earlier. On the other hand, some of Yelon's principles are most appropriate for particular types of ILOs, rather than being general principles. For example, we discuss modeling and active appropriate practice (the seventh and eighth principles, respectively) in the context of learning skills.

Here we discuss four of Yelon's principles, which we offer as general guidelines for designing teaching strategies regardless of ILO type, age of learner, educational setting, or subject matter. Our guidelines draw on Yelon's first, second, third, and ninth principles, though we use slightly different terms. Rather than describing them as principles, we discuss them as points to consider in creating an optimal environment or atmosphere for learning. Such environments include (but are not limited to) provisions for the following:

1. Goals

2. Feedback

3. Motivation

4. Risk taking

5. Learning style

6. Prior knowledge

Goals

Stop to think about some of your own significant educational experiences. It is likely that you or your teacher began with a goal or purpose. That goal may have been like a destination you were trying to reach, such as achieving a certain degree of skill in debating, playing the piano, or playing tennis. Or your goal may have been developing an understanding of a particular topic, or an idea, such as the gross national product. While still a novice, you probably had only a vague idea of what there was to be learned in a particular area. In fact, your initial goal might be described more as a direction than a destination. Students can begin to learn and teachers can begin to teach once they have some initial direction. As they progress, they will undoubtedly modify and clarify their goals. In addition, they will probably arrive at some initially unanticipated points. Their accomplishments will often result in a readjustment of their plans and a resetting of their goals.

It is important that students' conceptions of learning go beyond the narrow view that they are simply acquiring a discrete piece of knowledge or a skill. When schoolwork is seen as made up of independent elements of knowledge and skill, students will master the elements without being able to use the knowledge broadly or flexibly. They will not be able to transfer what they have learned to other contexts and situations. What they will have acquired is "inert knowledge" (Whitehead, 1916). Students' views of what they are trying to achieve should include a clear perspective on the use and usefulness of the knowledge or skill being taught. Good instruction takes explicit steps to help students achieve this perspective.

Feedback

Most successful educational experiences also require feedback. Feedback means getting information about progress toward one's goal. Good instruction includes such feedback. Besides guiding students personally and directly, teachers can set up situations that inherently provide students with feedback. Playing tennis against an opponent, clocking speed on a stopwatch, answering textbook questions while reading difficult material, working collaboratively with other students, engaging in a conversation about a new topic, and solving problems while studying new material all provide feedback for students. Feedback does not mean that the teacher judges the student's performance. Instead, feedback helps students in monitoring their own progress and in deciding for themselves how best to expend their energies. Good instruction teaches students to be skilled at self-assessment.

Motivation

For a host of reasons, people typically learn well what they want to learn. Although students can get a good grade in a boring course or in a subject in which they have little interest, significant learning is not likely when students are unmotivated (see Borich, 1992).

Motivation is an incredibly complex topic. Many factors contribute to the motivation of students, and all students are different. Interest, curiosity, competition, social reasons, parental pressure, the need to achieve, health, money, power, and fear are a few motivating factors. These act in complex combinations as well as alone.

Although there is much debate about the topic, motivation is best thought of as internal. That is, the attitudes, energy, concentration, and excitement that make up student motivation can be brought about only by the students themselves. Teachers don't motivate students, strictly speaking. Teachers' responsibility is to design environments that are likely to engage students so that students motivate themselves to learn. Among the most powerful instructional factors that teachers can employ is making instruction interesting and relevant to students' lives. At the same time teachers can design environments where student effort pays off in terms of successful learning. Teachers can draw attention to the fact that effort is important. Whether teachers' actions result in student motivation is always a question. Not all students will find the same material interesting or relevant. Teachers cannot afford to worry about motivating every student every single day. Motivation is best thought of as a long-term undertaking, not a day-to-day search for instructional gimmicks.

Risk Taking

Significant learning often occurs in a setting where it is safe to try. Learning always has beginning stages. Skill and understanding, depending on their complexity, can require much time and effort before any level of competence or mastery is attained. Learning, particularly in a group setting, can be a very threatening, high-risk venture. Yet students learn better when they take reasonable chances and do not restrict their output—when they make errors and learn from their mistakes. Instruction is improved by creating a learning environment in which students will take reasonable risks, where there is no danger of ridicule, and where errors are instructive, not embarrassing.

When thinking about evaluating or critiquing student work, teachers might consider rewarding certain kinds of mistakes. Mistakes that suggest students are trying new skills or approaches, formulating new ideas, putting old ideas together in novel ways, or otherwise taking intellectual risks could be rewarded. This would go a long way toward creating a supportive learning environment.

Learning Style

Students approach learning and problem solving in different ways and many attempts have been made to conceptualize and categorize different learning styles. Among these categories are field dependent/field independent, impulsive/reflective, and deep processor/surface processor. Instruments have been devised that attempt to measure learning preferences. However, there is no strong evidence that different learning styles can be reliably identified and systematically addressed through instruction. Snider (1990) suggests that teachers should be skeptical about the notion of learning styles. Nevertheless, it is a good idea to present information and have students process information in a variety of ways and through a variety of modalities. Certainly students should be encouraged to be reflective and process deeply. This represents good instructional practice. It is worth considering that rather than aiming at students' learning style or information-processing strengths, the point of varying approaches is to allow students to add new strengths to those already existing. Thus, if a student doesn't learn well from language, rather than abandoning language for a different modality, it is important to provide high-quality learning experiences that are language based. In this way, students can become more competent learners.

Prior Knowledge

Learning is a profoundly relative process. What students learn depends enormously on what they already know. The more one knows and is able to do, the more and more easily one can learn new material. Meaningful learning occurs when new and existing knowledge are related. Instruction, to be successful, depends on having students build on their existing knowledge. When students lack any point of reference, learning is relegated to rote memorization of information or procedures. This kind of learning is typically short-lived and not very useful. Thus, good instruction provides opportunities for teachers to gain some understanding of their students' current knowledge states. Having a conception of what students know helps teachers plan instruction that builds bridges between new and existing knowledge and, when necessary, provide opportunities for students to acquire background knowledge.

We raise these initial points in order to place instruction and instructional planning in perspective. Planning and carrying out instruction involves more than creating strategies directly aimed at achieving intended learnings. Instruction is not an independent, day-to-day collection of activities or tasks. We have met teachers who think instructional planning is writing objectives and designing activities the night before they are to be used. This is far too reductionist a view of instructional planning. Students do not learn in nice, neat daily bites; this is especially true if our intentions include cognitions. The details of daily plans may be formulated in this way but these daily plans ought to come from a general teaching strategy that takes a broader and more integrated view of the curriculum. Instruction also involves providing an effective and humane instructional context in which these activities take place. Keeping these initial points in mind can help create an effective learning environment.

ACADEMIC TASKS

Research in cognitive science suggests that a crucial determinant of learning is students' thinking or cognitive processing, and this processing is directly influenced by the kind of tasks in which students actually engage. Teachers think of schoolwork as the material they present and the work they assign. Sometimes, however, there is a difference between schoolwork as teachers plan it and the academic tasks and commensurate thinking in which students ultimately are engaged (Doyle, 1983, 1992; Posner, 1982).

This potential discrepancy means that teachers ought to think about not only what they will assign and present but also the qualities of student thought or engagement that they are seeking to engender. Doing so requires teachers to consider performances or products the students will formulate (for example, book reports, essays, comments during discussion, arithmetic worksheets), the operations used in this formulation (for example, memorizing, following correct steps, reading and synthesizing), and the resources students are provided for their work (for example, directions, books and other materials, knowledge they are presumed to have). Appearing to do the work is not enough—teachers need to hold students accountable for the desired quality of thought or engagement. Student accountability is conveyed through tests and other formal methods of evaluation and also through the questions teachers ask, the feedback teachers give, and all the other cues teachers provide that indicate and emphasize desired learnings. Whenever possible, learners should have a clear idea of the kind of learning for which they are accountable.

Being clear about intended learning outcomes does not mean one should simplify them. Ambiguity is a concomitant feature of academic work and the classroom accountability structure (Doyle, 1983). Some learning is relatively unambiguous. This is the case for cognitive skills, especially simple skills. For example, holding students accountable for multiplying decimals or recalling a set of definitions is unambiguous. Students know quite clearly what they will be asked to do. In fact, accountability and learning activities are often identical. However, accountability can require considerable ambiguity. This is typically the case for understanding and higher-level learning in general. If, for example, students are to understand "balance of trade," we do not want to tell them explicitly how they will be held accountable. We may ask them to explain balance of trade in their own words, provide examples of unfavorable and favorable balances, or describe an imaginary nation and ask for predictions about its trade balance. The learning activities that lead to understanding "balance of trade" also will be varied. They may be similar to accountability tasks, but should not be identical. If teachers describe accountability tasks or performances unambiguously, students are likely to learn only what the teacher has told them they will have to "do."

Students do not like ambiguity. They direct significant effort at reducing the ambiguity of tasks and expectations. Most teachers are familiar with questions students ask about how long assignments must be, whether material will be included on tests, and what the nature of tests or other performances will be. Teachers can help students realize that comprehension, understanding, and other high-level outcomes (i.e., cognitions), while difficult, are worth working for to achieve. Over time students will realize that understandings require learning strategies that go beyond memorization or narrowly focusing on the acquisition of a specific performance. Learning activities will require that students encounter and use content in many different ways. Accountability tasks will be ambiguous because they require novelty that goes beyond the learning tasks.

For example, a teacher may want to present material about the relationship of gas volume to pressure and temperature. If the intended learning involves comprehension of this relationship, students will have to understand how pressure and temperature affect molecular behavior. They will need to know or learn a model that allows them to picture molecules and understand the effects of changing energy states on molecules. Students should be engaged in tasks requiring inferences about how changing these variables affects molecular structure. Experiments that allow students to "play" with these relationships and begin to develop their own formulae expressing the relationships are desirable academic tasks. Too frequently, however, our tasks and accountability system emphasize solving problems that require the simple application of formulae (for example, $PV = nRT$). Students learn how to substitute numbers into a formula rather than gain the higher level of understanding originally intended. Teachers' questions, such as what happens to tire pressure when traveling at high speeds, or how a racquetball feels after being hit many times, would help students realize that they are accountable for more than applying a formula.

Bereiter and Scardamalia (1989) talk about intentional learning. Intentional learning occurs when students have a learning goal and view learning as problematic —problematic in that learning is effortful and requires a strategy to move from an initial state to one of having learned. Having learning goals means that students are able to move past a schoolwork perspective. Students take a schoolwork perspective when they view their goal as getting the work done. Any learning that occurs is entirely incidental. Intentional learning requires shifting the "point" of school from work to learning itself. Becoming an intentional learner calls on a rich mix of motivation, metacognitive skill, and more. An intentional learner needs a theory of knowledge, that is, a way—a set of ideas—for thinking about learning. Good instructional practice, then, must include learning as part of the classroom discourse. Typically and appropriately, instruction focuses on the content or "stuff" but does so to the exclusion of focusing on learning the "stuff." Instruction should make the learning process more visible and explicit. For example, teachers could note that the class is being asked to learn both understandings and skills. There could be discussion about what this distinction means and what learning strategies are best for understanding, which are best for developing skill. In this way, students can develop a theory and language of learning, relate this language to a growing set of learning strategies, and monitor and regulate their own learning processes.

TEACHING STRATEGIES

In this chapter you will design general teaching strategies (that is, the instructional events) for each of your course's units. These general teaching strategies are described in your course design at a level more general than daily lesson plans but more specific than a list of resource materials to be used. A teaching strategy is based on instructional foci (see Chapter 5) and thus covers a unit- or subunit-sized chunk of your course. An instructional focus identifies the "stuff" of a strategy but does not describe the pattern of interaction among the students, material, and teacher. This interaction (that is, who does or says what, with or to whom) is described in the instructional strategy.

Even the most elegantly organized course, designed for the achievement of the most worthwhile learning, can fail if the teaching strategies employed are inappropriate or insufficient for the desired learnings (Bellon, Bellon, & Blank, 1992; Greenwood & Parkay, 1989). A good deal of attention and effort has already been given to the categorization of intended learning outcomes. One of the reasons cited for this work was the fact that different kinds of learnings require different kinds of instructional strategies (see Bell-Gredler, 1986). Let us examine several special considerations for designing teaching strategies aimed at skills, cognitions, and affects.

Teaching Skills

In teaching a cognitive or psychomotor–perceptual skill, practice is a crucial learning activity. Instruction for skills typically includes a presentation or initial teaching of the skill and then opportunities to practice. Presenting the skill most effectively typically requires modeling, where the student has the opportunity to observe someone (typically the teacher) demonstrate the skill. Doing this is relatively straightforward with psychomotor skills. Cognitive skill, like problem solving, may require the teacher to think aloud while performing the skill in his or her head.

Skills are often broken down into simpler subskills for the purposes of presentation and practice. Complex skills should be subjected to a cognitive task analysis resulting in flowcharts or other specifications of substeps (see Chapter 2). Teachers can then decide what size chunks to teach. Skills need not be taught intact. That is, complex skills consisting of many substeps can be mastered incrementally. Students may learn the first several substeps before proceeding on to successive steps. Once the steps or substeps of a skill are presented, students need opportunities for practice. Instructional strategies that provide for practice need to consider goals, guidance, motivation, risk taking, and prior knowledge. All of these points are important, but motivation is crucial, since too often practice becomes unchallenging, boring, repetitive seat work.

Two additional factors teachers might consider when designing skill instruction are difficulty and transfer. Opportunities to practice skills can vary from easy to hard. Maintaining a single or narrow level of difficulty in practice activities is misleading to both students and teachers. For example, if students are learning how to outline, they can be given multiple opportunities to outline. Initially, material that is not too long or intricately structured can be outlined. Later practice could be based on longer, more complex material.

Transfer, too, is something teachers designing skill instruction can think about. Skill transfer tends to be quite specific. The more similar a situation or context is to that in which the skill was practiced, the more likely the skill will be employed properly. Unfortunately, knowing how to perform a skill does not guarantee that a person will know when to do so. If students are to know when to use skills and be able to use them in different contexts and in flexible ways, practice opportunities need to be varied. For example, students might outline a variety of material, such as fiction, journalism, technical text, and historical writing. In addition, students can be given practice opportunities where they use more than one skill and are not explicitly directed to use a certain skill. Students, for instance, may need to gather information for a debate. Outlining would be an appropriate skill to use. However, instruction or guidance would come after students had an initial opportunity to use their outlining skills spontaneously. Teachers could point out aspects of the situation that cue the utility of this skill to students who did not use outlining.

Sometimes students attempt to learn a skill by memorizing the skill's specific steps or substeps; their practice often takes the form of mental rehearsal or repetition. Rehearsal often is not the most effective strategy for remembering a skill's steps. Students would benefit greatly from explicit instruction that teaches them to use other strategies such as imagery, chunking, and various mnemonics. (See Bransford & Stein, 1984; Halpern, 1996; Mayer, 2002; West, Farmer, & Wolff, 1991.) Memorization may be an appropriate strategy for the early stages of skill acquisition. However, a learning strategy that relies exclusively on memory is apt to result in rote learning. Teachers should guard against rote learning of skills by making clear the reasons for the steps and by showing how a skill relates to other skills or ideas.

Teaching Cognitions

In teaching cognitions, the principal instructional consideration is providing for elaboration. Elaboration requires that students have multiple and diverse opportunities for engaging new content. When comprehension or understanding is the goal of instruction, students must integrate new knowledge with existing knowledge. To accomplish this, students must think about and think with the new material in a variety of ways. Listening, notetaking, explaining, analyzing, discussing, developing, critiquing, inventing, experimenting, comparing, arguing, defending, and justifying are some of the kinds of engagement that lead to elaboration. Teachers can design instruction that provides such opportunities. Time constraints often necessitate compromise. Teachers cannot include all the possible forms of elaboration. However, they can select activities that suit their content and audience. Keep in mind that to the extent that new ideas build on existing knowledge, students will have repeated chances to use their knowledge in a variety of ways.

Transfer and difficulty are important considerations when instruction focuses on elaboration. Transfer and varied difficulty are virtually built into the notion of elaboration. Nevertheless, they should not be taken for granted. Activities can be consciously designed to vary in difficulty and context. Clearly, teaching for cognitions is a slow process. The multiple learning activities required by an elaboration strategy take time. We believe that this is truly an instance where "less is more" (Sizer, 1984). The power, flexibility, and durability of meaningful learning are worth the time, and over the long haul, provide students with more lasting and worthwhile outcomes.

Course Design is not a book that is primarily focused on instructional planning. Explaining how to design instruction is an incredibly complex topic and one that we, as a field, are now slowly coming to understand. The breadth and sophistication of instructional approaches makes even cataloging approaches a formidable task. The expectation of *Course Design* is that by truly understanding what you want students to learn, you as teachers will be better able to make the complex and often extemporaneous instructional decisions you face. There are, however, some directions and instructional suggestions that are worth pointing out.

Beginning a Unit or Course

All instruction unfolds temporally. That is to say, courses and units have beginnings, middles, and ends. Certain types of instructional events ought to occur during these stages of an unfolding course. The beginning of a course ought to present the overall framework that students will subsequently encounter. This suggestion is not novel and has been offered by Ausubel (1968) and others. Ausubel developed the idea of an advanced organizer. The organizer was intended to be a bridge between the new knowledge being presented in the unit and the learner's existing knowledge. The importance of this bridge remains consistent with everything we know about meaningful learning. Collins, Brown and Newman (1989) in their description of ideal learning environments advocate global before local skills. They note that this allows students to build a conceptual map, which accomplishes two things. First, it helps learners make sense of the pieces they are learning and provides a clear goal toward which to strive. Second, it improves learners' ability to monitor their progress and develop attendant self-correction skills. Brown and Campione (1996) describe opening new units with a "benchmark" lesson, "which serves to introduce the class to the big ideas and deep principles they will be studying. Ideally the first benchmark centers around some common knowledge that the class as a whole has developed in preparation for the first benchmark" (p. 299). Anything teachers can do to provide a context that gives learners the "big picture" or a framework for what they are going to encounter is worth doing, and to serve this purpose, it should occur at the unit's beginning.

Too many units begin with a class discussion in which students are asked what they already know about an upcoming topic and what they want to learn about the topic. This practice is so widespread that we hesitate to question its value. Our observations of classrooms suggest that several perhaps unintended but nonetheless deleterious outcomes result. Fundamentally, it is the same students, the ones with the richest background knowledge, who tend to dominate these sorts of beginnings. The unmistakable message that is being sent to other, less-well-informed students, is that they are beginning the unit already in a deficit position. It will certainly seem to them that the same students seem to know everything even before instruction begins. In the same vein, we believe that students can only ask good questions about what they want to learn if they do so from a position of at least some knowledge. Thus, opening units in such a manner, while seeming to be "democratic" and immediately relating to what students know, may not actually have that effect.

Many teachers report that they like to find out what students know at a course's outset. This seems entirely legitimate and, in fact, *Course Design* urges teachers to take prior knowledge into account. Our contention is that finding out what students know at the time the unit actually begins is too late to effectively use the information in planning. Teachers ought to have conversations with students to ascertain their knowledge about an upcoming topic and to find out what sorts of questions they would like to pursue. However, this ought to happen well before the start of the unit and the information gathered, therefore, would be of greater use to teachers as they plan. Such conversations and discussion can but need not include the entire class. Teachers can get a very good sense of what students know and what they are interested in learning by judiciously sampling student knowledge and opinions. Sometimes it may make sense to start a unit with a discussion. We urge moderation in the use of discussion to open units and advocate for a beginning that really grabs student interest and attention while providing the framework for what is to come.

The story, devised as part of the curriculum planning process, can form the basis for this introduction. The story may have to be rewritten to serve this purpose and it should be illustrated with appropriate examples. The examples can be selected to appeal to the diverse interests of learners and to different styles of learning. The story and illustrations are precisely the common knowledge that Brown and Campione (1996) refer to. Thus, stories are not only tools for planning, they are instructional foci for the beginning of a course or unit. The story should be referred to by name, for example, the inquiry story, the dance story, the geology story. Students should know that part of the enterprise in which they are involved is constructing a version of the story that is coherent, developed, and understandable. The story should be revisited explicitly as the unit develops. Students should be aware of the growing elaboration of their story.

The Middle and End of a Unit or Course

The instructional variations that are both possible and desirable during a course or unit are too numerous to catalog. However, some excellent suggestions, many from the work of Brown and Campione (1996), which combine aspects of constructivist and social cognitive theory, are worth mentioning. Brown and Campione refer to an instructional approach they dub Forming Communities of Learners (FCL). A major component of FCL is to incorporate collaboration and discourse among learners as a regular feature of instruction. They base their approach on principles of learning and describe it as consisting of three essential components:

- Students engage in independent and group research, becoming expert on their topic.
- Students share their developed expertise with the rest of the class. Mastery of the entire body of content is the responsibility of all members of the class.
- Students engage in a consequential task that forms the conclusion of the unit.

The resulting instruction is extremely well suited for meaningful learning of ideas and concepts as well as many of the important metacognitive outcomes. FCL also lends itself to students being able to build on existing strengths and interests and can readily be used to make sure that content that represents the full range of learner diversity makes its way into the curriculum. What's more, the approach incorporates "cross talk," a way to ensure and structure classroom discourse and create a sense of a community of learners that is essential in an effective classroom.

Concluding courses or units with consequential tasks is a way for students to consolidate their learning. The best consequential tasks require students to transfer what they have learned in order to solve problems, perform, or create a product in a different context. Consequential tasks often involve communicating with an audience consisting of people outside the classroom community. Good consequential tasks also have evaluative payoff, although this is not their primary function.

Brown and Campione (1996) worry about what they call "lethal mutations of practice." These mutations occur when teachers employ instructional methods in a piecemeal fashion, often not fully understanding the reasons behind the various practices. It is not our intention to contribute to these mutations and so we urge teachers to read about FCL for themselves. We include it here because it provides one sound approach for thinking about powerful instruction aimed at understanding.

Another effort designed to create learning environments is knowledge building, developed by Scardamalia and Bereiter (2003). Knowledge building takes place when a community of learners collaborate to improve their collective knowledge. Being able to effectively participate in knowledge work is viewed as essential preparation for students to (later) participate in our knowledge society and culture (Scardamalia, 2002). Knowledge-building learning environments share some common features with FCL, other types of collaborative learning, and problem-based learning, but also have several distinctive features. The community must care about improving their understanding and to do so they must engage in consequential or authentic work. This work requires a culture and means of engagement with other members of the community.[1] We cannot possibly describe knowledge building in sufficient detail here. It is a promising instructional approach and perspective, one that you should learn more about.

Teaching Affects

The teaching of affects is a difficult area for which to provide guidance. In addition to cognitive engagement, affective learning usually requires emotional involvement and often some degree of personal commitment. The range of how people cognitively react to a situation is great, but it is probably much less variable than their emotional reaction. Combine this with the fact that educators disagree as to what affects are (let alone agreeing on acceptable instructional practice), and you will understand the dif-

[1]Scardamalia and her colleagues have developed a computer application, *Knowledge Forum,* that supports knowledge building work. (http://www.knowledgeforum.com)

ficulty of suggesting strategies for affective learning. We cite some samples of general instructional practices currently used or advocated for teaching affects.

1. Involvement in the learning experience is crucial to affective teaching and learning. Emotional involvement differs in some ways from intellectual or cognitive involvement; it involves strong feelings, some degree of risk, and a relating of the experience to the learner's personal life. If the learner is expected to attach positive value to a thing or person (for example, liking, enjoyment, value, respect), the learning experience must allow for positive emotion. The obverse is true for an ILO aimed at negative values or feelings.

2. An atmosphere of freedom and trust facilitates the willingness of the learner to take risks. Learnings that require self-understanding, self-knowledge, or beliefs and values involve varying degrees of personal risk. For example, learning whether or not to sample new recipes is much less profound and involves much less risk for the learner than learning whether or not he or she is prejudiced. When personal risk is high, the learner must trust and feel comfortable with the environment.

3. The depth or level at which the affective strategies can be used depends largely on the group (their age, maturity, size, trust, and respect for one another) and how comfortable the teacher is in leading these exercises.

4. Affective intended learnings usually have specific referents for the learner, such as respecting others' opinions, valuing clear writing, and being aware of one's attitude toward minority groups. The techniques we present are intended to give some idea of what teachers can do to involve learners emotionally. The referent or subject matter depends on the particular course, the learners, the teachers, and the milieu.

5. Many affects are best learned through modeling; that is, the teacher or fellow classmates act in ways that embody the affect and learners attempt to imitate or model themselves after these "significant others." Clearly, modeling accounts for much of our significant informal educational experiences. Parents, for example, have long realized that their children ignore suggestions to do as the parents say, not as they do.

What follows are suggestions for teaching affects. They represent a compilation of techniques that have been found to facilitate affective learning. These techniques include ways to structure learning situations and kinds of activities that may be used. The techniques are illustrative of the type of classroom situation or activity appropriate for teaching affects.

The techniques are organized into five categories. Each category represents a useful framework for thinking about these and other affective teaching techniques. In planning to teach an affective ILO, a teacher would probably want to use techniques from a number of categories rather than from only one type of category.

Feedback Situations   There are always ways in which to structure interpersonal interactions that facilitate the giving or receiving of feedback. Feedback is a response or return of information from one person to another. The response may be to an act performed by a person or simply to the person's presence. The response may be descriptive of what was seen, sensed, felt, and thought, or the response may be judgmental, that is, placing a value on the object or actor. Feedback is best accomplished in small group situations in which people are with the same group members for several meetings. Each time the group meets, exercises and activities should aim at building trust. Two- and three-person groups, referred to in much of the affective literature as *dyads* and *triads,* are often employed to help establish this feeling of trust.

Simulations   Techniques can be used to help students explore thoughts, feelings, and fantasies about themselves, others, or even places and things. The teacher often sets up the situation that people will explore either individually or as a group. This technique makes the experiencing or expressing of certain feelings or values easier, as the risks associated with simulation are typically less than those associated with reality.

Attending to the Present   Relatively straightforward techniques can be used to help students pay attention to present physical and emotional sensations and to feelings and values. They are an aid in helping students explore feelings and discovering how and when they block out the present. The techniques may be as simple as having students begin sentences with the word *now.*

Role-Playing   Techniques that involve students playing the role of another person or object can be used. Role-playing is related to fantasy explorations except that role-playing is more active; typically, students act out a role in front of others. These techniques allow students to try out behaviors, feelings, and values not usually a part of their repertoire. In this way they can add to their own behavior repertoire, as well as identify more easily with the behaviors and the feelings of others. Becoming an object or playing the role of another person, describing these experiences, and generally using theater games are all role-playing techniques.

Communication   This category is a broad one, encompassing a great deal of the interpersonal interactions of the students. It includes kinds of communication often ignored by students, such as facial expressions, body language, and other nonverbal forms of communication. This category also includes situations in which the content of communication is specified. Describing "things I like to do" is such a situation.

These categories are neither exhaustive nor mutually exclusive. They illustrate the range of considerations necessary when planning for affective learning. You will find many ideas and examples of the situations and exercises described above in Borton (1970), Brown (1971), Gordon (1966), Hawley and Hawley (1972), Morris (1978), Raths, Harmin, and Simon (1966), Schmuck and Schmuck (1974), Stevens (1971), and Weinberg (1972).

APPROACHES TO INSTRUCTION

Many theories, approaches, and models of instruction have been devised and presented to teachers. Some of these are short-lived fads while others endure. Some are content-specialized, such as process writing or whole-language instruction. Some are more general, such as mastery learning and individually guided instruction. While we cannot present even a fraction of the available instructional approaches, we would like to call your attention to some that are promising in that they incorporate many features that are essential for effective instruction. These approaches to instruction are not exclusive; many of the features that make an approach effective are shared.

Below is an annotated bibliography. Reading these items will provide you with some helpful background about instructional approaches. We include these readings in part because the references contained in each of them are extensive. You will find complete citations for this bibliography in the chapter's reference section.

References

Baron, J. B., and Sternberg, R. J. (Eds.). (1987). *Teaching thinking skills: Theory and practice.*
This collection is focused on incorporating thinking skills into classroom instruction. Teachers will find in these chapters many useful suggestions for engaging students in problem solving and critical thinking as part of regular content-based instruction. Of particular note is the chapter by Robert H. Ennis in which he provides a comprehensive taxonomy of critical thinking skills. "Critical thinking," "thinking skills," and "reasoning" are used so commonly, often with a lack of clarity. Ennis's chapter is a tonic for teachers who have wondered just what critical thinking is but have been afraid to ask.

Bereiter, C. (2002). *Education and mind in the knowledge age.*
This book presents a theory of mind and explores the educational implications of this new theory. The theory of mind is one that improves on existing theories—many of which have their origins in (what Bereiter refers to as) folk theory. Significant in the new theory is that ideas are treated as "real things"—conceptual artifacts—and understanding is defined by a person's evolving relationship to the idea. Bereiter develops the idea of knowledge building as key to establishing a meaningful understanding of the world. The book provides an important perspective for thinking about teaching and learning.

Charles, R. I., and Silver, E. A. (Eds.). (1988). *The teaching and assessing of mathematical problem solving.*
This is an edited volume sponsored by the National Council of Teachers of Mathematics. While especially applicable to teaching mathematics, many of the articles discuss problem solving in ways that have general interest and application. Several chapters discuss the use of social and collaborative structures to create a classroom culture that supports learning, problem solving, and intellectual discourse. Other chapters focus on metacognitive aspects of instruction, that is, helping students become more self-regulating learners.

A special issue of *Educational Psychologist* (Spring 1987).
This is a special issue devoted to school and classroom organization. Several contributions by Robert Slavin review and describe various approaches to grouping for instruction. Tracking, ability grouping, and hetero- and homogeneous grouping for instruction are important issues for teachers. This volume will help teachers think about these and other issues of instructional grouping.

Gardner, M., Greeno, J. G., Reif, F., Schoenfeld, A. H., diSessa, A., and Stage, E. (Eds.). (1990). *Toward a scientific practice of science education.*

A collection of articles about instruction in science. One section explores the social context of learning and how this can be taken advantage of and incorporated into instructional designs. An article by Brown and Campione explains explicit strategy instruction and reciprocal teaching. Teachers should be aware of both of these instructional strategies.

Halpern, D. F. (1996). *Thought and knowledge: An introduction to critical thinking* (3rd ed.).

A comprehensive and readable treatise on the key components of critical thinking. Compounds include deduction, induction, analysis of arguments, hypothesis testing, probability and uncertainty, decision making, and creativity. This is an excellent resource for teachers wishing to learn more about critical thinking. Each chapter presents a framework for thinking about and using an aspect of critical thinking. Chapters end with suggestions for applying the framework. These suggestions can be readily incorporated into instructional design.

Johnson, D. W., and Johnson, R. T. (1991). *Learning together and alone* (3rd ed.).

The latest edition of a popular book describing cooperative instructional environments. The authors' approach to group instruction is focused largely on motivational issues and is provided as an antidote to individualistic and competitive classroom environments.

Jones, B. F., and Idol, L. (Eds.). (1990). *Dimensions of thinking and cognitive instruction*.

This is an edited volume with chapters that span a wide range of instructional issues. The organizing theme is the integration of thinking and problem solving with traditional content and skill instruction. Chapters look at teaching in various content areas and at general issues of metacognition and creativity. A chapter by Bransford, Vye, Kinzer, and Risko explains the concept of anchored instruction, an instructional approach designed to foster transfer and make knowledge acquired in school more accessible to learners in "everyday" settings.

Liben, L. S. (Ed.). (1987). *Development and learning: Conflict or congruence?*

The theme of this volume is the relationships among development, instruction, and learning. The relative contributions of development and instruction have been the subject of considerable debate. This book will help teachers understand how instruction can be designed to take advantage of students' developmental levels. Any teacher who devalues the potential contributions of instruction or takes the opposite view, that a student's developmental level has little relevance to instructional planning, should read this book.

Rabinowitz, M. (Ed.). (1993). *Cognitive science foundations of instruction*.

This book is a collection of articles that make the connection between instructional decisions and cognitive theory. Topics range from cognitive task analysis, to a cognitive view of questions and their impact, to the design of integrated curriculum.

Resnick, L. B. (Ed.). (1989). *Knowing, learning, and instruction: Essays in honor of Robert Glaser*.

An edited volume in which most of the contributions focus on the problems of "inert knowledge," that is, knowledge that has little applicability for thinking about or solving problems in the "real" world. Of particular interest to instructional planners are the chapters by Brown and Palincsar and by Collins, Brown, and Newman. Brown and Palincsar describe reciprocal teaching, an approach for providing guidance and scaffolding to novice learners through the structured use of social supports. Collins et al. describe cognitive apprenticeship, a way to situate instruction in a more realistic and supportive context that serves to make learning more easily transferred and applied.

Resnick, L. B., and Klopfer, L. E. (Eds.). (1989). *Toward the thinking curriculum: Current cognitive research*.

This is an important and helpful volume for instructional planners. Each chapter is devoted to a different content area: reading, writing, mathematics, science, and problem solving. The chapters are well written and addressed to classroom teachers. Explicit instructional guidelines are presented. This volume is a high-priority read for teachers interested in the latest developments in instructional psychology.

Rosenshine, B., and Stevens, R. (1986). Teaching functions. In M. C. Wittrock (Ed.), *Handbook of research on teaching* (3rd ed.).

A review of research and explanation of an approach to teaching that has come to be known as "direct instruction," "effective teaching," "mastery teaching," and "explicit teaching," popularized by Madelaine Hunter. It emphasizes explicit objectives, clear explanations, opportunities for practice, and feedback on performance.

Steffe, L. P., and Gale, J. (Eds.). (1995). *Constructivism in education.*
This book is a large collection of work exploring the impact of constructivist theory on educational practice. The range of constructivist thinking is broad, including radical constructivists, Piagetians, and sociocultural approaches. Best about the volume is that theory is tied to instructional practice across a complete range of subject matter.

Voss, J. F., Perkins, D., and Segal, J. (Eds.). (1991). *Informal reasoning and education.*
The authors of the chapters in this book explore the realm of informal reasoning. Informal reasoning is contextualized reasoning as opposed to formal or mathematical reasoning. Informal reasoning occurs in all content areas as well as in nonacademic settings of the "real world." The volume makes a powerful case for including informal reasoning in the curriculum and examines instructional approaches that will help students reason more effectively.

SOME EXAMPLES

The examples that follow illustrate several general teaching strategies based on each unit's ILOs and the points and guidelines presented in this chapter. A rationale or introduction for each unit or subunit describing what the unit is about, what it builds on, and what it leads to is also included. The examples are not models to emulate. They demonstrate the variety and individuality of general teaching strategies for different grade levels and subject areas as conceived by different teachers. As you look at the examples, you should consider or discuss the following questions:

1. How does this strategy provide for an effective learning environment?
   a. Are the goals apt to be clear to the learners?
   b. Are opportunities for feedback provided? Does the feedback vary in its source and when it is available?
   c. Are students likely to be motivated? Is the material presented in an interesting, lively, and/or relevant fashion?
   d. Are students likely to take risks? Will they be rewarded for trying new behaviors or ideas?
   e. Are attempts made to ascertain what students already know? Is their prior knowledge incorporated into the unit's activities?

2. Do the academic tasks fit the kind of learning being sought? Are students, through assigned products and performances, likely to be held accountable for the features that reflect the kind of learning being sought?

3. Do students have opportunities to practice skills at varying levels of difficulty? Are students given opportunities and encouraged to transfer skills to new contexts? Are skills presented in ways designed to make them meaningful?

4. When students are required to understand, comprehend, or otherwise acquire new ideas, are they required to think about and work with these ideas in a variety of ways? Do students have opportunities to apply ideas in contexts and situations that are not identical to those in which the ideas were presented?

5. When students are learning affects, are they encouraged to take a stand on issues, defend their beliefs, encounter opposing beliefs, and otherwise become emotionally involved in their learning?

EXAMPLE 7.1: SUBUNIT TWO—WONDERS OF THE FOREST COMMUNITY

This is the second subunit of a first-grade science unit entitled "Forests."

Introduction

Once the students have become familiar with the attributes of a variety of forests, they will begin focusing on nearby deciduous woods to examine closely the forest ecosystems.

ILOs

COGNITIONS

1. Students will understand that forest communities are self-sustaining systems with basic features that allow energy and matter to flow through them.

2. Students will realize that animals depend on plants for their basic needs.

3. Students will understand that forest communities rely on the ability of plants to convert radiant energy into food.

4. Students will understand that plants have basic needs.

5. Students will understand that plants interact with their environment.

6. Students will understand that plants have properties that allow them to live, thrive, adapt, and meet their needs.

7. Students will realize that plants benefit from animals in meeting their needs.

COGNITIVE SKILLS

1. Students will be able to represent the layers of the forest.

2. Students will be able to recognize several species of trees based on their varying properties.

3. Students will be able to describe ways in which plants affect their environment.

4. Students will be able to illustrate the members of a food chain.

5. Students will be able to identify the parts of a plant and their purposes.

Instructional Foci

1. Forest walks

2. Forest mural

3. Examination of rotting log

4. *A Day in the Woods, Wonders of the Forest, Forests and Jungles, Once There Was a Tree, An Oak Tree Dies and a Journey Begins, The Dead Tree,* and various other books

General Teaching Strategies

This subunit begins with the teacher informing the students that they will be constructing a forest mural that depicts a nearby forest. They need to be as accurate as possible in their representation, so they will visit the forest and read books to promote accuracy. They will also be told that scientists who study the forest have identified several layers of the forest where different plant and animal activities take place. When they take their first walk to the nearby forest, they will try to recognize those layers. To help them understand the meaning of forest layers, they will look at pictures of large cities with different layers of buildings. The names of the forest layers will be given before the students take their walk. They will draw the layers that they can see and try to attach the appropriate label to each layer. When they return to the classroom, they will share their observations and decisions along with the reasons for their decisions.

Over the next two weeks, students will construct a forest mural. They should represent the forest in its current season. They can decide which time of day they want to depict, in order to make decisions about which animals should be visible.

Throughout the mural-building process, students will use books listed in the bibliography as an added resource for information about the growth forms and species they might include. The plant subunit, which is interspersed throughout the unit as a whole, will receive its primary emphasis during this subunit, relating the properties of green plants to properties of trees and forest plants.

The teacher will read *A Day in the Woods* to focus students on the abundance of animal life that finds shelter in the forest, as well as on the interrelationships between plants, animals, and environment.

Wonders of the Forest will also be read to relate the attributes of the forest that were presented in the previous subunit to the forest ecosystem. Students will also read along and listen to *Forests and Jungles* on an accompanying tape to gain further information. The students will then make decisions as to how they want to represent the elements of the forest ecosystem on their mural.

The students will identify the various feeding relationships they have encountered in their reading. The teacher will list these relationships on chart paper. Then the students will work in small groups to see if they can discover any feeding patterns—animals eating plants or animals eating animals, which animals and plants were involved in the various relationships, which layers of the forests were involved, and so on. The students will use the names of the plants and animals they have identified to create food chains. They will sort the animals into plant eaters and meat eaters. After considering questions such as "Where do plants get their energy?" and "What happens to animals when they die?" they will represent the relationships among producers, consumers, and decomposers on food chains that they will create in small groups. They will then assume the roles of the plants and animals in their chains. The teacher will connect the children with a ball of string as their relationships to the rest of the group emerge. The final product will represent a more complex food web.

The students will take a trip to the forest to compare their mural to the type of forest they are representing. They will also examine a rotting log and its surrounding environment. They will observe and record the animal and plant life they see on, under, and around the log. They will examine the forest floor around the log and examine the changes in materials from the leaves on the top of the forest floor to the matter several inches down. They will consider the log as nonliving matter being returned to the environment.

EXAMPLE 7.2: SUBUNIT TWO—RIVERS

This is the second subunit of an upper elementary unit on rivers.

Introduction

The first subunit ended by studying the major rivers of the world, geologically and geographically speaking. This unit begins by investigating the relationship between humankind and rivers. Many ancient civilizations developed in proximity to major river systems. Studying several of these river civilizations provides the basis for the next subunit where students will investigate the history and development of the Connecticut River Valley.

ILOs Emphasized

1. Students will know why rivers have such an impact on the development of civilization.

2. Students will comprehend the various steps in the development of civilization as influenced by rivers and their resources.

3. Students will recognize the historical importance of rivers as various resources to humans.

4. Students will recognize the various resources of rivers used historically by people.

5. Students will demonstrate the knowledge acquired from Subunit One (specifically flood plains, soil deposits, and sediment) during discussions.

6. Students will describe in chronological order the development of human settlements along rivers.

7. Students will identify the various functions of travel along rivers.

8. Students will explain the reasons humans first settled along rivers.

9. Students will identify the factors that lead a people to develop agricultural settlements.

10. Students will explain the development of towns and cities from those agricultural settlements.

11. Students will explain why it was beneficial throughout history for cities to be located along rivers.

12. Students will recognize the importance of rivers as a means of exploration and expansion during the settlement of North America.

13. Students will document the development of settlements in the Connecticut River Valley.

Instructional Foci

1. Pictures of historical settlements along rivers, ancient irrigation systems, historic forms of river transportation

2. Northfield Mountain Recreational and Environmental Center field trip—boat along river, slide show on Indian life in area

3. Library and historical society

4. Field trip to Old Deerfield Village

Teaching Strategies

This subunit begins with a teacher presentation of the time when humans first discovered rivers as a resource. The presentation should be filled with questions directed at students and use different forms of presentation (visual, oral, written). "Let's list some of the biggest cities in the world...." Point out that most of the cities on the list are built either along a river or on another body of water. Explain how the earliest agricultural settlements developed.

Through literature, students will further investigate this development. They will read about different forms of irrigation and how plant and animal life were domesticated.

In small groups, children will construct scale models of early agricultural settlements along the Hwang-Ho, Nile, Euphrates-Tigris, and Indus rivers. These models should incorporate the concepts covered in Subunit One, meaning that students should be discussing the flood plains, land formations, and life cycle when constructing the models.

Students will keep a journal of a fictitious character who lives in an early settlement. In the entries, the student should demonstrate what that person's life is like during the time and place. It is imperative that the teacher make the goal of the journal clear: Students should demonstrate knowledge of that particular time period, what it might have been like to live along that river then.

Further readings and teacher presentations are needed to cover the concepts of how settlements evolved along rivers. The teacher can begin by asking, "What resources did people get from rivers back in _____? Can you think of any examples of how these resources might have evolved to people using rivers in different ways?"

The topic can shift back to North America, with a discussion of how early explorers traveled, considering that there were no roads, only dense woods. There are many biographies on famous explorers of North America who traveled along rivers. Divide the children into small groups (could be based on choice of book, teacher's choice, etc.) and assign them a book to read, with discussion periods. The group makes a final presentation to the rest of the class, with accompanying visuals (map of explorer's journey, mural of scene from the book). The presentation could also be a dramatization of the explorer's story.

Students will develop a board game that somehow illustrates the chronological development of civilization along rivers. They can choose to work in small groups or individually. The game must incorporate the different aspects of the topic studied . . . flood wipes out village, go back to start; or enemy takes over fortress at opening of river and you lose your trading route, go back ten spaces.

Together the class will investigate the development of civilization along the Connecticut, perhaps focusing on one particular town. Again, area resources should be utilized: Jones Library, Amherst Historical Society, resident interviews, old newspaper clippings, museum visits. Perhaps the task could be broken up into smaller parts to be investigated by individual groups.

After the research is put together in the form of a report, perhaps each part presented orally or combined in a class book, the class goes on a field trip to Old Deerfield Village, along the Deerfield River. This gives the students the opportunity to see an example of an early settlement, to compare what they see to what they determined in the report.

Individually, each child will choose a town on another river to research historically, reporting on topics similar to the whole class project, although resources may be limited to books due to proximity constraints. The student should gather information about how and why the town was settled, who settled there, how the town developed, what resources were used, the residents' way of life, climate, and so forth. The children will publish these as information books, with illustrations.

EXAMPLE 7.3: SUBUNIT TWO—THE SOUNDS OF POETRY (1 ½ WEEKS)

This is the second subunit, "Sounds of Poetry," of a middle school unit, "Reading and Writing Poetry."

Introduction

Poetry is intended to be read aloud and therefore the poet writes with attention to the way the poetry sounds. Sometimes words can function onomatopoeically, having meaning in the sound of the word itself. At other times the sound or cadence of words can express emotion or change the pace and mood of the poem. Alliteration and assonance are examples of this use of language. Poets also choose to use sound and the description of sound for the connotation of emotions, colors, and attitudes. All three uses of meaning conveyed through sound will be examined in this subunit. Students will be challenged to think of noises as words. They will read poems by a variety of authors, attending to the sounds of the language chosen. They will write poems describing the sounds of a scene and the images inspired by listening to music.

ILOs

1. Students will be able to respond to the question," What is poetry?" They will realize that poetry expresses the voice of the poet in a way that differs from prose beyond the simple conventions of form.

2. Students will realize that people differ in their understandings of a poem, and know that poetry allows for more than a single interpretation.

3. Students will understand the importance of sound within a poem. They will recognize the use of and the significance of alliteration, onomatopoeia, and rhyme.

4. Students will be able to express their opinions and interpretations of a poem. They will be able to explain and give reasons for these interpretations.

5. Students will be able to use imagery in their poems.

6. Students will be able to write poetry using rhyme and free verse.

Instructional Foci

1. Poems include:
   "The Eagle" by Alfred, Lord Tennyson
   "Silver" by Walter De la Mare
   "The Peppery Man" by Arthur Macy
   "The Train" by David McCord
   "Poem to Mud" by Zilpha Keatley Snyder

2. Crumpling of paper/Clinking of glasses

3. Listening to music:
   the saxophone jazz of Kenny G
   Pachelbel's canon

Teaching Strategies

The first discussion will revolve around the use of alliteration, though this term need not be used. The teacher will read "The Eagle" by Tennyson aloud. Ensuing questions might include, What does the eagle look like? How do you know this? How would this poem be different if the poet had written "he held onto the rock with his sharp talons" instead of "he clasped the crag with crooked hands"? "Silver" by Walter De la Mare should also be read aloud with student attention drawn to the quick quietness alluded to in the repetition of sibilant sounds. Questions should demand progressively more introspection as students delve more deeply into poetic techniques.

Students will be asked to find adjectives to describe the sound of crumpling paper. Guidance should be provided with questions such as, What words did that crumpling sound like? If necessary the teacher can elaborate: Did it sound like "crumple" or more like "crackle," "crunch," "crinkle"? What other things can you think of that might sound like this? Again, examples can be given: crackers crunching under sneakers is the type of vivid image looked for here. Describing the clink of glasses will provide further practice in word choice. Students should be asked not only to think of descriptive adjectives but to think of words that evoke the sound but mean something different. An example given by the teacher as a starter might be "pink drink." In this way, using examples and demonstrations, the student will be encouraged to experiment with words that evoke noises and sounds in and of themselves.

The writing assignment following this lesson should be open-ended, reading something like this:

1. the sounds in your kitchen when dinner is being made

2. the sounds in your room as you are lying in the dark going to sleep

   Think about the scene, and how you feel in that place. You might write a poem in the midst of that activity!

The second section of this subunit will focus on expressing the mood of a piece of music through the art of poetry. Students will listen to one minute of upbeat jazz music. They will be asked to think about what mood the music conveys and what images it sparks in their minds. The second listening will be the basis for the next poem writing assignment; students will listen to Pachelbel's canon and then jot down ideas, feelings, colors, and scenes that come to mind. They will be encouraged to share these associative ideas. They will eventually illustrate these music poems, showing the interrelations possible among music, art, and writing.

Oral reading of "The Train" and "Poem to Mud," and the ensuing discussion, should serve as review for the techniques of alliteration and onomatopoeia. The poetic terms should not be used, instead letting students describe the techniques through their own observations.

EXAMPLE 7.4: SUBUNIT ONE—THE CAMERA

This is the introductory subunit for a high school art unit on black-and-white photography.

Introduction

This subunit introduces the basic functions of a 35-mm, single-lens reflex camera. Vocabulary and identification of the parts of a camera are introduced. The concept of a camera as a controller of light is accompanied by lessons on how to select appropriate shutter and aperture settings. The concept of depth of field is introduced here.

ILOs

1. The students will understand how the uses and technology of cameras have evolved over the past 150 years.
2. The students will understand the processes and techniques involved in photographing, developing, and printing black-and-white film with a 35-mm camera.

Instructional Foci

1. 35-mm camera

2. Textbook, Upton & Upton, *Photography,* pp. 37–85

3. Charts and posters in demonstration area

4. Many examples of shutter and aperture priority photographs

5. Vocabulary list on bulletin board as well as given in handout form to each student

6. Student folder

7. Current shows and exhibits on board

8. Photography journals, numerous books, and examples

Teaching Strategies

The teacher demonstrates with 35-mm camera while the students get hands-on practice using the controls and features of their own cameras. It is crucial at this point to mix in some aesthetic and creative elements with the technical aspects. The teacher should show quality examples of master artists' work and previous students' work highlighting the different features of the camera. The teacher initiates a discussion about how the camera features were manipulated to attain different images. The students are encouraged to comment on the images' visual impact, strengths, and weaknesses, and whether they feel they are effective. This is a great warm-up activity to introduce "critique" vocabulary while getting students familiar with this type of group discussion and evaluation process. Students are asked to keep an "eye" out for photographs from any source that would be good discussion material for the class in the technical and/or creative aspects. The teacher gives an assignment called "The Different Ways of Seeing: The Ten-Step Assignment."

This assignment is a great first photography exercise. You begin at one of the doors of your home. You stand in one place and look around until you find something that you frame (a slice of the world that looks interesting); you then take ten steps toward it to frame it (or part of it) at a closer perspective. You walk another ten steps and repeat this procedure. The rules of this assignment are that after each ten steps you must look up, down, left, right, straight ahead, and behind you, and try to explore every angle and perspective you can to frame something you believe to be interesting. This enables the photographer to experience a bird's-eye view or a worm's-eye view (squatting or lying down) and get a different "handle" on some familiar territory. Another important point is to try to remember to experiment with the vertical as well as horizontal orientation of your 35-mm camera.

INTRODUCTION AND TWO SUBUNITS FROM A HIGH SCHOOL ALGEBRA UNIT ON COORDINATE GEOMETRY

Introduction

The goal of the overall teaching strategy for this unit is to get students thinking in terms of practical application of newly learned mathematical concepts. This should be accomplished through class discussions and practice working with realistic examples both individually and in small groups. Any time group or individual practice is called for, the work should be submitted with written explanations of all operations. That is, any significant steps in the work should be fully explained in terms of what is being done and why. It is important that the groups comprise different members each class period in order that each student's ideas, views, and skills be shared with all of the others. The primary instructional focus for the entire unit will be the application of newly learned concepts and skills to "real-world" data and examples provided by both the teacher and the students. The students should keep all of the distributed examples in a notebook, neatly organized and available for use in class each day. The two most critical intended learning outcomes to be emphasized in every subunit are the following:

1. Students will understand that real-world data can be represented graphically and quantified and idealized by mathematical formulations, which can be used to draw conclusions from a graph.

2. Students will be able to interpret mathematical relationships from graphs and make generalizations and predictions regarding their behavior both quantitatively and qualitatively.

EXAMPLE 7.5: SUBUNIT THREE—GRAPHING TWO-DIMENSIONAL LINEAR EQUATIONS

This is the third subunit from a high school algebra unit on coordinate geometry.

Central Concepts

- linearity
- slope of a line
- midpoint of a line
- forms of linear equations
- parallel lines and intersecting lines
- intercepts
- systems of equations

Principal ILOs

1. The students will understand the meaning of and uses of linear equations.

2. The students will recognize and be able to manipulate linear equations in order to find pertinent information regarding the graph of each equation.

3. The students will understand how performing operations on linear equations affects graphical representation and interpretation.

4. The students will understand the concepts of interpolation and extrapolation and how to use them for predictions.

5. The students will understand the structure of the Cartesian coordinate system and the use of ordered pairs for graphing linear and nonlinear equations.

6. The students will understand the mathematical relationships between parallel, intersecting, and perpendicular lines.

7. The students will understand the derivation and use of the distance and midpoint formulas.

Teaching Strategy

This subunit should begin with a class discussion on the topic of linearity. The students should be clear on the difference between linear and nonlinear relationships, and the examples should be reviewed and classified into linear and nonlinear categories in small work groups. This should be followed by the introduction of the concepts of slope, parallel lines, intersecting lines, and midpoint. Class discussion should focus on the relationship of the midpoint and midpoint formula to the concept of interpolation and the usefulness of slope for extrapolation. The groups can then practice finding and comparing the slopes of various lines in the examples and discuss the meaning of the differences.

At this point the students should have a fairly strong grasp of the structure of the Cartesian coordinate system. Working in small groups, the students should discuss ideas for relating and describing the points in a graph (i.e., a linear equation). Each group should present its ideas to the class, with the ensuing discussion centering around the merits of each. At this point, the concept of a linear equation may be formally presented to the class. Additionally, some attention should be given to the relationship of the roots of an equation to the intersection of a line with the axes on a graph (the intercepts). Variations on the equation of a line such as standard, point-slope, and slope-intercept form should be discussed with an emphasis on the benefits of using a particular form for a specific application. Students should then have an opportunity to practice finding and interpreting equations of lines from the examples, in groups and individually. Additionally, they should practice interpreting meaning from an equation describing some data.

Once the students are proficient and comfortable working with the equation of a line, the idea of graphing systems of equations can be introduced. The class should discuss the significance of graphing several lines simultaneously on one graph and the relationship to solving systems of equations. Special attention should be given to the meaning of the intersections of lines in a graph of simultaneous equations. The students should have group and individual practice with the examples to solve systems of equations using graphs.

EXAMPLE 7.6: SUBUNIT FOUR—OPERATIONS OF GRAPHS

Central Concepts

- translation and rotation of axes
- reflection
- symmetry and inverses
- angle of intersection

Principal ILOs

1. Students will understand how performing operations on linear equations affects the graphical representation and interpolation.

2. Students will recognize and be able to manipulate linear equations in order to find pertinent information regarding the graph of each equation.

Teaching Strategy

At this point, the students should be quite adept at working with and interpreting linear equations and graphs. The concepts of translation, rotation, and reflection should be introduced as methods of altering the visual presentation of data. Care should be taken during class discussions to ensure that the students understand that these operations change the way data is perceived but do not actually change the data itself. The discussions should also cover symmetry, inverses, and angles of intersection as additional tools for interpreting and evaluating graphs and equations. The students should work in groups, examining the examples to see if any of the graphs have been or should be altered for clarification and readability. They should also experiment with actually altering the graphs of the examples to see how that affects perception and interpretation.

COURSE PLANNING STEPS

Course Planning Step 7.1   Develop each of your selected instructional foci into a description of general teaching strategies. This description should be based on your ILOs and on the points and guidelines presented in this chapter. Pay particular attention to the high-priority unit ILOs. Avoid using the passive voice in your descriptions. (For example, do not say: Terraria are constructed.) Instead, make it clear who is doing what in the strategy. (For example, do say: Students construct terraria by following instructions the teacher hands out.)

Course Planning Step 7.2   For each of your units write a brief (25–100 word) description, introduction, or rationale of the unit. Include what your unit contains, why it is important, how it builds on previous units (if it does), and how (if at all) succeeding units build on it. The introductions accompanying the River, Poetry, and Camera units are good examples.

Course Planning Step 7.3   Reconsider your total instructional plan in the light of your rationale, checking for internal consistency and comprehensiveness. Add to the completed units any ILOs you had not thought of previously.

QUESTIONS FOR DISCUSSION: GENERAL TEACHING STRATEGIES

1. Did you add, change, or eliminate any ILOs in the process of specifying a general teaching strategy? Which ones, and why?

2. Which of your units at this point seem to be most complete, most appropriate, or simply best? Why?

3. Which of your units at this point seem to be least complete, appropriate, or perfected? Can you say why?

4. Compare your brief unit rationales with your course rationale. Do the units as described seem to support the course rationale fully? Does this comparison suggest that the course rationale be rewritten?

5. With your instructional plan in hand, could someone else now teach this course (assuming practical teaching experience and a knowledge of the subject matter)?

6. Of your ILOs, which two or three do you now feel most confident about accomplishing? Are there any you feel uneasy about? Why?

REFERENCES

Ausubel, D. P. (1968). *Educational psychology: A cognitive view*. New York: Holt, Rinehart and Winston, Inc.

Baron, J. B., & Sternberg, R. J. (Eds.). (1987). *Teaching thinking skills: Theory and practice*. New York: W. H. Freeman.

Bell-Gredler, M. E. (1986). *Learning and instruction: Theory into practice*. New York: Macmillan.

Bellon, J. J., Bellon, E. C., & Blank, M. A. (1992). *Teaching from a research knowledge base: A development and renewal process*. New York: Merrill.

Bereiter, C. (2002). *Education and mind in the knowledge age.* Mahwah, NJ: Lawrence Erlbaum Associates.

Bereiter, C., & Scardamalia, M. (1989). Intentional learning. In L. B. Resnick (Ed.), *Knowing, learning, and instruction: Essays in honor of Robert Glaser.* Hillsdale, NJ: Lawrence Erlbaum Associates.

Borich, G. D. (1992). *Effective teaching methods* (2nd ed.). New York: Merrill.

Borton, T. (1970). *Reach, touch, and teach.* New York: McGraw-Hill.

Bransford, J. D., & Stein, B. S. (1984). *The ideal problem solver: A guide for improving thinking, learning, and creativity.* New York: W. H. Freeman.

Brown, A. L. & Campione, J. C. (1996). Psychological theory and the design of innovative learning environments: On procedures, principles, and systems. In L. Shauble & R. Glaser (Eds.), *Innovations in learning: New environments for education.* Mahwah, NJ: Lawrence Erlbaum Associates.

Brown, G. (1971). *Human teaching for human learning: An introduction for confluent education.* New York: Viking.

Charles, R. I., & Silver, E. A. (Eds.). (1988). *The teaching and assessing of mathematical problem solving.* Hillsdale, NJ: Lawrence Erlbaum Associates.

Collins, A., Brown, J. S., & Newman, S. E. (1989). Cognitive apprenticeship: Teaching the crafts of reading, writing and mathematics. In L. B. Resnick (Ed.), *Knowing, learning, and instruction: Essays in honor of Robert Glaser.* Hillsdale, NJ: Lawrence Erlbaum Associates.

Doyle, W. (1983). Academic work. *Review of Educational Research, 53*(2), 159–199.

Doyle, W. (1992). Curriculum and pedagogy. In Philip W. Jackson (Ed.), *Handbook of research on curriculum.* New York: Macmillan.

Educational Psychologist. (Spring 1987). *22*(2).

Gardner, M., Greeno, J. G., Reif, F., Schoenfeld, A. H., diSessa, A., & Stage, E. (Eds.). (1990). *Toward a scientific practice of science education.* Hillsdale, NJ: Lawrence Erlbaum Associates.

Gordon, W. J. J. (1966). *The metaphorical way of learning and knowing.* Cambridge, MA: Synectics Education Systems.

Greenwood, G. E., & Parkay, F. W. (1989). *Case studies for teacher decision making.* New York: Random House.

Halpern, D. F. (1996). *Thought and knowledge: An introduction to critical thinking* (3rd ed.). Hillsdale, NJ: Lawrence Erlbaum Associates.

Hawley, R. C., & Hawley, I. L. (1972). *A handbook of personal growth activities for classroom use.* Amherst, MA: Educational Research Associates.

Johnson, D. W., & Johnson, R. T. (1991). *Learning together and alone* (3rd ed.). Englewood Cliffs, NJ: Prentice-Hall.

Jones, B. F., & Idol, L. (Eds.). (1990). *Dimensions of thinking and cognitive instruction.* Hillsdale, NJ: Lawrence Erlbaum Associates.

Liben, L. S. (Ed.). (1987). *Development and learning: Conflict or congruence?* Hillsdale, NJ: Lawrence Erlbaum Associates.

Mayer, R. E. (2002). *The Promise of Educational Psychology, Volume II: Teaching for Meaningful Learning.* Upper Saddle River, NJ: Merrill Prentice-Hall.

Morris, J. (1978). *Psychology and teaching: A humanistic view.* New York: Random House.

Posner, G. J. (1982). A cognitive science conception of curriculum and instruction. *Journal of Curriculum Studies, 14*(4), 343–351.

Rabinowitz, M. (Ed.). (1993). *Cognitive science foundations of instruction.* Hillsdale, NJ: Lawrence Erlbaum Associates.

Raths, L. E., Harmin, M., & Simon, S. B. (1966). *Values and teaching.* Columbus, OH: Charles E. Merrill.

Resnick, L. B. (Ed.). (1989). *Knowing, learning, and instruction: Essays in honor of Robert Glaser.* Hillsdale, NJ: Lawrence Erlbaum Associates.

Resnick, L. B., & Klopfer, L. E. (Eds.). (1989). *Toward the thinking curriculum: Current cognitive research.* 1989 Yearbook of the Association for Supervision and Curriculum Development.

Rosenshine, B., & Stevens, R. (1986). Teaching functions. In M. C. Wittrock (Ed.), *Handbook of research on teaching* (3rd ed.). New York: Macmillan.

Scardamalia, M. (2002). Collective cognitive responsibility for the advancement of knowledge. In B. Smith (Ed.), *Liberal education in a knowledge society.* Chicago, IL: Open Court.

Scardamalia, M., & Bereiter, C. (2003). Knowledge building. In *Encyclopedia of education* (2nd ed.). New York: Macmillan Reference, USA.

Schmuck, R. A., & Schmuck, P. A. (1974). *A humanistic psychology of education: Making the school everybody's house.* Palo Alto, CA: National Press Books.

Sizer, T. R. (1984). *Horace's compromise: The dilemma of the American high school.* Boston: Houghton Mifflin.

Snider, V. E. (1990). What we know about learning styles from research in special education. *Educational Leadership 48*(2), 53.

Steffe, L. P., & Gale, J. (Eds.). (1995). *Constructivism in education.* Hillsdale, NJ: Lawrence Erlbaum Associates.

Stevens, J. P. (1971). *Awareness, exploring, experimenting, experiencing.* New York: Bantam Books.

Voss, J. F., Perkins, D., & Segal, J. (Eds.). (1991). *Informal reasoning and education.* Hillsdale, NJ: Lawrence Erlbaum Associates.

Walker, D. (1990). *Fundamentals of curriculum.* New York: Harcourt Brace Jovanovich.

Weinberg, C. (Ed.). (1972). *Human foundations of education.* Englewood Cliffs, NJ: Prentice-Hall.

West, C. K., Farmer, J. A., & Wolff, P. M. (1991). *Instructional design: Implications from cognitive science.* Englewood Cliffs, NJ: Prentice-Hall.

Whitehead, A. N. (1916). The aims of education. Address to the British Mathematical Society, Manchester, England.

Yelon, S. L. (1996). *Powerful principles of instruction.* White Plains, NY: Longman.

PLANNING A COURSE EVALUATION

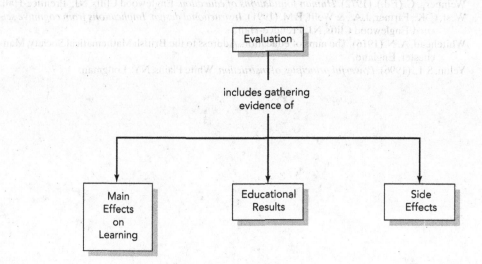

After completing this chapter, you should be able to:

1. Comprehend the meaning of the terms *actual learning outcome, main effect,* and *side effect.*

2. Specify appropriate behavioral evidence for any given ILO.

3. Specify likely side effects that may result from a course.

4. Gather and analyze behavioral evidence using a troubleshooting approach to course evaluation.

PERSPECTIVE ON EVALUATION

To this point, course planning has been concerned with setting up a focused, justifiable, interesting, feasible, and coherent course. But a course must also be effective, and as planners we need to know how effective it is. Typically, we need information about the course's effectiveness in order to make decisions about the course. Such information gathering and subsequent decision making comprise an evaluation aimed at course improvement.

Assessment has supplanted *evaluation* as the most widely used term referring to the process of gathering evidence and using it to make judgments about educational practice. We consider the two terms synonymous.[1] Standards-based reform has stimulated a great deal of interest in and writing about educational evaluation. Much of what is new has to do with the use of standards to improve education. As far as the theoretical and conceptual foundations for educational assessment, we continue to find the work of Scriven (1967) and Cronbach (1963) sound sources. We do believe that one facet of evaluation that is new and important is having students play more of a role in their own assessment. To a great extent, this has as much to do with instruction, having assessment become a tool for learning, as it does with making judgments about and improvements in curriculum and instruction. Brown and Campione (1996) and Campione, Shapiro, and Brown (1995) discuss the potential benefits and provide interesting illustrations and guidelines for how students can become involved in their own assessment. For our purposes in *Course Design,* we focus on evaluation or assessment that serves to improve curriculum and instruction.

The Uses of Evaluation

Evaluations can be used for many types of decisions. For instance, Cronbach (1963) identified three uses for evaluation: (a) course-improvement decisions, (b) decisions about individual students, and (c) administrative regulation. Evaluation for course improvement involves gathering information that will be useful in deciding which curricular and instructional aspects of a course can and should be improved. Evaluation aimed at decisions about individual students consists of gathering information to be used in assessing student needs or in the grading, grouping, or selection of individual students. Evaluation for administrative regulation is directed toward assessing the merit of schools, curricula, materials, teachers, and so forth.

Cronbach (1963) argues that using evaluation for course improvement contributes more toward improving education than do the other uses of evaluation. This argument has been debated most eloquently by Scriven (1967), who points out that decisions on the merit or worth of a course ("summative" decisions) are as important in improving education as decisions aimed at course improvement ("formative" decisions).

---

[1] *The New Oxford American Dictionary* (2001) uses *evaluate* in its definition for *assess* and uses *assess* in its definition of *evaluate.*

As mentioned, this chapter deals with course evaluation aimed at gathering and analyzing information that will be used for course-improvement decisions. That is, a formative evaluation is emphasized. This emphasis was not chosen because summative decisions are unimportant. But if the course is irremediably bad, this fact should become evident during the formative evaluation. The course can be abandoned on the basis of such data. On the other hand, courses can almost always be improved.

Range of Outcomes

Cronbach (1963), in discussing evaluation for course improvement, emphasizes the need for an evaluation to describe the broadest possible range of course outcomes. On this point Cronbach is in substantial agreement with others such as Scriven (1967), who also emphasize the description of course consequences.

Scriven (1967) elaborates further on the *range* of course outcomes to be examined. He distinguishes between two related but distinct enterprises, which he labels *evaluation* and *goal estimation*. Goal estimation (goal-based evaluation) focuses entirely on the extent to which a course has achieved its *stated goals or objectives*. Evaluation, on the other hand, requires gathering information on the *full range of course outcomes or consequences*. Goal estimation, as well as being more limited in focus, is viewed as less desirable than evaluation because goals are often unrealistic and thus an inadequate basis for information gathering.

Scriven's (1967) emphasis on evaluations that examine a full range of course outcomes has led him to propose *goal-free evaluation* as a radical alternative to goal estimation or goal-based evaluation. Goal-free evaluation views a course as an educational or instructional "treatment" and attempts to gather data on *likely consequences* of that treatment irrespective of stated goals and objectives. In contrast, a goal-based evaluation focuses only on stated goals and objectives.

This chapter combines goal-free and goal-based approaches in attempting to identify the important course consequences. ILOs are used to guide the collection of evidence that will determine whether or not intended learnings are actually achieved. The extent to which the course's ILOs are actualized constitutes the *main effects* of the course. A second aspect of the evaluation is an examination of materials, methods, and other factors likely to result in consequences or effects that we did not intend or even consider. These unintended (and sometimes undesirable) outcomes are referred to as the *side effects* of the course. Once we collect information regarding both main and side effects, we can use it to make course-improvement decisions.

Using Information for Course Improvement

It may be helpful to think about course evaluation in the same way a TV repairer thinks about a broken TV. The repairer finds whether or not the set works by plugging it in, turning it on, and evaluating the quality of picture and sound. Assuming there is something wrong with the set, the repairer is faced with troubleshooting the problem. This process consists of setting up a series of probes that result in evidence pertaining to the operation of particular components of the set. The troubleshooting procedure allows the repairer to isolate that aspect of the system that is malfunctioning.

While troubleshooting a course is analogous to electronic troubleshooting, it is far more complex. The likelihood of identifying a single course component as *the* problem is slight. But if we want to be able to use the information gathered in an evaluation to improve the course, we have to relate particular kinds of information to particular course components.

The troubleshooting scheme presented in this chapter is largely based on the intended learning outcomes of the course. Guidelines for gathering evidence are presented first, followed by questions that facilitate the processing of this evidence.

To summarize, actual learning outcomes (ALOs) are those things learned by students during, or as a part of, the course. These ALOs consist of those learnings that were considered important and were thus stated as ILOs (that is, main effects) and those learnings that were not considered important or were thought to be undesirable and were thus not stated as ILOs (that is, side effects). These main and side effects, together with an assessment of educational results, form the basis of course evaluation presented in this chapter. The considerations important in this evaluation include the following:

Do all the intended learning outcomes turn out to be actual learning outcomes?

If not, which ILOs were and which were not achieved?

What ALOs were not planned for in the course?

Are the side effects desirable or undesirable?

To what extent were the educational goals achieved and were the ILOs relevant to the achievement of those goals?

The answers to these questions must then be applied in a troubleshooting approach in order to make course-improvement decisions. Applying the evidence for decision making involves thinking about the relationship between the evidence gathered and the various course components (for example, teacher behaviors, instructional foci, and the organization of units). To do this, evidence of learning must first be gathered.

GATHERING EVIDENCE ON MAIN EFFECTS

The course's ILOs refined in Chapter 4 are of four types: cognitions, cognitive skills, affects, and psychomotor–perceptual skills. The task of evaluation planning for these ILOs is one of specifying what will constitute acceptable evidence; that is, evidence that will indicate whether or not an ILO has actually been learned. Evidence is defined as an outward sign; therefore, by definition, evidence of learning must be observable. Since the evidence will be gathered from students, we look for this evidence in observable student behaviors or observable products of student work.

In the ensuing discussions we will focus the evaluation on high-priority ILOs. We believe that a course evaluation should emphasize these ILOs over less important learnings. Typically, time and resources limit the scope of an evaluation; evidence of highest-priority ILOs may be all the evidence you can gather. These ILOs have been identified and asterisked in Chapter 4 (Course Planning Step 4.6).

One way to conceptualize the differences between the types of ILOs from the standpoint of evaluation is to consider the extent to which the content or behavior is circumscribed or defined in a particular ILO. A behavior such as "explain in your own words" is more narrowly focused or limited than "grasp the meaning of." Content such as "the key provisions of the Magna Charta" is more focused or limited than "interesting topic sentences." A useful rule of thumb is: whatever portion of the ILO was not circumscribed in Chapter 4 now receives the greatest attention in specifying behavioral evidence. For a cognition, the content was highly circumscribed when stating the ILO; therefore, we now focus on the specification of sample behaviors that will serve as evidence. For a cognitive or psychomotor–perceptual skill, the behavior or performance was probably highly circumscribed when stating the ILO, and we must now specify sample contexts (that is, content) for those behaviors. Each type of ILO is treated separately in the following sections.

Cognitions

A cognition is an understanding and has no *directly* observable referent. Therefore, no *one* behavior constitutes acceptable evidence of understanding. The understanding of an idea has numerous and varied exemplifications. The evaluation task, therefore, is to specify a set of behaviors that together will constitute acceptable evidence of understanding. A useful question to ask is, "If someone demonstrates these specified behaviors, would I be willing to say that the person has achieved the intended understanding?"

When faced with the problem of gathering behavioral evidence on the extent of knowledge acquisition, caution is advised. The ability to verbalize an idea (for example, to give a definition or give a label for an object) does not mean that the learner has necessarily understood the idea. It is possible both to recite definitions of ideas that have never been understood and to be unable to formulate a definition of an idea that has indeed been understood. These caveats notwithstanding, the course or unit story can be useful from the standpoint of assessment. Asking students to tell, in their own words, the geology, inquiry, literature, symmetry, or whatever story can be very revealing. Having students devise examples or cite situations or experiences that correspond to parts of the story has also provided insights into student thinking. Many teachers have said that students have applied stories to other contexts and subject matter. For example, a teacher who worked with the inquiry story reported that her students used the ideas of evidence and hypotheses while discussing literature. This sort of transfer is extremely powerful evidence of understanding.

Indicators that students have learned ideas that are classes or categories of objects or events (see p. 104) include the ability to identify an object by placing it into a category and the ability to recognize a nonexample (that is, an object that bears a "family resemblance" but is not a member of the set—for example, recognizing that a frog is not a reptile). Other behaviors such as defining, stating attributes, and describing relationships serve as evidence for these cognitions. The selection of behavioral indicators for cognitions depends, in part, on whether the cognition requires memory, comprehension, or justified belief:

1. The primary kinds of observable behavior that may indicate memory are stating (either wholly or partially) and recognizing the idea.

2. The primary kinds of behavior that may indicate comprehension include translating, paraphrasing, and explaining. Other behaviors that may be used include comparing, describing, and distinguishing.

3. Behaviors indicating justified belief include verbally justifying, defending, supplying evidence, arguing, and choosing an appropriate course of action based on specific information.

Knowing which properties relate to a particular cognition is a first step toward the specification of evidence. For each relevant property several behaviors should be specified.

Wiggins and McTighe (1998, Chapter 4) offer a useful rubric for assessing understanding. They make the point that understanding is not an all-or-nothing affair and that by looking for various sorts of evidence, teachers can get a sense of students' levels of understanding. The rubric has the following six facets:

1. *Explanation: sophisticated and apt explanation and theories, which provide knowledgeable and justified accounts of events, actions, and ideas.*

2. *Interpretation: interpretations, narratives, and translations that provide meaning.*

3. *Application: ability to use knowledge effectively in new situations and diverse contexts.*

4. *Perspective: critical and insightful points of view.*

5. *Empathy: the ability to get inside another person's feelings and worldview.*

6. *Self-Knowledge: the wisdom to know one's ignorance and how one's patterns of thought and action inform as well as prejudice understanding.*

Example 8.1

ILO: The student should understand that regular medical checkups are an essential aspect of good health. (This ILO involves the properties of memory, comprehension, and justified belief.)

Evidence of memory (recalls the assertion): When asked, "What is an essential aspect of good health?" the student responds, "Regular medical checkups."

Evidence of comprehension (comprehends the assertion): The student can explain in his or her own words some aspects of good health.

Evidence of justified belief (has evidence for the assertion): The student can argue the benefits of regular checkups. The student can explain the consequences of not having these checkups. The student can explain the reasons regular checkups are beneficial.

Example 8.2

ILO: The student understands the idea of gravitational force.
Evidence of understanding the idea: The student defines "gravitational force." The student describes the relationship between gravitational force and other forces.

The student points out phenomena that cannot be explained by gravitational force. The student explains relevant phenomena using the idea of gravitational force.

Example 8.3

ILO: The student understands the relationship between an organism and its environment.

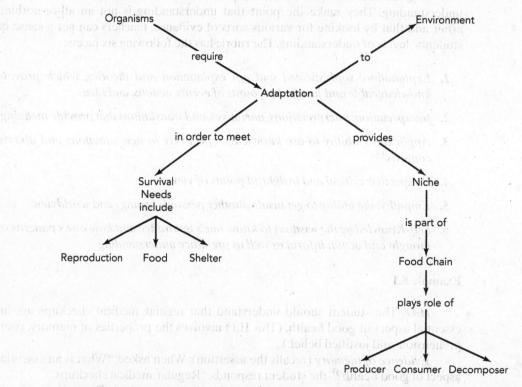

FIGURE 8.1   Student's conceptual map showing relationships between an organism and its environment.

Evidence of understanding the relationship: The student is able to create a map showing how the following terms are related. The student can label relationships where appropriate. (Note: There will be differences between your map and student maps as well as differences among student maps. This evidence should be interpreted with an emphasis on the relationships depicted. A sample answer is shown in Figure 8.1.)

organism	shelter	food
reproduction	adaptation	environment
niche	decomposer	survival needs
producer	food chain	consumer

Course Planning Step 8.1 If one or more of your high-priority ILOs are cognitions, write them down on a separate sheet of paper entitled "Evidence of Main Effects." Then, for each of these ILOs, write down two or more observable behaviors that will count as evidence that the student has acquired these cognitions.

Affects

How an individual manifests an affective skill or understanding varies greatly from person to person and situation to situation. It may not always be reasonable to expect a person who has learned an affect to supply behavioral evidence of that affect on demand. Therefore, a useful strategy of course evaluation for affects is to keep your eyes open and observe behavior unobtrusively. The following guidelines should be helpful in using this strategy:

1. Describe what behaviors would evidence an individual's having a particular affective skill or understanding.

2. Consider the context or circumstance in which these behaviors would be likely to occur. That is, during what occasions, and in what places or situations, might a person behave in the desired manner?

3. Consider which of these circumstances arise in the educational setting and would thus permit you to observe a student demonstrating that affect-related behavior.

With these guidelines, you can become sensitive to the opportunities that arise where manifestations of these affects can be observed. The following examples illustrate how you might use these guidelines.

Example 8.4

ILO: The student should act in a caring and sound manner toward the environment. (Affective skill)

Evidence of affect (behaviors, actions): The student doesn't willfully disturb any aspect of the environment. The student leaves natural conditions as they are found. The student instructs or reminds others of proper actions. The student states valid reasons for any intrusion he or she makes on a natural setting.

Circumstances: school grounds, field trips (nature hikes).

Example 8.5

ILO: The student should recognize his or her tendency to either believe or disbelieve statements made by others. (Affective understanding)

Behaviors: The student can give an accurate description of his or her reaction to others.

Circumstances: The student accepts outlandish arguments without questions, is overly argumentative, or questions all statements made by others during class discussions and during interactions with peers outside of class.

Some affective skills and understandings can be evaluated more straightforwardly. That is, you can devise a means of gathering evidence that can be administered to students in a direct manner. The examples that follow illustrate this.

Example 8.6

ILO: The student should understand how commercials and advertisements affect consumer behavior. (Affective understanding)

Evidence of affect: The student can explain how commercials try to appeal to individuals. The student can point out examples of consumer behavior where consumers pay more for an advertised product that is entirely equivalent to a less expensive unadvertised product. The student can give examples of how his or her own consumer habits are personally affected by commercials. The student can explain the difficulties in overcoming commercial "hype" surrounding certain types of consumer goods.

Example 8.7

ILO: The student should be able to respond to another person's comments with empathy and without altering the content of the message. (Affective skill)

Evidence of affect: Given several transcripts of client comments, the student will write down responses. These can be judged for degree of empathy and how closely the client's meaning was understood.

Course Planning Step 8.2   If one or more of your high-priority ILOs are affects, write them down on a sheet of paper entitled "Evidence of Main Effects." Then for each of these ILOs write down two or more observable behaviors that will count as evidence that the student has acquired the affect. Finally, write down a set of circumstances or contexts in which the behaviors are most likely to be observed.

Cognitive Skills

Cognitive skills are typically stated in terms of specific though not directly observable behaviors. Because the behavior is often circumscribed, which leaves less room for varied interpretations, the specification of behavioral evidence is generally more straightforward than for cognitions or affects. Two ideas that are helpful in thinking about the specification of appropriate content (or context) in which to demonstrate a skill are *difficulty* and *transfer*. Difficulty refers to the complexity of the content. For example, outlining a long and complex article is more difficult than outlining a shorter article; constructing a convincing argument is more difficult for a position with which you disagree than for one with which you agree.

Transfer, while related to difficulty, refers to the degree of similarity between the content used for learning the skill and the content used for supplying evidence of the skill. For example, outlining a story or scientific article involves transfer if the learning tasks focused only on outlining newspaper items; having students use *Psychological Abstracts* to locate information when their learning tasks focused on the *Current Index to Journals in Education* also requires transfer. Whenever possible, the kinds of evidence you gather for a cognitive skill should vary in terms of difficulty and transfer. This will provide more useful information for making decisions aimed at improving your teaching. The following examples illustrate the process of specifying evidence for cognitive skills.

Example 8.8

ILO: The student should be able to plan a nutritionally balanced meal.

Evidence of cognitive skill: The student should be able to plan a nutritionally balanced meal for: a person with a large caloric requirement, a person who plans to be very active on a hot and humid summer day, or a child on a cold winter morning.

Example 8.9

ILO: The student should be able to propose ways to test a hypothesis.

Evidence of cognitive skill: The student should be able to explain, in writing, two different experiments to test a given causal hypothesis. The student should be able to state verbally the qualities of a testable hypothesis. The student should be able to describe empirical and nonempirical modes of hypothesis testing.

Course Planning Step 8.3   If one or more of your high-priority ILOs are cognitive skills, write them down on a sheet of paper entitled "Evidence of Main Effects."

Then write down two or more descriptions of behavioral evidence or indicators for each of these ILOs.

Psychomotor–Perceptual Skills

Psychomotor–perceptual skills are skills and abilities of a behavioral nature. The concern in specifying acceptable evidence is again in the *context* of the behavior. As with cognitive skills, students must be given sufficient opportunity to exhibit the behavior.

Example 8.10

ILO: The student should be able to discern the sounds of orchestral instruments.

Evidence of psychomotor–perceptual skill (aural discrimination): The student should be able to match the names of 15 different instruments to the sound of each instrument (assumes the student has previously memorized the names). The student should be able to name the instruments he or she hears used in a particular symphonic piece (specify the piece or criteria for selecting the piece).

Course Planning Step 8.4   If one or more of your high-priority ILOs are psychomotor–perceptual skills, write them down on a sheet of paper entitled "Evidence of Main Effects." Then write down two or more descriptions of behavioral evidence or indicators for each of these ILOs.

GATHERING EVIDENCE OF EDUCATIONAL RESULTS

Educational results are overall course outcomes; they are due to the complex and cumulative effects of actual learning outcomes and other factors acting on students. Educational results are attributes, conceptions, or characteristics of the well-educated person. Anticipated or intended educational results are described by the course goals. Assessing and evaluating educational results are extremely difficult. Results may not be readily observable; or, being broad, they cannot be judged by a single behavior. Typically, results cannot be exhibited on demand. In fact, many results do not materialize until after the course is over. In spite of all these difficulties, if we are serious about our educational goals, we have an obligation to evaluate the educational results of our course.

Evaluating results for some courses means actually gathering evidence of these effects. The results of a driver education course can be assessed by looking at the driving records of students. A course aimed at helping teenage drug abusers can keep track of the students to see if they get and keep employment, succeed in school, and otherwise cope with life more successfully. Evidence of results for high school honors courses can be gathered by looking at what students take in college, what they major in, and how well they do. The results of many courses may be found in how well prepared students are for subsequent learning and by seeing how they fare in these courses.

Short of actually looking for course results, teachers should be receptive to the kinds of evidence that would indicate the effects a course has had. It is, after all, the anticipated results (that is, goals) that justify a course. We owe it to both our students and ourselves to try to determine how sound our justification is.

Although we have not included a course planning step concerned with gathering the evidence of educational results, we wish to alert you to the importance of this aspect of course evaluation. If evidence is available, it should be gathered.

One reason such evidence is rarely gathered is our preoccupation with traditional assessment methods. Traditional assessment has legitimate uses, but also serious limitations. The major problem with traditional assessments is that the tasks comprising traditional assessment are often trivial and contrived. The types of tests on which schools typically rely, especially short-answer and multiple-choice tests, are unique to schools. School-type tests are typically substitutes (or "proxies") for assessments that could determine whether or not students can actually use their knowledge to accomplish tasks they encounter in their lives. Outside of schools, people are more typically assessed in terms of their success in accomplishing tasks necessary for carrying out their work, for example the persuasiveness of a speech, the effectiveness of a marketing plan, the workmanship in a carefully crafted cabinet, or the successful diagnosis of a disease. That is, outside of schools people rely on more "authentic" means of assessment.

AUTHENTIC METHODS OF ASSESSMENT[*]

The concept of *authentic assessment* is not new. In fact, it is already well established as a successful standard in some less "academic" disciplines. Recitals, plays, art exhibits, and athletic events are all examples of assessments that students often eagerly anticipate. Preparing students for performances and exhibitions of these sorts is commonly regarded as equivalent to teaching the discipline. This is the case because the performances and exhibitions are not contrived strictly for the purpose of assessment. Instead, they are considered in our culture to have value in their own right, as evidenced by the fact that not only the teacher but also parents and the general public attend these performances and exhibitions.

In order to address the problem of triviality with traditional assessment in schools, more authentic assessment methods seek to situate problems and tasks in real-world contexts (Archbauld & Newman, 1988). For example, instead of the traditional end-of-year final examination in a high school economics course, Wiggins (1989) offers the following scenario for students to elaborate:

*Portions of this section were written with the help of Christine Cunningham.

You are the chief executive officer of an established firm. Your firm has always captured a major share of the market because of good use of technology, understanding of the natural laws of constraint, understanding of market systems, and the maintenance of a high standard for your product. However, in recent months your product has become part of a new trend in public tastes. Several new firms have entered the market and have captured part of your sales. Your product's proportional share of total aggregate demand is continuing to fall. When demand returns to normal, you will be controlling less of the market than before.

Your board of directors has given you less than a month to prepare a report that solves the problem in the short run and in the long run. In preparing the report, you should: (1) define the problem, (2) prepare data to illustrate the current situation, (3) prepare data to illustrate conditions one year in the future, (4) recommend action for today, (5) recommend action over the next year, and (6) discuss where your company will be in the market six months from today and one year from today.

The tasks that must be completed in the course of this project include

- deriving formulas for supply, demand, elasticity, and equilibrium;
- preparing schedules for supply, demand, costs, and revenues;
- graphing all work;
- preparing a written evaluation of the current and future situation for the market in general and for your company in particular;
- preparing a written report for your board of directors;
- showing aggregate demand today and predicting what it will be one year hence;
- showing the demand for your firm's product today and predicting what it will be one year hence. (p. 710)

Authentic assessment is particularly relevant to your highest-priority ILOs. How can you be assured that students in your course can really use their knowledge outside of the classroom unless you provide them the opportunity to show you what they can do in a context that approximates situations they will encounter after they leave your course?

There are three major formats used in authentic assessment: paper-and-pencil tasks, performances, and portfolios. Paper-and-pencil tasks most closely resemble traditional evaluation methods. They generally consist of a written question and a written response. What makes them more or less authentic is the extent to which they afford the opportunity for students to use their knowledge and skills in accomplishing tasks they might encounter outside of school. The economics project described above is one example of a set of authentic paper-and-pencil tasks. A set of tasks taken from a ninth-grade earth science final examination is more conventional than the economics project, but nevertheless more authentic than most exam questions:

TOPIC: pH

1. Test the pH of a sample of water collected from a recent local rainfall.

2. Then, compare the acidity of the sample in this test with those of two other samples from recently recorded rainfalls at the same site.

3. Then, describe the expected effects of rainwater of this pH on plant and animal life.

TOPIC: ROCKS

1. Find, in grams, the mass of the river rock sample.

2. Then, determine whether the rock sample is igneous, sedimentary, or metamorphic. Describe the characteristics of the rock that lead you to this conclusion.

3. Then, describe the likelihood that this rock originated within this school district, giving two reasons to support your answer.

In both sets of tasks, students must not only use knowledge learned in the course to solve a problem but must also relate that knowledge to their own environment.

Performances can encompass a diversity of media, including oral presentations (e.g., speeches and debates), the performing arts, multimedia presentations, and demonstrations. Performances may also require practice and polishing and may take a long-term effort to produce. They also tend to emphasize integration of skills and understandings, collaborative group work, and student choice and design. The economics test presented above could have provided for a performance if it had asked students to present their reports to a "board of directors" in a role-play.

Portfolios (Mitchell, 1992) are not mere collections of student work. Although, like collections, they might include written pieces, video productions, drawings, and constructions, what distinguishes them from mere collections is their reflective component. Students themselves select work they want to include and actively assess and document their own progress. Teachers may guide this selection process by suggesting criteria. For example, the ninth-grade earth science course mentioned above gives students the following guidelines:

Each student chooses his/her best four pieces of work. Students may remove, replace, or improve pieces throughout the year. Any drafts must be included. Each piece will be a coherent, multidimensional, inventive effort. The piece will be connected to an activity or some action carried out in class. Each piece will include one or more of the following elements:

- a detailed explanation of applications to the real world of understandings gained from a class activity

- a discussion of the student's recognition of a pattern or of patterns shown in the class activity

- diagrams and/or drawings

- major implications that may be drawn from the activity

- a related investigation carried out by the student or by a group of students

- connected art, storytelling, narrative, poetry, letters, or music

- extensions, such as computer work or the creation of a simple instrument

- connected writing and work: from another class or from an out-of-school experience

---

In addition each portfolio piece must include reflections on both the student's performance and the student's learning.

In a volume on portfolios published by The National Council of Teachers of Mathematics (Stenmark, 1991), items were identified that signified (a) growth over time, (b) mathematical connections, (c) student views of themselves as mathematicians, and (d) the problem-solving process. These items included the following:

- a table of contents
- excerpts from a student's daily journal
- draft, revised, and final versions of student work on a complex mathematical problem
- a problem made up by the student
- work from another subject matter that relates to mathematics
- a report of a group project, with comments about the individual's contribution
- a solution to an open-ended question done as homework
- a mathematical autobiography
- teacher-completed checklists
- notes from an interview—by the teacher or another student
- papers that show the student's correction of errors or misconceptions
- a photo or sketch made by the student (or teacher) of a student's work with manipulatives
- a letter from the student to the reader of the portfolio, explaining each item

These portfolios have the potential to provide the richest evidence of the course's main effects.

Authentic assessment techniques address one major deficiency of evaluation as we have presented it thus far. When gathering evidence of main effects ILO by ILO, there is the risk that learning in the course will be fragmented. Authentic assessment techniques we have discussed here attempt to provide a more integrated view of student learning. By this we mean not only learning among course topics, but also learning of content with use of that content in solving real-world problems. Furthermore, the more we attempt to assess the latter, the closer we approach assessment of those educational results that go beyond specific learning outcomes.

Rubrics

It is one thing to collect authentic assessment data and another thing to analyze it. One of the reasons teachers shy away from more authentic assessment techniques is the perception that this data is very difficult to analyze, much less quantify. That is, once we collect it, what do we do with it? Scoring rubrics represent an attempt to assign numbers to this highly qualitative data on student learning. A scoring rubric makes explicit the criteria used to evaluate student work. For example, one teacher, Jerry Sherman from Millbrook High School (New York), used four criteria to assess portfolios:

1. *Purpose:* The degree to which the student establishes and maintains a clear sense of purpose, demonstrates an awareness of the task, and shows effort and perseverance toward goal attainment.

2. *Achievement:* The degree to which the student exhibits an understanding of key concepts, development of essential skills, and a feel for the subject matter.

3. *Application and Continuity:* The degree to which the student connects new understanding to previous learning, shows an ability to link concepts, discovers underlying rules or principles, and applies those rules or principles.

4. *Reflection:* The degree to which the student has looked at his/her own learning process, has monitored that process and has self-assessed, sees herself/himself changing with the acceptance of new understandings, and connects himself/herself to the ideas and concepts expressed.

Sherman then specified four levels for each criterion:

1. exemplary
2. proficient
3. minimally competent
4. little evidence of competence at this time

The scoring rubic in Figure 8.2 on page 212 resulted from combining the four criteria with the four levels.

The World Wide Web has many resources for creating rubrics, including an enormous number of ready-made rubrics. The following three web sites are portals that provide a good start for exploring these resources:

- school.discovery.com/schrockguide/assess.html
- www.teach-nology.com/currenttrends/alternative_assessment/rubrics/
- www.exemplars.com/rubrics/assessment.html

Course Planning Step 8.5 Examine your course's educational goals and review your highest-priority ILO. Now, design a set of authentic assessment techniques for gathering evidence of what the students can do with the knowledge in the real world.

GATHERING EVIDENCE OF SIDE EFFECTS

Another important kind of evidence is that of side effects. To reiterate, side effects are those outcomes that were not intended and perhaps not even considered when planning the course. Gathering evidence on side effects is difficult because there are no statements that serve as guides for the evaluation. It is doubtful whether the full range of course side effects should ever be assessed. Even if it were possible, the effort

IN ASSESSING, CONSIDER	PURPOSE	ACHIEVEMENT	APPLICATION AND CONTINUITY	REFLECTION
☞	The degree to which the student • establishes and maintains a clear sense of purpose • demonstrates an awareness of task • shows effort and perseverance toward goal attainment	The degree to which the student exhibits • an understanding of key concepts • development of essential skills • a feel for science and for the value of science	The degree to which the student • connects new understanding to previous learning • shows an ability to link concepts • discovers rules or principles underlying the relationships between ideas, concepts, or objects, and applies those rules or principles when identifying and solving problems	The degree to which the student • has looked at his/her own learning process, has monitored that process, and has self-assessed • sees herself/himself changing with the acceptance of new understandings • connects himself/herself to Planet Earth and to the ideas and concepts expressed
performance levels ✍				
EXEMPLARY 9 1/2–10	• establishes and maintains a clear purpose • demonstrates a clear understanding of task • shows a high level of effort and perseverance toward goal attainment	• exhibits keen understanding of key concepts • shows superior development of essential skills • shows outstanding feel for science and for the value of science	• readily connects new understandings to previous learning • is most adept at linking concepts • readily discovers underlying rules and principles and applies those rules	• carries out extensive self-assessment and examination of own learning process • regularly sees self changing with the acceptance of new understandings • makes strong personal connections to the planet and to the concepts and ideas expressed
PROFICIENT 8–9	• establishes a purpose • demonstrates an awareness of task • shows effort and perseverance toward goal attainment	• understands the key concepts • has developed the essential skills • has a feel for science and a grasp on the value of science	• connects most new understandings to previous learning • frequently links concepts well • frequently discovers underlying rules and principles, and often applies them	• frequently carries out self-assessment and examination of own learning process • often sees self changing with the acceptance of new understandings • often connects self to the subject of the piece
MINIMALLY COMPETENT 6 1/2–7 1/2	• tries to establish a purpose • shows some awareness of task • shows some effort	• shows some understanding of key concepts • shows some development of the essential skills • grasps some of the value of science	• makes some connections between new understandings and previous learning • attempts to link concepts • sometimes discovers underlying rules and principles; sometimes applies them	• sometimes carries out self-assessment and examination of own learning process • sometimes sees self changing with the acceptance of new understandings • sometimes connects self to the subject of the piece
LITTLE EVIDENCE OF COMPETENCE AT THIS TIME 5–6	• does not establish a purpose • shows little awareness of task • shows little evidence of effort beyond "getting it done"	• lacks clear understanding of the key concepts • shows little development of the essential skills • is not in touch with the value of science	• tries to make connections between new understandings and previous learning • rarely finds links among concepts • rarely finds underlying rules and principles; no evidence of application	• generally does not examine own learning process, does not self-assess • rarely sees self changing with the acceptance of new understandings • rarely makes connections between his/her life and the subject of the piece

FIGURE 8.2   Earth Systems portfolio assessment criteria.

Source: Jerry Sherman, Millbrook High School (NY).

necessary to accomplish such an assessment would be enormous. Therefore, only the most likely or probable side effects must be identified in order to guide the evaluation.

Moreover, since time and resource constraints are great, the side effects examined should be limited to those deemed undesirable. Given the goal of course improvement and the constraints typical of an evaluation, the probable undesirable outcomes are most in need of attention. If the situation permits, however, you may also want to assess desirable side effects in order to plan for and optimize their occurrence (in which case they may become intended learning outcomes).

Considering side effects is important when viewing your course because the discovery of potential side effects will probably change what you do in the course. It is particularly important to consider how likely the side effects are to occur and how undesirable they will be if they do occur. For example, a common side effect of an introductory psychology course is a sense of power on the part of the student. Some students may begin to "analyze" their friends and the social interactions in which they take part. Students might also decide that they can become "amateur therapists." If these side effects are likely and viewed as sufficiently undesirable, you might make changes in the course to head them off. For example, maybe all students should experience the discomfort of being "analyzed."

It is conceivable that some side effects are unavoidable and are so undesirable that the course should be abandoned. On the other hand, you might want to go through with the course but with an increased sensitivity toward the probable side effects. In the consideration of side effects, you get a chance to "stand outside" your course and become your own critic.

The most effective method for identifying side effects is to examine the instructional plan carefully. The instructional plan is composed of planned interactions between learner and teacher, instructional foci, and the organization of course units in the context of various institutional factors. A few of these course components are examined in the following sections.

Learner interaction with teacher refers to what teachers do in the course, how they interact with, or behave toward, their students. There are many descriptors of teacher behavior; they include authoritarian, child-centered, and traditional. The important question is: What might students be learning as a result of the exhibited teacher behaviors? From a teacher who constantly emphasizes right and wrong answers, for example, students might learn that a particular subject is clearly defined with no gray areas or areas of debate, that knowledge is factual and either true or false.

There are almost always affective consequences of any prolonged type of interaction between teacher and students. Attitudes about self, school, and subject matter should be examined as possible side effects.

Instructional foci constitute the focal points of the learning experiences in the course. As focal points they can limit as well as enrich learning and can produce biased views of the content with which the course deals.

For example, learning entirely through the use of printed materials, a student might learn that a particular subject (or even learning in general) is a passive enterprise and that personal efforts of experimentation, discovery, or discussion do not lead to legitimate knowledge or learning. (This may apply to the exclusive use of any *one* kind of instructional focus.)

Instructional foci may also lead to undesirable learnings in that they are biased. Bias is evidenced by a particular treatment of certain societal groups (for example, minorities) or by stressing a particular ideology (for example, environmentalist views of the environment to the exclusion of other views).

Organization of course units may result in unintended learnings stemming from the relationships among the course's units. Considerations here focus on the sequence and grouping of units, that is, relationships implicit in the course organization.

For example, a history course organized on a chronological basis may lead the student to assume a cause–effect relationship. That is, a particular event occurred, which caused the following event, and so on. A chronological organization may hinder the student's learning of recurrent themes in history or important historical ideas (for example, nationalism). Or a botany course organized around plant parts in such a way that a student learns about the root, then the stem, seeds, leaves, and flowers in that order may result in the student's viewing a plant as a group of individual structures rather than as a single organism with specialized tissues forming its various parts.

Other factors bear on course outcomes. Such factors range from how students are seated (possibly the mere fact that they are seated) to the scheduling of units (for example, are interesting units lumped together or interspersed with other less interesting units?).

Examining the instructional plan in order to assess likely side effects is a complex task. The examples above should be helpful in pointing out the range of areas to investigate. Two general guidelines may be of further use in assessing side effects:

1. Examine the attitudes of students toward the subject, toward how it is being taught, and possibly toward school in general.

2. Examine the course for those features that are stable (that is, significant strategies, materials, or behaviors that the student experiences daily). These features should form the basis for answering the question: What might students be learning as a result of this?

Focusing the search for side effects on attitudes and other outcomes likely to result from the prominent aspects of the course places this search in a realistic perspective. The examples that follow may help prepare you to gather evidence of side effects.

Example 8.11   Mr. Harris is teaching the senior honors section in world history for the first time. Mr. Harris values this opportunity highly and spends an entire summer preparing for the course, which will focus on "Revolutions of the World." His goal is to have students understand the historical forces that caused people to revolt and to relate these forces to current societal forces.

Rather than use available books, which Mr. Harris feels are inadequate, he bases the course on a carefully prepared series of lectures. Outside readings will be employed occasionally. The course focuses on the American, French, and Russian revolutions.

What effects might a lecture presentation have on students? How might students characterize revolution as a result of using the American, French, and Russian cases as examples? Are there other kinds of revolutions that are not violent or not political? Do revolutions occur in non-Western countries? Do revolutions always result in stable political–social arrangements? Do the rebels always win? What role does ideology play?

Example 8.12   Ms. Cole had taught junior English for several years. The course had always focused on a set of novels and plays read by the class in the same sequence. Ms. Cole had led discussions about the books and had found herself doing most, if not all, of the discussing. To remedy this, she decided to take a nondirective role in the course. She provided a long list of readings to students on the first day of class. Students were free to read any six books they selected. During class, small groups were formed in which students discussed common readings. Often these groups were made up of only two or three students. One large group of students (about 17 pupils) always read the same book and were thus in the same group. Ms. Cole did not intervene and required only a written synthesis in which students described their reaction to the reading and group discussion.

By being nondirective, might Ms. Cole give students the impression that "expert opinion" has no place in discussions of literature? Is a student's choice of reading always a wise choice? Are aspects such as style and genre likely to be considered in these types of discussion? Can students distinguish good or great literature from lower-quality work?

These questions and those accompanying Example 8.11 illustrate a few side effects that seem likely as a result of these courses. These examples should point out the perspective needed when looking for side effects.

Course Planning Step 8.6   Examine your course's planned interactions between the learner and (a) the teacher, (b) the instructional foci, (c) the organization of course units, and (d) the institutional setting of the course. On a sheet of paper entitled "Possible Side Effects," list unintended undesirable learnings that you as a teacher and course planner should be wary of as you teach the course.

TROUBLESHOOTING

Course planning has, at this point, ended. Troubleshooting, which consists of using the information gathered during evaluation for making course-improvement decisions, is done after the course has actually begun.

In evaluating a course, you should know whether the course's high-priority ILOs have been achieved. You should also be aware of any major undesirable consequences of the course. You may have some evidence that bears on the educational results of your course. The task now is to use this information to improve the course. Several authors discuss ways to use evaluation to improve teaching. Among these are Dick and Carey, 1990; Eby, 1992; Glatthorn, 1987; Hill, 1987; Kindsvatter, Wilen, and Ishler, 1988; and Kourilsky and Quarana, 1987.

Pinpointing the aspects of a course in need of improvement presents many problems. Assume, for example, that as a result of an evaluation you determine that one or two important ILOs have not been achieved. Does this mean that the instructional focus was inadequate? the teaching strategy faulty? the ILO unlearnable or unteachable? a prerequisite unprovided for? Any number of these factors could be involved. The following is a scheme for systematically trying to determine which course aspects need improvement:

1. *Gather all the evidence you can.* How many students failed to achieve a particular ILO? Which students were they? What did these students do differently? Did anything else distinguish these students from those who did learn the ILO? How "close" did these students come to learning the ILO? *If you have evidence of an unachieved ILO, then*

2. *Examine the ILO.* Are prerequisites provided for? Does the ILO fit in with the other ILOs that were achieved? *If the ILO appears satisfactory, then*

3. *Examine the course organization.* Did the ILO receive proper emphasis in the unit? Was it preceded and followed by appropriate ILOs? Was the instrumental content appropriate for teaching the ILO? *If the course organization is satisfactory, then*

4. *Examine the general teaching strategies for the ILO.* Did the instructional focus provide the focus necessary for this ILO? Was the instructional focus interesting? Was the teaching strategy appropriate? Was enough time spent on this ILO? Was the ILO emphasized sufficiently? *If the instructional plan is satisfactory, then*

5. *Examine the instruction.* Was the instructional plan actually carried out? What details may have changed? Was the plan adequate to hold students' attention and interest? Did outside disturbances, unexpected events, scheduling changes, or other factors interfere with instruction?

If you have gathered evidence on your course's educational results, you will want to include this information in your troubleshooting. Since educational results are due to a variety of interacting factors (some of which are entirely outside the course), improvement decisions are difficult. However, depending on the importance of an unachieved goal or the undesirableness of an obtained result, course changes may be very necessary. Troubleshooting here will have to include external factors. Has something occurred in the school, city, or neighborhood that could affect course results? What other sorts of things are students involved in at this time? Much of the troubleshooting you have already done will apply here. Perhaps the problem is several unachieved ILOs, or maybe discipline problems in the class caused you to employ unusual or harsh measures. If all your high-priority ILOs were achieved, and the course went smoothly, yet the results were disappointing, you will have to ask some questions about whether your intended learnings are as appropriate for your goals as you had initially thought.

One further useful way to troubleshoot a course is to administer a questionnaire to the students. Questionnaires can ask students about a wide range of topics. The questions can be specific and detailed or they can require general and overall views. They can ask about the effectiveness of administrative and instructional procedures or about the students' reaction to personal characteristics of the teacher; they can inquire about ratings of current practices or they can ask for suggestions of new practices. Obviously, it is difficult to know what to ask and where to stop. A useful criterion in developing questionnaires is to limit them to questions that will help inform course-improvement decisions.

As you develop questions, center the questions on those areas in which you are willing and able to make changes. Then design your questions so that they solicit information useful in making those decisions. Don't waste your students' time with questions that do not or cannot lead to course improvements. For example, asking students to rate your overall performance as a teacher gives information too general to be useful and has the potential only to inflate or deflate egos. On the other hand, the students' reaction to the size of their within-class group may well be valuable information.

By carefully and systematically making changes and continuing to evaluate the course each time it is taught, the course should become more and more refined. As noted, troubleshooting cannot be carried out while a course evaluation is being planned. But when the course is actually taught, troubleshooting should be incorporated as a useful scheme that aids course improvement.

SUMMARY

This brings to a close the planning of your course. In a sense, course planning never stops but continues to evolve. Unless a course is scrapped or radically altered, further planning often takes the form of refinements based on the evidence gathered during evaluations as well as on "gut" reactions. To some extent, we can know what we want to accomplish only as we try to implement preliminary plans. Thus, ILOs, educational goals, and other course components will be altered as you or others actually teach the course.

We hope that you have worked through, rather than around, the book to arrive at this summary. Much of what you have read and what you have been asked to do may have seemed highly technical. We recognize that a considerable amount of actual course planning also involves common sense and a great deal of creativity. What needs to accompany these two ingredients, however, is the talent for asking the right question at the right time and having the understandings and skills necessary to answer (and ask) these questions.

QUESTIONS FOR DISCUSSION: COURSE EVALUATION

1. Troubleshooting involves using evidence to think about course components. The links between various course components are often important to consider when

deciding where to make course changes. In what ways are each of the following course components linked: (a) rationale–general teaching strategies, (b) ILOs–instructional foci, and (c) unit organization–ILOs?

2. Discuss any course you may have taken in which side effects or unintended learnings were of greater significance than the espoused aims of the course. What may have contributed to this?

3. In trying to improve a course, what is the benefit of making systematic improvements instead of "wholesale" course revisions?

4. What type of information would lead you to abandon a course?

5. What are the differences and similarities between course evaluation as presented in this chapter and pupil evaluation as you have experienced it?

REFERENCES

Archbauld, D. A., & Newman, F. M. (1988). *Beyond standardized testing.* Reston, VA: National Association of Secondary School Principals.

Brown, A. L., & Campione, J. C. (1996). Psychological theory and the design of innovative learning environments: On procedures, principles, and systems. In L. Shauble & R. Glaser (Eds.), *Innovations in learning: New environments for education.* Mahwah, NJ: Lawrence Erlbaum Associates.

Campione, J. C., Shapiro, A. M., & Brown, A. L. (1995). Forms of transfer in a community of learners: Flexible learning and understanding. In A. McKeough, J. Lupart, & A. Marini (Eds.), *Teaching for transfer: Fostering generalization in learning.* Mahwah, NJ: Lawrence Erlbaum Associates.

Cronbach, L. J. (1963). Evaluation for course improvement. *Teachers College Record, 64,* 672–683.

Dick, W., & Carey, L. (1990). *The systematic design of instruction* (3rd ed.). Glenview, IL: Scott, Foresman.

Eby, J. W. (1992). *Reflective planning, teaching, and evaluation for the elementary school.* New York: Macmillan.

Glatthorn, A. A. (1987). *Curriculum leadership.* Glenview, IL: Scott, Foresman.

Hill, J. C. (1987). *Curriculum evaluation for school improvement.* Springfield, IL: Charles C. Thomas.

Kindsvatter, R., Wilen, W., & Ishler, M. (1988). *Dynamics of effective teaching.* New York: Longman.

Kourilsky, M., & Quarana, L. (1987). *Effective teaching: Principles and practice.* Glenview, IL: Scott, Foresman.

Mitchell, R. (1992). Portfolios. In R. Mitchell, *Testing for learning: How new approaches to evaluation can improve American schools* (pp. 103–131). New York: Free Press.

Scriven, M. (1967). The methodology of evaluation. In R. W. Tyler, R. M. Gagné, & M. Scriven (Eds.), *AERA Monograph Series on Curriculum Evaluation. Volume 1: Perspectives on curriculum evaluation.* Chicago: Rand McNally.

Stenmark, J. K. (1991). *Mathematics assessment: Myths, models, good questions, and practical suggestions.* Reston, VA: National Council of Teachers of Mathematics.

Wiggins, G. (1989, May). A true test: Toward more authentic and equitable assessment. *Phi Delta Kappan,* 703–713.

Wiggins, G., & McTighe, J. (1998). *Understanding by design.* Alexandria, VA: Association for Supervision and Curriculum Development.

EPILOGUE

Our central message in this book has been that when we teach, we should teach with a purpose. Further, our purposes should be made explicit in the form of educational goals and intended learning outcomes. There are no hard-and-fast rules for explicating our purposes; we must think for ourselves about our students, our subject matter, and our assumptions about education, and then express our purposes appropriately. We have to discipline ourselves to take our purposes seriously so as not to lie to ourselves. If we want students to learn to solve problems, mere content coverage just won't suffice. Our instructional planning must be appropriate for our purposes. These are the major lessons to be learned from this book.

Although the major purpose of designing a course has been to learn how to develop a curriculum, this was not our only concern. An unstated but nevertheless important benefit of working on this project was to learn what to look for in a curriculum, to begin the process of becoming a curricular "connoisseur" (Eisner, 1985). Developing a curriculum gives us a different perspective on curricula developed by others. This perspective enables us to look at curricula and talk about them more intelligently, precisely, and profoundly.

Often educators compare the educational enterprise to another activity, that of travel. In such an analogy, the student does the traveling, teachers serve as travel guides, educational goals and intended learning outcomes are considered destinations, and instructional plans specify the means of transportation and the itinerary.

But there is a constant danger inherent in the planning of educational itineraries and the means of transportation; there is much more to a journey than arriving at the destination on time and unharmed. People also embark on journeys for the experience of traveling. A trip through France is not undertaken just to arrive in Paris. The French countryside, the French people, the French wine and food, and the enjoyment of a traveling companion are all as important for the "success" of the journey as the arrival in Paris. Nor should a kindergartner embark on an educational journey merely to receive a high school diploma or to learn the three R's. Thus, there are compelling reasons for expecting the educational process not only to help children become "well educated," but also to meet a set of criteria relating to the intrinsic, rather than instrumental, aspects of the process. The educational process should not only accomplish goals but also be human, rational, engaging, enjoyable, and personally gratifying, to mention just a few such criteria. The most compelling reason for this requirement is not that such humane education is most efficient or effective (it may not be), but, instead, that schooling constitutes a substantial portion of people's lives and life should be lived in such a manner.

One final caveat in using this guide must be mentioned. In all our planning, research, and evaluation it is easy to forget that educational journeys are for the student-traveler, not for their teacher-guides, nor for the travel-agent administration. The educational travel industry is simply intended to help the student-traveler along on an educational journey; as much as we want to, we cannot make the journey for the student. We can only act as guides. It is in this spirit that this book is intended to be used.

REFERENCE

Eisner, E. (1985). *The educational imagination: On the design and evaluation of school programs* (2nd ed.). New York: Macmillan.

COLONIAL AMERICA: SOCIAL STUDIES CURRICULUM FOR GRADE 5

Kerry Nappi

The examples included in these appendixes represent courses or units that vary in subject matter and grade level. As has been the case for all the examples throughout Course Design, *these are not presented as models to emulate. Instead, each design reflects one teacher's way of addressing the requirements faced when planning for a particular age group and subject matter. Most importantly, each design reflects the individuality of the teacher-planner.*

COMMENTS

This is an excellent unit. While planned for fifth graders, the unit could easily be adapted for students in middle school by including more sophisticated readings and increasing the amount of student research that is expected. The unit's Introduction and Notes to a Teacher emphasize the importance of understanding the nature of history as well as learning about colonial America. The general teaching strategies make extensive use of group and collaborative learning activities.

INTRODUCTION

Generally speaking, nine- and ten-year-olds have reached a developmental stage at which they are ready to understand peoples and lands that are removed both by distance and time. In other words, they are ready to learn history. Up to this point, elementary social studies curricula usually focus on local or very familiar topics (Our School, Our Community) and may use those as background for study of modern cultures (Our Neighbors, Mexico and Canada). By fourth grade, students can transfer the structure of social "studies" to a historical perspective, particularly if the unit is constructed so as to take advantage of students' sense of and experience with history, even their own family's. For most of them, knights, pilgrims, and pharaohs are already ideas they know, even without an understanding of the time periods in which they lived and the cultures from which they developed.

History is chronological by nature. There are commonalties by which eras and peoples can be studied. The Smith College Campus School social studies curriculum considers both of these factors in the sequencing of its units. The study of history begins in fourth grade with Ancient Rome. Fifth grade covers Medieval Europe and The Age of Exploration and Discovery. This unit, Colonial America, is designed to fit after these and to precede Industrialization in the United States. The unit could be isolated from this scheme, but it would have to be modified; understandings of medieval Europe are clearly necessary to learn it as is. Either fifth or sixth grade would be an appropriate level, but the expository texts suggested for the activities are sophisticated in several instances, making it difficult for grades lower than these.

In developing the unit, I have endeavored to make history real and exciting for students. Whenever possible, we simulate conditions and situations of the colonial period of the United States. Basal texts are used as only one of a variety of reading materials; in fact, as often as possible, students read about events and people from the primary sources available to "real" historians. These replicated authentic documents are more difficult to read, but they are far less "watered down" than social studies books. Another outstanding opportunity for students at the Campus School is a visit to Plymouth Plantation, where the *Mayflower II* is docked as its predecessor might have been in 1621 and the plantation is as it was in 1627.

If no other goal is met I would hope that students remain or become excited about the study of history and see it as a rich and relevant body of knowledge. Perhaps they will feel encouraged to discover the truths about their families' backgrounds. This is an age by which students have moved away from the egocentricity of young childhood; it is an age at which they can most appreciate the need for asserting one's independence and living out one's sense of adventure. What better people to study than the early colonists of America?

Notes to a Teacher

The order of the subunits in this unit is partly due to time schedules and may therefore need to be changed according to your schedule. A pivotal subunit seems to be the one focused on the field trip to Plymouth Plantation. If students go in the beginning of the unit, the benefit is high intrigue and interest. The downfall is lack of prior knowledge. Students with no formal instruction in the period who go to Plymouth tend not to ask good questions of the role characters, nor do they seem to remember much of the historical details. When they go with at least an introduction, and at least a spattering of reading (historical and biographical fiction, nonfiction, etc.), they remember names and events connected with characters, ask relevant questions about the period, and begin to know the historical figures more intimately. Ideally, the subunit should come early in the unit, though not first, and certainly with enough time left after the trip to take advantage of their new information, understandings, and excitement.

Subunit I is another that I considered inserting in other sequences for different purposes. I hope that when students study colonial America, they come to an understanding of what a colony is, not just colonial America but all colonies, past and present. To accomplish this goal, we must provide a structure for understanding "colony," including an accepted definition of the term, knowledge about a ruling country, reasons for and results of colonization, and aspects of typical colonial lifestyles. I chose to let the accumulated knowledge of colonial America stand as a basis for looking at the defining features of colonies and for comparison with other recognized colonies. It is just as reasonable, I think (though more boring for fifth graders, I suspect), to study "What is a colony?" first and then look at colonial America as an example.

One place where I am particularly unsure about the structure of the unit is in its lack of sequence. Historically, would it have been more sound to study the settlements in the order in which they occurred? I don't know, but I decided not to worry about order so much as a general sense of the period; in other words, I care less that students remember that Jamestown came 13 years before Plymouth than I do that they understand what made them colonies and the important aspects of colonial life.

A final word about materials: Wherever possible, I have indicated exact resources and even included some page references. This is because this unit plan's function is as a working document by which teachers will instruct. A teacher of the unit should realize, though, that there are vast numbers of books, tapes, videos, filmstrips, and people with huge stores of information on the subject. I have picked and chosen, given my knowledge of this year's students and the general student population at S.C.C.S. However, while the resources may change, I would like to share with you my own "hidden agenda" for teaching history. I chose texts, often, because of (and not in spite of) the fact that accounts differed. I want students to know that a part of history, and part of a historian's job, is speculating. I want them to read in one book that 102 passengers came aboard the *Mayflower,* and from another that 101 came. I want them to be part of the process of looking at data, considering the source, checking in three places for more evidence, and still not knowing for sure what's right. In other words, I want them less impressed by the "correctness" of historical fact and more interested in the search for "the best that we can tell is . . . ."

CONTENT OUTLINE

I. The Thirteen Colonies
- A. Why colonists came to America
  - European conditions
  - religious freedom
  - immunity for prisoners
  - adventure
  - promise of riches
  - missionaries
  - expansion of trade
- B. Early settlements
  - Roanoke, the "lost colony"
  - Jamestown
  - Plymouth Plantation

    C. Development of colonies
        land conditions
        villages and towns
        plantations in the South
    D. Relationships with Native Americans
        early assistance to colonists
        contributions to a mixed culture
        particular Native Americans

II. Society and Government
    A. Colonial society
        occupations
        religious influence
        family life; roles of men, women, and children
    B. Government
        Mayflower Compact
        Connecticut Charter
        Massachusetts Bay Charter
        voting requirements
        law enforcement
        famous leaders

III. The Home
    A. Houses
        materials
        shapes
        barn-raising parties
        common houses
        furnishings
    B. Clothing
        woolens, linens, breeches, stockings, leggings
    C. Food
        staples, regional differences, growing
    D. Health
        the "starving time"
        diseases and malnutrition
    E. Recreation
        games played
        social gatherings
        taverns

IV. The Church and School
    A. The church
        prominent religions
        freedom or not
        blue laws
    B. School
        availability of free, public schools

tutoring and apprenticeships
books used
V. Arts and Sciences
   A. Literature
   B. Painting
   C. Science
VI. Economy
   A. Farming
     tobacco farms
     need for labor, slavery
   B. Trade and industry
     whaling
     fur trapping
   C. Crafts
     pewter
     candle dipping

CONCEPTUAL MAP FOR UNIT ON COLONIAL AMERICA

In the conceptual map for this unit (Figure A.1 on page 226), "American Colonies" is central on the page, and also in the unit. We begin the unit by exploring one of these as an example and then go on to look at how the history and culture of European nations affect its development.

The subsections of "American Colonies" (culture, government, land, economy) are focal points of instruction through which higher-level understandings of the concept of colonization are made.

"American Colonies" and "European Nations" ought to be the flexible factors— that is, they're central to the unit, but only one of the two major cognitions[1] is contingent upon them; the other[2] should be able to use a very similar map to study any colony.

Sequence of Subunits

   A. Coming to the New World
   B. Reasons for coming and reactions to life in the New World
   C. An early settlement: Plymouth Plantation
   D. Daily life in settlements and regional differences
   E. Government
   F. Religion in the colonies

[1]Students will understand how colonial America both reflected medieval and Renaissance Europe and created a culture of its own based on the conditions, lifestyles, individual colonists, and desire for a different kind of life.
[2]Students will understand what a colony is, the characteristics of most colonies and their ruling powers, some reasons for colonization and opposition to it, and benefits to both the ruling country and its colony.

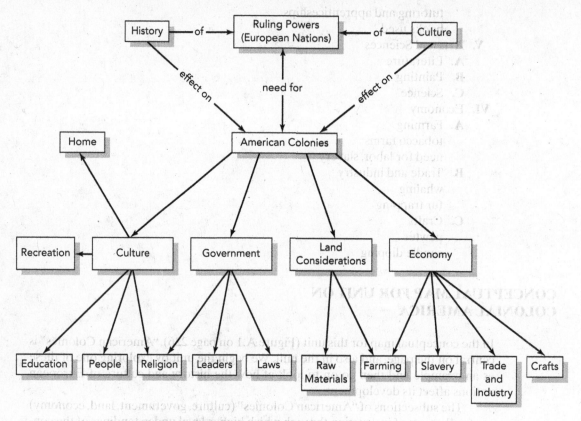

FIGURE A.1 Conceptual map for unit on colonial America.

    G. Relationships with Native Americans
    H. Indentured servants and slavery
    I. Why do we call them colonies?

SUBUNIT A: COMING TO THE NEW WORLD

Intended Learnings

- Students will understand various reasons for coming to the New World as early colonists and the conditions that led to the immigration.
- Students will understand what colonists found upon arrival in the New World and their reactions to the realities here.
- Students will be able to describe conditions (particularly spatial) aboard the *Mayflower*.

Instructional Foci

"The Voyage of the *Mayflower*," "The Adventure Begins," "appraisement and valuation of the *Mayflower*'s tackle" (replicas of documents), discussion, estimation and measurement of the main deck of the *Mayflower*

General Teaching Strategy

Many students of this age and grade will already know that the *Mayflower* was the ship that carried Pilgrims to the New World. Some will know the year, or at least the era, and names of specific settlers or colonies. While encouraging these students to share their information, let it be clear to the class that students of history often begin study of an era without many specific facts; as fifth graders at the Smith College Campus School, they can be counted on to have solid understandings of the history preceding colonization of America; that is, they've all studied medieval Europe. Prompt a discussion of the religious and political foundations set in medieval and Renaissance Europe, and development of the technology invented just after those "Dark Ages" they know so well. Give students the opportunity to summarize the general political and religious atmosphere present in Europe at that time. As discussions go on in this unit, look for ways in which connections to that knowledge can be made, or acknowledge the connections made by children.

In the beginning of this subunit (which also serves as the introductory lesson to the larger unit), help students understand the size of the *Mayflower* and the space available to its passengers and crew by having them (1) listen to a variety of historical accounts of the ship and her crossing, and (2) physically enclose themselves in an area akin to that of the *Mayflower*'s main deck.

Any nonfiction reading that describes the above could be used for the first purpose. The two I've chosen are "The Voyage of the *Mayflower*" by Patricia M. Whalen, *Cobblestone,* 1989, and sections of "The Adventure Begins" from "The *Mayflower* and the Pilgrim Fathers" jackdaw packet. I particularly like these two as they contain the necessary information, but not quite exactly; I lead discussion into the discrepancies between the two sources.

For today's purposes, I ask students to listen for two things:

1. details about living conditions aboard the ship (things the crew and passengers saw, heard, brought . . .)

2. details about measurement that will help us reconstruct close approximations of the space aboard the main deck

They listen with better intent to what is important and filter out what information is nonessential now if I give these directions before the reading.

The important data to glean from students before going on to the next activity is:

90' × 25' at the waist (Just what is the waist of a ship? Will we consider that?)
102 people aboard

"Space about the size of a modern day twin-size mattress"
five feet of head room

The idea of the activity is to mark off bow and stern points on a surface such as a blacktop. In a class of twenty students, each will have to represent about 5. They may be able to use chalk to mark off "their" square footage—the space allocated, theoretically, to five people aboard the ship. Much cooperation is needed for the measuring and marking part. The result should help students visualize the space available and mentally place themselves back in their spots for later activities.

Independently, students begin composing a list of items they think colonists would have brought with them. It is helpful to discuss beforehand the time period and availability of resources, the knowledge Pilgrims had of the land to which they were traveling, and what was important to survival and culture. By doing this activity independently at first, students are more apt to think about, and be able to defend, their choices. Back in small groups, they may rethink their choices, combine their space for common provisions, or decide to fit it all in.

The class reconvenes to compare lists and consider space and needs. These lists can be reconsidered at other points in the unit, directly or indirectly, by students or the teacher.

Other Possible Activities

1. This would be an appropriate place to start the reading of Patricia Clapp's *Constance,* a historical novel depicting the life of a real *Mayflower* Pilgrim, starting on the deck of the ship. Students will have immediate reactions to the comparison between fiction and nonfiction accounts of the story.
2. Scale models of a cutaway of the *Mayflower* may be drawn. Additional discussion about cross-section and scale may be necessary.

SUBUNIT B: REASONS FOR COMING AND REACTIONS TO LIFE HERE

Intended Learnings

- Students will understand various reasons for coming to the New World as colonists.
- Students will understand what it was that different colonists found upon arrival in the New World.
- Students will be able to differentiate between and define primary and secondary resources.

Instructional Foci

Expository texts, both primary and secondary, regarding reasons for coming to the New World, and colonists' reactions to conditions during early months; small group reading, discussing, listing; whole class discussions

General Teaching Strategy

Have students name several resources one might go to in doing research on a topic or person. As they name them, list on the chalkboard under categories you recognize (but do not yet name) as primary and secondary. Note that some will fit under both, and others under one only. When the list seems quite complete, ask students to distinguish between the categories, and go on to discuss the differences between primary and secondary sources, their availability, and their validity.

Ask students which of them have had experience with keeping diaries or journals (if your class is like mine, they have already done so in a variety of contexts); they should be able to name several purposes for keeping such records. Tell students that they will be getting the chance to investigate some of the diaries, journals, and early letters of colonists. Ask how this kind of reading might differ from reading a social studies book.

Before explaining the tasks for the next activities, read the introduction to Samuel Sewall's diary. This particular explanation tells of the religious reasons some colonists had for this kind of careful record keeping; that is, a record of occurrences that could later be examined for indications of having found favor or disfavor with God. This will be students' first direct experience with the Puritans' view of religion and its profound influence over their lives. Point out, too, the different purposes a ship's captain or colony governor might have for keeping a journal.

In random groups of four, have students read a sampling of primary and secondary resources. The task is to compile a list of reasons different settlers came to America, divided into the categories religious, political, economic, and social. Cite several examples that do not fall clearly into one or another, and explain that students should be able to justify whatever category they choose.

For this first part of the small group activities, students may struggle with the breakup of the task. Some will decide to split up the reading and do the list together, others to do all individually and compile at the end, still others to read each piece aloud with a recorder to keep track of ideas. The teacher may decide to have groups run all one way, or to continue to let them figure it out on their own. It is important, however, to have the whole class share their methods, so that groups have a chance to share with each other.

When the class reconvenes, the lists are shared aloud and recorded on class charts. Groups should appoint one spokesperson to do the sharing, but all must be involved in the listening. I ask all who are not speaking to do two things: (1) listen to the reasons being shared and mentally note whether or not their group got it, and (2) decide whether the reason could be paraphrased for better understanding. This keeps them accountable for the listening; I also can check the paraphrasing of their own or others' words to see if they've really understood.

This is also the appropriate time to make the distinction between primary and secondary sources vivid. Students can practice pointing out differences and also try to specify authors' purposes.

The second half of the subunit involves the same groups and similar types of readings. The groups are given a little background by the teacher in excerpts from William Bradford's journal and other letters. The groups are asked to read several other documents to find the positive and negative aspects of life in the New World. This is a chance for them to further practice group responsibility for understanding a text and for reading early American writings (which are characteristically full of invented spelling and much jargon of the day).

We meet as a class again to share and discuss colonists' ideas about this new land they've settled.

Many of the issues that arise in this subunit are repeated within more specific subunits elsewhere. The context is broad, yet the experience with this method of inquiry and understanding of the general atmosphere of the colonies is critical. There has been no specific instruction of times, dates, or names, but when they appear in sources we make note of them.

SUBUNIT C: AN EARLY SETTLEMENT: PLYMOUTH PLANTATION

Intended Learnings

- Students will be able to describe conditions aboard the *Mayflower*.
- Students will understand the roles of men and women in the colonial period.
- Students will understand a typical lifestyle of colonists.
- Students will understand how Plymouth Plantation arranged its houses, central buildings, protective structures, and farmland for safety and usefulness.

Instructional Foci

Books, pamphlets, brochures, maps, and photographs regarding Plymouth Plantation; field trip to Plymouth Plantation and the *Mayflower II;* letters, discussion, sense chart

General Teaching Strategy

This subunit relies on scheduling to fit so perfectly into unit plans. If, in fact, it will not fit at this time, students may need different kinds of preparation or follow-up activities for the trip. The goal of the trip is to really "see" what it is we've been reading about, to make the information more understandable, and also to provoke further thoughts and questions about colonial life.

Before the trip, have students prepare in several ways:

1. Using the "street plan" in *Constance,* have students sketch their own maps with family names written next to their cottages.

2. Students should be fairly familiar with colonists' names by this time through reading the novel, but in any case, have each student choose one family or individual to be in charge of gathering specific information about during the trip. Have them prepare by researching as much as they can before meeting them, and preparing a list of questions they will ask. Students may have to rely on neighbors of the colonists as not all of them are represented at all times.

3. Have all students read the "interviews" with Sarah Morton and Mistress Fuller found in *Cobblestone,* November, 1989. Several students who are comfortable with the reading could volunteer to play the parts of Sarah, Mistress Fuller, or the interviewer.

4. Read aloud to students other nonfiction accounts of the plantation.

5. Tell students some of the general categories under which the rest of the unit will be studied: government, religion, relationships with Native Americans . . . . They will have a better sense of the kinds of questions to ask with a structure for study already set in their minds.

During the course of the trip, remind students about these points of interest; help them ask questions that will elicit specific information as well as a general sense of the life of these Pilgrims. Students who have a clear purpose, enthusiasm and motivation about a subject, and a willing adult can usually lead themselves to where they want and ought to be. Life on the plantation is full of chance occurrences of daily life; it is impossible to prepare students for these, but help them get the most out of them. For instance, one year a lamb was born moments before we arrived. We returned to its yard several times over the course of the day, watching the afterbirth, the mother feeding, and attempts at first steps.

Upon returning to the classroom, all of the preparations must be accounted for, their purposes fulfilled. Students need the chance to talk about everything. A "sense chart" hung on a bulletin board is one way to share. Sections can be divided into "I tasted . . . ," "I smelled . . . ," "I saw . . . ," and so on. During the subsequent days, give students the opportunity to add to this board.

Our class makes it a habit to write letters of appreciation to people who share things with us or teach us. For these letters, students have someone specific to write to: the person about whom they were gathering information. Encourage students not only to thank them but also to share learnings and ask questions; students need every opportunity to see learning as ongoing.

SUBUNIT D: DAILY LIFE AND REGIONAL DIFFERENCES

Intended Learnings

- Students will understand how colonial America both reflected medieval and Renaissance Europe and created a unique culture based on the conditions, lifestyles, individual colonists, and the desire for a different kind of life.
- Students will understand the differences between colonies of the northern, southern, and middle Atlantic regions.
- Students will understand the roles of men and women in the colonial period.
- Students will understand a typical lifestyle of colonists.
- Students will understand the religious influence on many colonists and on the culture of the early colonies.
- Students will be able to name some of the religious laws of the colonies.

Instructional Foci

Nonfiction books, magazines, tests, filmstrips, historical fiction, simulated journals

General Teaching Strategy

This subunit is the most research oriented of the subunits. It has been placed in this sequence because the activities involved in subunit C serve as models for the product (a simulated journal such as a book read aloud, *Sarah Morton's Day*), but it could be used at this or any later point.

Before beginning independent research, have all students read the text section on different regions. Distinctions must be made between land conditions, weather, industry, and commerce.

Following this introduction, the students will be creating a simulated journal such as the above example. They will be assigned a gender and region but must make choices for other topics. Some of the information they must include is time of year, fictional name, occupation, and colony/town. They must also include information regarding religion, some laws and leaders guiding them, activities of their daily lives, and some of their personal hopes and dreams. Illustrations should accompany the text.

Assign roles randomly, posting lists so students can use each other as resources, especially among same-region characters. Set aside a sharing time once journals are complete, and save for evaluation purposes.

SUBUNIT E: GOVERNMENT

Intended Learnings

- Students will understand how governments and the ideals of governing grow from one another.
- Students will name several laws that governed early colonists.

Instructional Foci

Magna Charta, Mayflower Compact, nonfiction resources, discussion

General Teaching Strategy

To begin the whole class discussion, the teacher will either read aloud or have students preread "Mutiny on the *Mayflower.*" The focus of interest for this part of the lesson is twofold: events and atmosphere leading up to the writing and signing of the Mayflower Compact and actual provisions of the document. Students will be questioned as to how they understand conflict to have been the predecessor to that document, and how its development was, in effect, conflict resolution between two factions of people and a multitude of opinions. In a similar way, the Magna Charta will be reexamined by the class (all of whom have previously studied the Middle Ages) for similarities. It is the "spirit of the law" students should be asked to respond to, as well as the dissatisfaction with situations that led to each.

In smaller groups of three to four, students will look for evidence of the laws of the colonial period being carried out in everyday life. They will post the examples found in a variety of nonfiction resources so that the class can use them as examples. Some recognition should be made at this point of the heavy weight religion was given during this period, even in civil laws. Through an evaluation piece associated with the above intended learnings, this will become even clearer.

SUBUNIT F: RELIGION IN THE COLONIES

Intended Learnings

- Students will understand the influence of religion on many colonists and on the culture of the early colonies.
- Students will understand the irony of the persecuted becoming the persecutors, most especially in this subunit, as illustrated by the hypocrisy of those who came seeking religious freedom and denied others the freedom to worship or not as they chose.
- Students will be able to name some of the religious laws of the colonies.
- Students will be able to explain the history of witchcraft and its significance during the witch crazes of the colonial period.

Instructional Foci

Chart of laws from subunit E, books, magazines, video movie, social studies textbook

General Teaching Strategy

In the first part of this subunit, many connections are made to the understandings of religion in Europe during the Middle Ages and after. Students will need a chance to remember, or even reconstruct, these understandings throughout the subunit.

The class together should reconsider the list of laws that groups found and displayed on chart paper in the last subunit. A student or teacher can color code or underline those which the class decides are religiously based. Independently, have students read the text sections about religion, keeping track on a prepared note chart of differences among the colonies' religious states. The teacher should choose excerpts that differentiate among the 13 colonies and how religion often determined founding.

In the discussion to follow, have students recognize where and when church and state acted as one, asking for instances in which that is no longer true. Students may be on the lookout for current news events that illustrate the separation taken for granted or challenged even today.

The second part of this subunit focuses on the much-publicized witchcraft of the colonial period. The teacher should give students a historical background of witchcraft, from ancient Greece and Rome, noting societal attitudes toward it and commonly accepted uses of it.

After a preliminary discussion of conceptions of witches from their historical fiction reading and other exposure to the ideas of witches, show students the movie *Three Sovereigns for Sarah.* Excerpts may be sufficient to give students the idea of cultural pressures, greed, and ignorance as partly responsible for the crazes. Have students read several fictional pieces as well as several nonfiction pieces about witches and witchcraft. The class will then be able to distinguish, orally and in writing, among the images presented.

Many students are intrigued by the subject and opt to do additional reading. Provide a variety of accounts of witchcraft in the American colonies; some are in script form that students can present to the rest of the class.

SUBUNIT G: RELATIONSHIPS WITH NATIVE AMERICANS

Intended Learnings

- Students will understand the contributions of Native Americans to the survival of European settlers.
- Students will understand the speculative nature of history, and the role of historians and readers of history in making inferences.

Instructional Foci

The Double Life of Pocahontas by Jean Fritz, textbook, charts

General Teaching Strategy

This novel was chosen specifically because of the style in which it was written; Fritz makes it very clear to the reader that she had to make guesses about history given what information she had available to her.

The activity is structured to be understood in its totality; all groups provide pieces of a story told in sequence to the class. Groups of four students will be asked to read one chapter of the book. Probably the most effective use of time would be for individuals to read ahead of class time and then collaborate in the classroom. Groups are to record main events and characters in the chapter they read so that, retold to the class, all will get a comprehensive and chronological story of Pocahontas's life. The groups should choose a storyteller, with all to add details before the next group begins.

The other focus of the activity is to look for evidence that Jean Fritz, historian, had to make guesses. Direct quotes from each of the chapters will be posted for the class to see.

The same groups will have a second chance to work together after the story of Pocahontas has been told and discussed. Using the history texts, students will read about early life in the colonies, noting contributions made by Native Americans. Postreading discussion should center around those contributions as well as the ultimate "thanks" these groups of people received. This will give students a chance to make connections to their fourth-grade study of Native Americans.

SUBUNIT H: INDENTURED SERVANTS AND SLAVERY

Intended Learnings

- Students will understand how the different land conditions of the colonies of the North and South meant the South had a greater need for laborers.
- Students will understand the irony of the persecuted becoming the persecutors, specifically in this subunit, the landowners' use of humans as things.
- Students will be able to explain the roles of indentured servants and slaves during the colonial period.
- Students will be able to trace and explain the slave triangle between Africa, the West Indies, and colonial America.

Instructional Foci

Various books, stories, articles, and a play; broadsheet of slave notices; role-playing

General Teaching Strategy

Many people do not connect slavery with early colonial America. Students will have many opportunities to read about, act out, and discuss the common situations during this period throughout the subunit. Their most recent common experience with indentured servants is in hearing about two examples of such servants through the read-aloud *Constance*. Discussion could begin with the conditions recognized through this historical fiction piece and go on to a nonfiction account of indentured servants from the earliest colonies. *Meet the Real Pilgrims* is one such example, but there are several. Also share with students copies of a real indenture and have the class interpret it together.

Small groups of students will then read together a mock trial of an indentured servant, each presenting an excerpt of that script to the rest of the group. All through this first half of the subunit, emphases should be placed on the attitudes and conditions of life of indentured servants. This will ultimately serve as a contrast to the same for slaves.

Tell students they will be participating in some role-playing for which there are no scripts. Ask them to identify some information they would think important if they were to play the part of another person. Share the broadsheet of slaves being auctioned off with the whole class. A teacher-led discussion should again come back to living conditions and the attitude that it was acceptable to own, buy, and sell people. The teacher prepares realistic scenarios for small groups of children to read, discuss briefly, and then improvise the action of in front of the class. For example, a slave couple celebrating the birth of another child is interrupted by the arrival of their master. He has come to congratulate them, and at the same time inform them that their oldest child, a strong teenage boy, has been sold.

The students will then read a complete account of a slave's travels from Africa to slavery in America. They will keep a simulated journal of the important events of his life, his fears, hopes, and dreams, and the travels he takes. Where possible, actual maps will be included. These rather real-life accounts will be compared to other non-fiction resource information on early slavery.

The teacher should lead students to an understanding of the extent of slavery in the South, greatly due to the large plantations that needed to be worked. The group as a whole should discuss major differences between indentured servants and slaves. Primarily, that indentured servants chose their lot, were of many races, and had realistic hopes for the future were the factors that separated them from African slaves taken by force and kept for a lifetime against their will.

SUBUNIT I: WHY DO WE CALL THEM COLONIES?

Intended Learnings

- Students will understand what a colony is.
- Students will understand the characteristics of most colonies and their ruling power.
- Students will understand some reasons for colonization and opposition to it.
- Students will understand benefits to both the ruling power and the colony.

Instructional Foci

Discussion, record of comments, encyclopedia, group notes

General Teaching Strategy

So what will students think of colonies after many weeks of concentrated study? The teacher is now in a position to ask. This is no longer prior knowledge, but very current knowledge. It is, however, unlikely that it has been synthesized in quite this way.

For the whole class, the teacher leads a discussion with some of the following questions:

So, we've studied Plymouth and Jamestown, and . . . what are we calling them?

What, then, do we want to say a colony is? (It will take some time and argument to decide on some defining features of colonies.)

What would make a country like England want to pour all that money into a colony? Or any powerful country for example? Let's make a list of some viable reasons for colonizing.

Why would anyone go? What are their responsibilities to England (or whatever ruling country)?

In this way, all the major defining points of colonization are discussed prior to giving any formal definition. The students have American colonies as a common background, and their arguments will demonstrate some of the discrepancies that are, in fact, not clear in considering American colonies.

The students, though, will want and deserve some answers. Give groups the encyclopedia entry for colonization. Have groups decide what makes a colony a colony. Their second task is to make a two-sided argument giving evidence that we were, indeed, colonies . . . and that we were not, alas, really colonies.

Back as a class, read through all groups' arguments, discussing once again the uncertainty in the final analysis. Students should reach a level of comfort in understanding of colonization to acknowledge both sides. They will need this reinforced in looking back through the various subunits, as it is one of the most important cognitions of the unit. If, in fact, the "American colonies" and "European nations" aspects of the unit's conceptual map are flexible, this is the understanding that should be the strongest, the one most able to stand when memory of the 102 passengers has faded.

EVALUATION

The evaluation piece of the unit here addresses only the two main cognitions. Other understandings as well as cognitive skills do need to be evaluated to gain a sense of students' progress through the subunits and at the conclusion of all subunits.

1. Students will understand what a colony is, the characteristics of most colonies and their ruling power, some reasons for colonization and opposition to it, and benefits to both the ruling power and the colony.
   a. Given a description of a modern so-named colony, students will write an essay explaining how it truly is a colony (as we understand the term) and how it is not. Their skills in brainstorming, organizing ideas, developing arguments, and other essay-writing steps will be crucial. To eliminate the disparity between what students know and what they can express in writing, an oral interview on this same topic would work, but it would be very time-consuming.

b. Students will write two letters to government officials, one urging colonization by the United States and the other protesting it. The letter should include comments on our history as colonies, reasons for/against, possible benefits/drawbacks, and ethical considerations.

2. Students will understand how colonial America both reflected medieval and Renaissance Europe and created a unique culture based on the conditions, lifestyles, individual colonists, and the desire for a different kind of life.

    a. Besides a formal evaluation, the teacher should make note of individuals' understandings of the connections between medieval Europe and colonial America. It is clearly stated in the introduction that this is a crucial connection for students at the Campus School, given their previous studies.

    b. Given a list of general topics related to culture, living conditions, and so on, students will fill out a chart showing similarities and differences in these areas between medieval life and colonial life. In addition, they still will be asked to give examples to support their ideas.

A SURVEY OF WESTERN ART

Margaret Timmerman

COMMENTS

This is a very well-conceived design for a yearlong art history course aimed at high school juniors and seniors. Students would have to have some background in the history of Western civilization. The course could serve nicely as an elective in humanities or history. The use of flowcharts to explain the complex skills of analysis and research in art history is very helpful. The course, while designed as yearlong, does not contain exhaustive lists of ILOs or overly detailed general teaching strategies. Individual teachers are given clear direction and guidance but also have considerable freedom to select the artworks that will serve as examples and the specific learning activities that will achieve the desired learnings. These features are strengths for teachers who know this material. At the same time, anyone without a solid background in art history would find teaching this unit difficult.

RATIONALE

Historians often point out that during times of upheaval the arts are usually on the front line of change. Because art is produced by individuals, rather than by institutions, art can react more quickly to the social climate and is thus seen as heralding future conditions. Change itself is one of the predominant aspects of life today, and it is important for society that its citizens be able to keep up with the rapid fluctuations in culture and technology. Citizens who have knowledge in a variety of fields, including art, will be better able to cope in such a rapidly changing society.

Art history is an important means of understanding our cultural heritage, and the diverse societies that produced that heritage. It can serve as a balance to the increasing importance of technology in our society. And it is a way of training people to see beauty in a world that is growing increasingly ugly. With such training, people may be aroused to fight against the aesthetic decay that surrounds them.

For the learner, art can be an interesting introduction or adjunct to the study of history. It can inform one about our cultural heritage and provide a means of understanding past societies, from which our modern society is derived. It provides the learner with both the sensitivity and the vocabulary to be aware of and describe his or her own feelings and reactions to pieces of art. It also can provide the student with a chance to refine the use of language. By both reading and writing about art and aesthetics, the student will be able to understand and communicate subtle differences in expression. He or she will also be able to apply the vocabulary of art to the world.

Usually, the study of art history is not begun until the student has reached the college level. However, the benefits that derive from this field are such that I think it is important to offer it at the high school level. For those students who then go on to study it further in college, it will provide them with a head start and allow them to do more advanced work in the field. For those who do not go on to college, or choose not to study it in college, this course will at least offer them a basic understanding of the concepts and methods used in the discipline. Thus they will at least accrue the benefits outlined above, whatever their opportunities for further study.

INTRODUCTION

This course is designed as a survey of Western art for eleventh and twelfth graders. It is a full-year course, and although it could be shortened somewhat this is not recommended due to the amount of material covered. The course assumes that the students are not familiar with the study of art history, and thus there are no prerequisites. However, students will find it useful to have had at least one basic studio art course.

The material in the course is sequenced chronologically. This sequence was chosen deliberately, for two reasons: (1) an understanding of the art of ancient Greece and Rome is necessary for the study of all subsequent Western art, and (2) any artistic style is usually related to the artistic events that preceded it, thus necessitating a chronological approach. The units employed cover fairly large time spans, in the hope that this will make it easier for the student to relate the various eras and grasp the overall flow of history. In order to achieve this it is also necessary for the teacher to deal with the material in a cumulative manner, whenever possible making comparisons with the art of earlier periods.

This course attempts to answer three central questions:

1. How is an artwork related to the culture in which it is produced?

2. Are there any artistic traditions evident in the history of art, and if so, when and how are they manifested?

3. How does the viewer objectively evaluate a work of art? This final question is part of a larger, more general goal of making the students sensitive to their own likes and dislikes in art. If students are aware of how they react to an art-

work and are also aware of the criteria generally used to designate a good piece of art, then it is hoped that they will be able to appreciate many kinds of art. Appreciation and enjoyment do not always go hand in hand.

The intended learning outcomes (ILOs) are derived from these central questions. The ILOs for this course are pertinent for every unit, and the teacher should feel free to emphasize different ones at different times.

ILOs

Primary ILOs

1. Students will understand the relationship of major styles to the cultures in which they were produced and will know what thoughts and events influenced the development of these styles.

2. Students will be able to identify major pieces in the history of art, giving the artist, style, and approximate date, and will be able to give a justification for their identification.

3. Students will know about the recurrence of certain traditions in the history of art and will be able to point out when and why these recurrences appeared.

4. Students will be able to use the vocabulary of art to clearly analyze the formal elements in an artwork.

Secondary ILOs

5. Students will know something about individual artists and what makes them important in the history of art.

6. Students will be able to conduct basic art historical research.

In order for the teacher to have a clear idea of what he or she wants the students to learn, it is also helpful to group the ILOs according to the type of learning outcome, that is, into cognitions, corresponding cognitive skills, psychomotor–perceptual skills, and affective understandings.

COGNITIONS AND COGNITIVE SKILLS

1. Students will be able to identify major pieces in the history of art and give a justification for their identification. Corresponding cognitive skill: Students will be able to recognize some of the masterpieces in the history of art. "Recognition" here implies a kind of memorization of visual stimuli and does not necessarily mean the student would be able to give reasons for the identification.

2. Students will understand the relationship of major styles to the cultures in which they were produced. "Understand" here implies that the student will be able to point out some cause–effect relationships.

3. Students will know many of the vocabulary words used when discussing art. "Know" here implies that the student will be able to give a definition of the words. Corresponding cognitive skill: Students will be able to use the vocabulary of art to analyze formal elements. "Use" here implies that the student will be able to apply specific vocabulary to any number of different examples.

4. Students will have an understanding of artistic traditions. "Understanding" means that the student will be able to give examples of works from different periods and discuss how they are similar.

PSYCHOMOTOR–PERCEPTUAL SKILLS

Students will be able to do basic art historical research. This implies that they know the steps involved and will be able to carry them out in a logical sequence.

AFFECTIVE UNDERSTANDINGS

Students will have an appreciation for many kinds of art. Appreciation indicates that they know why the artwork is significant, regardless of whether or not they like it.

Figure B.1 is a conceptual map that shows the major ideas that the course will cover and the relationships among these ideas. In this course it is possible to make a more specific map for each of the periods covered, as the example for Prehistoric Art shows. These specific maps, while time-consuming to make, would be useful for the students to have, as they would serve as a concise synopsis of the course. The flowcharts in Figures B.2, B.3, and B.4 on pages 244–246 outline the steps involved in primary and secondary ILOs 2, 4, and 6 listed previously.

INTRODUCTION TO THE COURSE

One Period

The introduction to the course as a whole is designed to give students an idea of what art history is. This is important, because at this age few have been exposed to a systematic study of art. For those students who are unsure of what the course is about, the introduction should let them know if they are really interested in this subject.

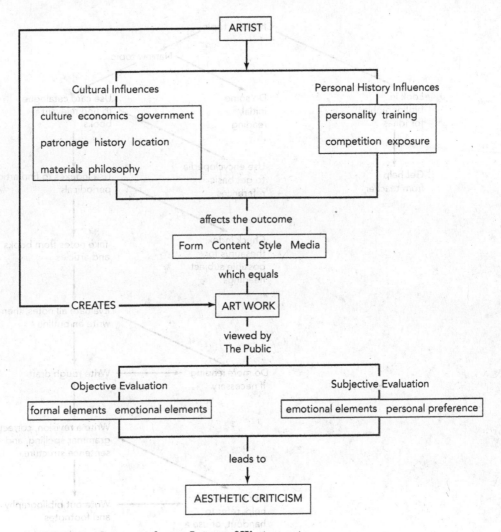

FIGURE B.1   Conceptual map: Survey of Western art.

Teaching Strategies

During this period, the teacher should outline the content to be covered, the materials and techniques that will be used, and what is expected of the students. It would be useful to give each student a copy of the course conceptual map and discuss it with them. The teacher should then go through a series of slides representing the major periods that will be covered. During this presentation, the teacher should introduce some of the basic vocabulary, the major historical periods, and the concepts outlined

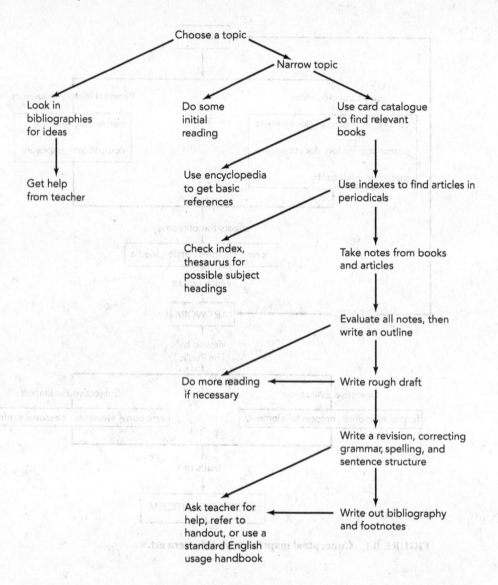

Choose a topic

Narrow topic

Look in bibliographies for ideas

Do some initial reading

Use card catalogue to find relevant books

Get help from teacher

Use encyclopedia to get basic references

Use indexes to find articles in periodicals

Check index, thesaurus for possible subject headings

Take notes from books and articles

Evaluate all notes, then write an outline

Do more reading if necessary

Write rough draft

Write a revision, correcting grammar, spelling, and sentence structure

Ask teacher for help, refer to handout, or use a standard English usage handbook

Write out bibliography and footnotes

FIGURE B.2   Flowchart for cognitive skill six: Doing basic art historical research.

on the map. Then the teacher should tell the students what instructional devices will be used in the class, including slide lectures, class discussions, worksheets on the readings, quizzes, museum trips, art projects, and a short research paper. This list is flexible, and the students should know that if they come up with good suggestions these can be incorporated into the class structure.

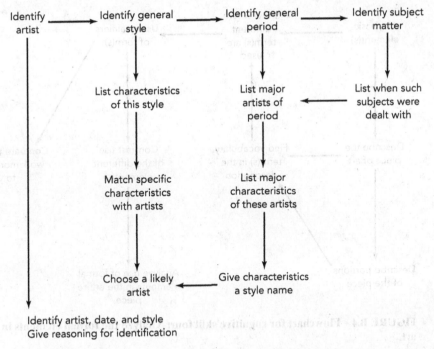

FIGURE B.3   Flowchart for cognitive skill two: Recognition of major masterpieces.

UNIT ONE: THE ANCIENT WORLD

This unit covers a very large time span and a variety of countries and styles. These can be broken down into three groups: (1) prehistoric, Egyptian, and the ancient Near East; (2) the Aegean, and ancient Greece and Rome; and (3) early Christian art. The unit will concentrate primarily on painting, sculpture, and architecture but will also introduce students to mosaics and pottery. The emphasis will be placed on the Greek, Roman, and early Christian works, and how these influenced all subsequent Western artists until the twentieth century.

ILOs

Numbers 1–4

Instructional Foci

Slide lectures, class discussions, quizzes, worksheets on the readings, a museum visit

Teaching Strategies

For the primitive period, the teacher should concentrate on the transition from a nomadic society to an agricultural one. Concepts should include nomadic living,

FIGURE B.4   Flowchart for cognitive skill four: Analyze the formal elements in a work of art.

hunting and gathering, communal living, domestication of plants and animals, and what we mean by civilization.

Another major area should be religion and the effect it had on the arts. Students should understand ideas such as ritual, monarchy, divine rule, monotheism, and polytheism. They should also know when religions became organized for large groups of people.

During the Greek and Roman periods the emphasis should be on the flourishing of civilization, the rise of large cities, and the development of various forms of government: democracy, republic, and empire. The students should understand the impact of trade in diversifying the economy and acquainting the people with other cultures. Once again religion is very important, and the students should know the major gods and some of the stories associated with them. (Readings outside of the text, such as Edith Hamilton's *Mythology,* should be utilized.) Another important consideration is that of the philosophic systems developed during this period: rationalism, Epicureanism, Stoicism, individualism, and empiricism should all be outlined. Finally, students should be aware of the development of mathematics and geometry, and of the reemergence of writing and the importance of literature and drama as art forms in these societies.

The early Christian period is included in this unit because these new art forms emerged in Imperial Rome. Students should be shown the similarities to pagan art, but should understand the new synthesis of symbolism that was achieved in biblical representations. They should also understand the basic differences between the

Christian religion and the Greek and Roman religions that preceded it. Students should know of the conversion of the emperor Constantine in the early fourth century, and the significance for art of Christianity's becoming the official religion. Emphasis should be placed on catacomb paintings, funerary sculpture, and the development of a Christian architecture.

Special Notes

1. In first introducing students to art history, teachers must stress the flexibility of stylistic names. We use names such as "archaic" or "hellenistic" in order to make it easier to discuss various general characteristics. However, seldom is a work solidly of one style; usually it will have attributes of several periods. Such stylistic names are convenient handles but should not be regarded as rigid. This is an important point to make at the very beginning, because these names become even more nebulous in the nineteenth and twentieth centuries.

2. If the students seem to have a good grasp of the formal characteristics of Greek art, it would be good to try to discuss the archaic–classical–baroque sequence that is evident. This is a pattern that recurs in the history of Western art, always reflecting the original qualities in these three Greek periods.

UNIT TWO: THE MIDDLE AGES, 5–6 WEEKS

This unit can be broken down into four parts: (1) Byzantine, (2) Carolingian and Ottonian, (3) Romanesque, and (4) Gothic. The works studied will concentrate on the spread of Catholicism and its influence on art. Forms included will be panel paintings, manuscripts, architecture, and architectural decoration (sculpture and mosaics). Special care should be taken to show students that this art, in general, was based on entirely different ideas than the art of Greece and Rome. However, they should also be shown where the classical influence appears during this period.

ILOs

Numbers 1–4

Instructional Foci

Slide lectures, readings, class discussions, quizzes, short opinion papers, a field trip to a museum or to look at local architecture, if applicable

Teaching Strategies

For the Byzantine period, the teacher should make clear the similarities and differences between this and early Christian art. The students should have a clear understanding of the Byzantine Empire: where it was, how long it lasted, why it was important, what brought about its collapse. They should understand the importance of official church patronage and the effects of the Iconclastic Controversy, including the split between Roman Catholicism and the Greek Orthodox Church. They should be aware of how church architecture was synthesized to fit the liturgical needs of the religion.

In dealing with Carolingian and Ottonian art forms, students should learn about the emergence of the monastery as a self-contained community. They should know the basic facts about Charlemagne's empire and its successors, and Charlemagne's attempts to restore the Holy Roman Empire. Students should be able to identify the major manuscripts of the period and understand how illumination became an art form. They should be aware of the importance of writing and literature within the hierarchy of the nobility and the church. They will be able to relate the invasions that periodically swept across the European continent, and the gradual shift of power from southern parts of Europe to those farther north. Especially important is the concept of revivalism.

In studying the Romanesque period, students should be aware of the triumph of Christianity throughout and beyond Europe and the growing sense of religious enthusiasm. They should understand that Romanesque refers to many regionally distinct yet related styles that sprang up across Europe. It did not have a central source and thus differs greatly from the two court styles that preceded it. Other important concepts include the revival of Mediterranean trade routes, a regrowth of commerce and manufacturing, and the subsequent flourishing of city life. At this time, a middle class composed of merchants and craftsmen also developed and had a large impact on medieval society. Students should be able to distinguish between the many regional variations in Romanesque style and also note their similarities. In sculpture and painting, they should be able to point out Byzantine influences.

When introducing students to Gothic art, the teacher should make clear that the style originated in the area around Paris, gradually spread and mutated until it became international, and then waned in importance. Students should also understand that the characteristics of the style first appeared in architecture and only later took hold of sculpture and painting. Another art form that should be introduced at this time is stained glass. In church philosophy, the students should be able to distinguish the basic differences between the patristic theology of the early church and the scholastic doctrines of the Gothic age. They should also understand the structure of feudalism and why it was important economically and politically.

Special Notes

1. At this point in the course it is important to make sure the students are thinking about the material in a cumulative fashion. Lectures and quizzes should include slides from the ancient world for the purpose of comparison. It is necessary for the teacher to point out the reappearances of older styles, for this link will otherwise often be missed by students. Only if they get in the habit of thinking about works they already know will they be able to view the history of art as a somewhat coherent series of developments.

2. If field trips are being planned, it is good if the teacher knows what pieces will be on display. Then he or she can assign short oral reports in which each student discusses a particular work. These reports could cover topics such as history of ownership, iconography, identification or forgery problems, media used, or special innovations or techniques. This will give the field trip more focus, make it more interesting, and take the burden of explaining off the teacher.

UNIT THREE: THE RENAISSANCE, 5–6 WEEKS

This unit covers a somewhat shorter time span, but a vast number of major artists and artworks. It can be broken down into three phases: (1) the early Renaissance, (2) the High Renaissance, and (3) mannerism. Emphasis is primarily on painting, sculpture, and architecture, although if possible it would be good to expose the students to some drawings and graphics at this time. Once again the art is based on that of classical antiquity, although the premise of the Renaissance artists was quite different from that of those who tried to revive antiquity during the Middle Ages. During this period, the artists tried to compete with the classical ideal. This is an important distinction. Finally, students should know that during this period the north and south of Europe followed two essentially different stylistic paths.

ILOs
Numbers 1–4

Instructional Foci

Slide lectures, readings, class discussions, quizzes, and an art project. (If possible, have the students briefly explore the development of painting techniques, including tempera, fresco, and oils.)

Teaching Strategies

The early Renaissance was marked by a specific aim: understanding the visible world. This desire produced very different effects in the north and the south of Europe, which should be understood by the students. In the north, the period is usually called "Late Gothic," and is characterized by extreme detail, disguised religious symbolism, the device of atmospheric perspective, and the development of a new relationship between the picture space and real space. Students should be aware of the impact of the development of the oil painting medium on the art of this period. They should also know about the invention of printing and its effects on both books and pictures. Students should have an understanding of the processes involved in woodcut, engraving, and drypoint. In the south, the important ideas were individualism and humanism, which lead to a new acceptance of art as the work of the creative mind rather than mere handicraft. This led to an increase in portrait painting and the signing of artworks. The Italians also invented linear perspective, just one example of their rational, scientific approach to the world around them. Another important concept is that of the rise of the vernacular and the decline of Latin. Finally, students should know the basics about Neo-Platonism, the philosophy developed to fuse the Christian faith with ancient mythology.

The High Renaissance applies only to Italy, and only to the work of six men. Students should be aware of how this art was a culmination of early Renaissance ideals but also how it differs from those ideals. Especially important are the concepts of genius, divine inspiration, and visual effectiveness. Students should understand why this "period" was so short-lived, and yet why it had such a powerful impact on following artists.

What is called the northern Renaissance occurred because of a sudden influx of Italian influence. This influence varied from area to area, producing a diversity of styles that have primarily a period of time in common. Important concepts include the Reformation and the attitudes of Protestant leaders toward art, the desire to assimilate Italian art, and the development of new subject matter that was not religious.

Mannerism is a recently coined term that covers the art produced in the second two-thirds of the sixteenth century. It appeared in both the north and south and was based on two conditions: First, it was an artistic reaction to the instability produced in Europe by the Reformation. Second, it was a reaction against the ideals of the High Renaissance. Artists knew they could not hope to imitate that style and thus chose to concentrate on other aims. Most expressed an inner vision that was not dependent on nature or the classics. Students should be aware of the formal elements that make this art so "unclassical."

Special Notes

1. If they are not already, students should be made aware of the origins of the style names that are used. If they understand what the name refers to it should help them remember the characteristics of the style, and also make clearer why such names are inexact.

2. From the Renaissance on, we become aware of the names of individual artists, including those who were women. It is important to try to include slides and reproductions of the work of female artists, so that the students get a sense of their contribution to our artistic tradition. It is also important to discuss why there were, historically, fewer women than men engaged in this pursuit.

UNIT FOUR: THE BAROQUE AND ROCOCO

This unit covers what are designated as the dominant styles during the seventeenth and eighteenth centuries. These styles were prevalent throughout Europe and England, with variations between north and south. Emphasis will be placed on painting, sculpture, and architecture, but attention should be paid to the use of "mixed media," which reached a new height. The baroque is a problematic period in terms of its sources, and students should try to decide if the style was a culmination of Renaissance ideals (like the archaic–classical–baroque sequence in ancient Greek art), or whether it was unrelated to the art that came before it.

ILOs

Numbers 1–4

Instructional Foci

Slide lectures, readings, class discussions, quizzes, field trip to a museum

Teaching Strategies

The baroque in all of Europe was influenced by three things: the renewal of the Catholic faith, the absolutist state, and new discoveries in science.

In the southern parts of Europe, the baroque style was based on the Counter-Reformation. It was an attempt by the Church to lure people back to it, by making the concepts of the religion easier to understand. The main idea was that of bringing the divine down to earth, in order to make God comprehensible to the common man. Students should know about the rise of Spanish power and should understand the causes and effects of the Sack of Rome. They should be aware of the Council of Trent, the Universal Inquisition, and the foundation of new Catholic religious orders, all aspects of the reform of the Church.

Central Europe was eliminated by the rise of France and the development of art forms suited to the aristocracy. Art became a weapon of propaganda for the state and helped glorify national power. Students should understand the effects of a lack of competition among patrons of the arts and how dependence on government commissions led to a standardization of art. They should also know about the growth of academies, in literature and music as well as in painting and sculpture.

In the northern parts of Europe, the middle class was the dominant force in government and economics. The impact of Protestantism forced artists to find patrons, and subject matter, that were not church related. Students should understand the effect of this free market system on painting and sculpture and should be aware of the kinds of buildings that were needed by the middle class. They should also understand the emphasis on the home during this period.

All these aspects of the baroque found a sort of synthesis in England. Here the opposing views of tradition and of modernism managed to coexist. The important concepts are: an earth-centered versus a sun-centered universe; theoretical political unity versus practical political diversity and balance of power; philosophy of the supernatural versus that of naturalism; reliance on religious faith versus reliance on scientific experimentation; and the unity of Christianity versus the rise of many religious sects.

The rococo was essentially an extension of the aristocratic baroque style, tempered so as to be suitable for domestic buildings as well as palaces. The most important idea to emerge during this period was that of rationalism, which led to this being called the "Age of Enlightenment." Students should understand the spread of this philosophy to the middle classes and its effect on the arts. Students should also see how this relatively calm era led to the revolutionary nineteenth century.

Special Notes

The baroque style is usually considered an acquired taste. Thus, this unit should pay special attention to the general goal of helping students define what they like, and why. It is important for them to see the baroque in its wider context, which may help them appreciate it even if they do not particularly like it.

UNIT FIVE: THE REVOLUTIONARY AGE, 5–6 WEEKS

This unit covers all of the nineteenth century and can be broken down into four major styles: neoclassicism, romanticism, realism, and impressionism. Students should be aware of the diversity of revolutions that occurred during this period—industrial, social, technological, political, scientific, and cultural—and should know how these affected the arts. Emphasis will again be on painting, sculpture, and architecture, including what was happening in America.

ILOs

Numbers 1–4

Instructional Foci

Slide lectures, quizzes, readings, class discussions, a field trip, and an art project (if possible)

Teaching Strategies

The neoclassicists based their art on that of republican Rome. Rome itself thus became a symbol for revolutionary protest, and neoclassicism became a way of life rather than just an artistic style. The ancient classics and histories were widely read. This revival was different from any previous classical revival, however. Students should understand the ideas of archeological accuracy, heroism, simplicity, and self-sacrifice.

By contrast, romanticism was eclectic; it embraced a number of past styles, including the classics, the Middle Ages, and the East. Romantic artists were interested in emotion for its own sake. This art was based on close observation of nature, as opposed to the conventions of neoclassicism. An especially important concept was that of the sublime, that is, awe in the face of the unknown and the unknowable. This notion had a large impact on the early landscape painters in America.

The realists based their art on the Dutch and Flemish naturalists of the seventeenth century. Most of these artists were for a new social order based on the needs of the middle class; many of them were thrown in jail for their participation in social movements. Students should understand why this unpretentious art was not immediately accepted by the critics, and also how it led to the work of the impressionists.

Impressionism was the first complete artistic revolution since the start of the Renaissance in Italy. These artists were interested in capturing a fleeting moment, and based their attempts on the effects of light. The students should learn the basics of color theory and understand the idea of optical mixing. It is important to discuss the subject matter that the impressionists chose to portray and the reasons for their great popularity.

The postimpressionists were a loosely formed group who agreed with the impressionists' desire to capture a fleeting moment, but not with the means they used to achieve this. The postimpressionists were divided into two camps: those interested in achieving permanence of form and those who gave primacy to emotional expression. Students should understand the change in the structure of the art world, from one of many artists working in a similar style with similar ideas, to one in which artists became increasingly individualistic and difficult to classify.

Special Notes

1. During the study of impressionism it would be interesting to have each student produce a small painting, using what they have learned of color theory and optical mixing. This project could take two to three class periods and would give the students firsthand experience with the effects these artists were trying to capture.

2. At the beginning of this unit, the teacher should assign a research paper, which the students will have six to eight weeks to complete. The teacher should set up a timetable and check each student's work every week, to make sure they are learning the processes involved. The timetable could include tasks such as choosing a topic, narrowing the topic, researching in books, researching in periodicals, writing an outline, writing a rough draft, and doing a revision. This will familiarize the students with the processes and formats used in research. It is also an exercise that will force them to study several points of view and then come to their own conclusions. (This project can be modified in scope according to the library facilities available to the students.)

UNIT SIX: THE TWENTIETH CENTURY, 5–6 WEEKS

The twentieth century must be viewed differently from the preceding artistic periods, due to the rapid nature of change in society and the arts. Three ideas are especially important: (1) local artistic traditions gave way to international trends, (2) the artistic capital shifted from Europe to America, and (3) the process of creating became at least as important as the actual final product. The unit should focus on architecture (especially the impact of new building materials), sculpture, and painting, but should also expose the students to some more minor forms: photography, drawing, stained glass, graphic arts, "found objects," and "happenings." Special attention should be paid to gaining an understanding of the philosophies behind the various art movements and to understanding if, when, and how these forms are related to previous styles.

ILOs

Numbers 1–4

Instructional Foci

Slide lectures, class discussions, quizzes, readings, a visit to a contemporary art gallery, and a lecture by a visiting local artist (if possible)

Teaching Strategies

This unit does not break down into convenient time periods, so it is probably easiest to deal with the material in one of two ways. The first would be to break it down according to medium, so that painting, sculpture, and architecture are dealt with separately. The second would be to break it down according to artistic movement. I would recommend the first treatment, keeping in mind that it is necessary for the teacher to point out parallels among the media. If the teacher does not do this, it will be difficult for the students to see the relationships among the various art forms.

Students should also be reminded that twentieth-century art movements are not at all clear-cut. Some artists did not belong to any organized movement, while others belonged to several. Some movements were spontaneous, while others were planned. The various styles often overlapped and borrowed from each other, and the dates of none of them can be pinpointed with exactitude. Such characteristics should be related to the rapidly changing, increasingly complex world in which we live.

Like the baroque, many modern styles are an acquired taste. Students should at least be able to appreciate the incredible vitality and ingenuity that characterizes the art of our age, even if they do not personally enjoy it.

This leads to the idea that much modern art is ugly or inane. This would be a good time for students to reassess their notions of what art is. They should be asked to explain their ideas on aesthetics, beauty, and the purpose of art.

Special Notes

1. One way to make this unit more interesting to students is to include some study of the contemporary art scene in their town or city. This could include a trip to a local gallery, a lecture (and/or demonstration) by a local artist, a visit to an artist's studio, or a trip to a museum that has a modern art exhibition.

2. This unit also lends itself to two possible group art projects: having the class make a piece of art out of "found objects" (each could bring one thing), or

having the class create a "happening." (The rest of the school could be invited to this, if it were properly planned.) Both these activities could lead to significant discussion among the students about the nature of art and how it is created.

3. If a final is planned for the end of the year, three or four days should be set aside for in-class review and questions.

COURSE EVALUATION

EVIDENCE OF MAIN EFFECTS—HIGH-PRIORITY LEARNING OUTCOMES

1. Students will understand the relationship of major styles to the cultures in which they were produced.
   a. The student can state, in oral or written form, how a work reflects the philosophy of the culture in which it was produced.
   b. The student can outline the basics of the form of government and the economic system of a period and show how these affected the arts.
   c. The student will know the major religions of various places and periods, and how these affected the arts.
   d. The student can state broad general differences between the art of two places and/or periods.

2. Students will be able to identify major masterpieces in the history of Western art and will be able to give a justification for their identification.
   a. The student can look at an artwork (which he or she may or may not have seen before) and state who did it, when it was done, and what style it is.
   b. The student can justify that identification by comparing the piece to other works by the same artist and noting similarities.
   c. If the student does not recognize the specific artist, he or she can state the style of the work and justify the choice by comparing it to other works of the same period.

3. Students will have an understanding of artistic traditions, and when and how these are manifested in the history of art.
   a. When shown an artwork, the student can state past influences that are visible in the piece.
   b. When shown an artwork, the student can state how it influenced subsequent artists or styles and can give two or three examples.
   c. The student can write a short essay tracing the development of a specific style over a long period of time. Once again, he or she should be able to refer to specific examples.

4. Students will be able to use the vocabulary of art to analyze the formal elements of a piece.
   a. When shown an artwork, the student can point out the use of specific elements (e.g., color, line) when asked to do so.

b. The student can compare and contrast two works of similar or different styles and state how they are the same or different in their use of specific elements.

c. When presented with a style name, the student can state the formal characteristics that are used to define that style.

The evidence of all the above learnings will show up in class discussions, on quizzes and worksheets, and during museum trips.

EVIDENCE OF MAIN EFFECTS—SECONDARY LEARNING OUTCOMES

1. Students will be able to say what they like in an artwork, and why it appeals to them.
   a. The student will understand and be able to explain the emotive elements in a work.
   b. The student will be able to explain why a particular piece, style, or subject appeals to him or her, in both its formal and emotive elements.
   c. The student will know that different kinds of artworks appeal to different people.

2. Students will develop an appreciation for many kinds of art.
   a. The student will be able to state why a certain work or style was important in the history of art.
   b. The student will be able to say why some works are classified as masterpieces and others are not.
   c. The student will be aware of the changing concepts of beauty and aesthetics throughout the history of art.

3. Students will be able to do basic art historical research.
   a. The student can write down or state the major steps one takes in doing research.
   b. The student can present the results of each step as he or she completes it (e.g., show an outline or a rough draft).
   c. The student should be able to present a properly documented paper five to ten pages in length, using standard research format.
   d. The student will be able to present diverse points of view and then reach his or her own conclusion about an issue.

POSSIBLE UNDESIRABLE LEARNING OUTCOMES

1. Those that result from interaction with the teacher:
   a. The student may get the feeling that all essay and identification questions have a right or wrong answer, rather than realizing that the justification is the important point.
   b. The student may notice the teacher's own bias for or against certain artistic periods and may feel that these biases are correct.

2. Those that result from the choices of instructional foci:
   a. The student may feel that all great artists are male.

     b. The student may decide that only those pieces that are considered master-pieces are worth studying.

     c. The student may become dependent on reproductions and not know how to react to an actual work (especially true of architecture).

     d. The student may develop a passive attitude toward art and not be able to understand the actual act of creation.

3. Those that result from the organization of the course:

     a. The student may get locked into the chronology and not be able to make comparisons that cover large time gaps.

     b. The student may not be able to see broad relationships through long periods of time.

     c. The student may come to believe that stylistic names are absolute.

     d. The student may remember the different forms of government in the various periods but not the religions, the philosophic systems, and the cultural aspects of the different eras.

4. Those that result from the institutional setting:

     a. The student may have trouble developing a concept of beauty if the room is messy or run-down.

     b. If there are not a lot of visual stimuli around (posters, books, slide viewers), the student may have trouble learning to memorize visual elements.

     c. The student will not be able to develop a true appreciation for art if he or she does not have some chances to see actual pieces rather than just reproductions.

A NOTE ON COGNITION

This course requires that students study, learn, and memorize a lot of visual information. For some this comes fairly naturally; for others it is very difficult. There are three things the teacher can do to improve the students' visual cognitive capacity:

1. Expose students to many, many pieces of artwork. The more they see, the more likely they are to remember broad characteristics or even small details. Every time they look at a work, they are getting practice at sharpening their visual skills.

2. Expose students to actual pieces, not just reproductions. Being face to face with a painting, sculpture, or building is a different experience from looking at a slide, and the students are likely to remember more from it. They will also be able to recall it more easily.

3. Make the students talk about what they see: the elements used, what they like or dislike, what is successful and what isn't. Talking or writing about art often helps students remember the pieces they have seen.

IMMIGRATION: A SOCIAL STUDIES UNIT FOR SIXTH GRADERS

Michelle Chang

COMMENTS

This is an ambitious unit that attempts to convey an understanding and appreciation of our country's cultural diversity by examining immigration. It has been said over and over that the United States is a country of immigrants; this unit attempts to bring this understanding to upper elementary students. The unit could be easily adapted to a middle school or junior high school audience. Among the unit's strengths are its coverage of immigration over a rather long historical span, the personal connection of exploring one's own heritage, and the explicit consideration of culture and the interplay of one's native culture in the process of assimilation.

INTRODUCTION

Coming to America has been a dream for generations of people around the world. The English began small settlements in the New World in the 1600s and were followed by people from all over Europe. Many immigrants left their families and friends behind and endured great hardship coming to America. They believed America was the "promised land" where you were granted the freedoms of life, liberty, and the pursuit of happiness, and money grew on trees. Many immigrants came to the United States expecting to stay only for a brief time and then return to their homeland with something to show for their hard work in the States. More often than not, these immigrants never returned to their native land. In the latter part of the twentieth century, the United States has been the destination for an increasing number of people from Asia and Latin America who have left their homelands for many of the same reasons as earlier immigrants.

Immigration has long played an important part in the settling and development of this country. Successive generations of immigrants have climbed the socioeconomic ladder. As money seems to be a major requirement for acceptance or approval by established Americans, those immigrants who have experienced financial success are more quickly accepted by previous immigrant groups. New groups of immigrants have been feared and ostracized by those people already settled because they are different. However, it is those differences brought to the United States by immigrants that make this a unique country. The United States is a nation of immigrants.

Today, of the many problems our nation faces, several can be traced back to ethnic differences. Courts across the country must grapple with cases involving racism every day. Affirmative action hiring policies have been debated by employers and employees. Segregation in schools and housing patterns have plagued politicians and concerned citizens for decades. Though many steps were taken by the government in the 1960s to address the injustices of inequality in this country, there is still a great distance to go before these problems will be adequately resolved.

Currently most elementary school social studies curricula focus on the local community, the state, and the history of the United States. The theory is to start with what is familiar, the local community, and expand the sphere of study as the child progresses through the grades. Some schools incorporate a unit on the history of black Americans or study famous black Americans in the month of February, which has been named Black History Month. Many schools also study Native Americans. However, few social studies curricula examine the variety of ethnic groups that have immigrated to the United States and, more importantly, the experiences of these groups of people. Thus one must search for appropriate materials, as few can be found in prepackaged social studies curricula. Many hope that future generations will be able to put an end to ethnic tensions in our country, but this task seems absolutely impossible unless children learn about the different groups that make up this ethnically diverse country. Studying immigration provides a vehicle for gaining knowledge about ethnic groups and helps students understand the conflicts and tensions between various groups in the country and in the world. This knowledge will perhaps provide students with the insight needed to resolve some of the aforementioned problems in this country.

This nine- to ten-week unit on immigration is designed for sixth graders but could certainly be adapted for other grade levels. Forty-five minutes to an hour a day is the recommended instruction time for this unit, with more time being spent when needed for field trips or guest speakers. Although the concepts surrounding the subject of immigration are complex, I believe this unit can be taught effectively to sixth graders. Eleven- and twelve-year-olds are relatively idealistic and thus it may be hard for them to see different sides of issues. Nevertheless, I think the subject of immigration will fascinate sixth graders. Immigration also provides a vehicle to study one aspect of social studies in the United States that is currently underplayed in most social studies curricula. The students must have relatively strong reading skills, as a fair amount of information will be gained by reading. Students must also be able to put themselves in someone else's position, not an easy task for an egocentric child. Students must be able to work together. They must also be able to articulate their ideas orally and in writing. This unit promotes the use of problem-solving skills, which sixth graders are developing. It would be helpful if students had some understanding of the history of the United States (U.S. social studies is currently taught in the fifth grade in a great number of schools), but it is not essential, as this unit could be expanded. Immigration could be taught as one part of a year-long study of the

United States. Students knowledgeable in the history of the United States will have a context for the study of immigration and thus will better understand factors affecting immigration.

As students study U. S. immigration it is hoped that they will gain an appreciation for individual immigrants', refugees', and various ethnic groups' contributions to American society and culture. It is also hoped that by putting themselves in an immigrant's or refugee's shoes, students will gain an appreciation for their struggle between assimilation and maintaining their own culture. Ours is a nation of immigrants, and it is important that students understand and appreciate the important roles immigrants have played and continue to play in American history.

CONCEPTUAL MAP

Figure C.1 details the major learnings of this unit. It does not include all the details surrounding these main concepts; rather, it is designed to be read in conjunction with the entire unit plan. For details refer to the content outline. The map is meant to be read from top to bottom. Students will study the factors that pull immigrants to the United States and push refugees out of their homelands. Students will also study the laws and regulations of the sending countries and the United States that pertain to immigrants and refugees. There are several factors that affect the success and failure of immigrants and refugees once in the United States. At this point some people may return to their homeland. If they choose to stay, immigrants and refugees must struggle to find a balance between assimilation and maintaining their own culture. This conceptual map is designed to accommodate the study of any of the immigrant and refugee groups that have come to the United States throughout the history of this country.

INTENDED LEARNING OUTCOMES

Cognitions

1. Students will know characteristics of different immigrant and refugee groups from Northern Europe and Scandinavia, Central and Eastern Europe, Asia, and Latin America.

*2. Students will understand factors that pull immigrants to the United States and push refugees out of their homelands.

*3. Students will understand factors affecting immigrants' and refugees' success and failure in the United States.

4. Students will understand the concept of assimilation.

5. Students will understand the process of immigration.
   a. Students will understand the relationship between immigration patterns and the laws and regulations that pertain to immigration.
   b. Students will understand the relationship between U.S. foreign policy and U.S. immigration laws and regulations.

*Learning outcomes of greatest importance.

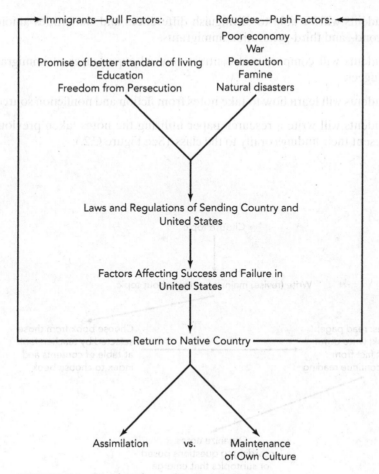

FIGURE C.1   Immigration unit conceptual map.

6. Students will understand the "average" experience of an immigrant.

7. Students will understand their own family history of immigration.

Cognitive Skills

*1. Students will compare and contrast characteristics of different immigrant groups.

2. Students will be able to distinguish between push and pull factors and how these affect immigration.

3. Students will identify the contributions immigrants have made to American society.

4. Students will compare and contrast the characteristics and experiences of "old" and "new" immigrants.

*Cognitive skill of greatest importance.

5. Students will be able to distinguish differences and similarities among first-, second-, and third-generation immigrants.

6. Students will compare and contrast general experiences of immigrants and refugees.

7. Students will learn how to take notes from fiction and nonfiction sources.

8. Students will write a research paper utilizing the notes taken previously and present their findings orally to the class. (See Figure C.2.)

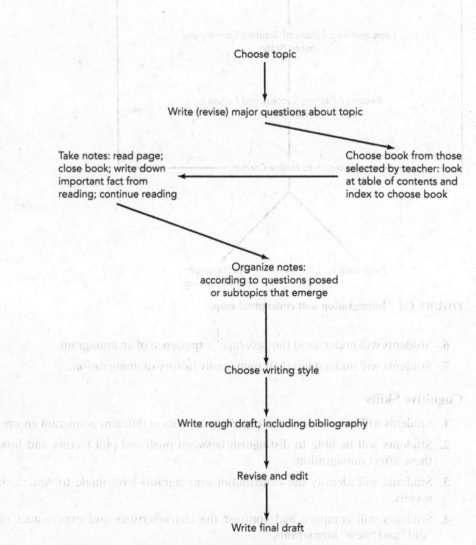

FIGURE C.2   Flowchart for complex skill: Writing a research paper.

CONTENT OUTLINE

   I. Why Come to the United States?
     A. Immigrants and pull factors
       1. promise of better standard of living
       2. education
       3. freedom from persecution
     B. Refugees and push factors
       1. persecution
       2. poor economy
       3. war
       4. famine
       5. natural disasters
     C. Examine own heritage
     D. Patterns of immigration
       1. Northern Europe, Scandinavia
       2. Southern and Eastern Europe
       3. Latin America
       4. Asia
  II. U.S. Laws and Regulations Pertaining to Immigration
     A. Period of open immigration
       1. immigrants by choice
       2. picture brides
     B. National Origins Quota System—1920s
     C. War brides—1945, McCarran-Walter Act—1952
     D. 1965 legislation
     E. 1980 Refugee Act
     F. Present policy
 III. Factors for Success and Failure of Immigrants
     A. How immigrants came—boat, plane, walking
     B. What they came with
       1. money
       2. skills
       3. education
       4. language
       5. friends and family vs. alone
     C. Where they settled
       1. community's attitude toward immigrants
       2. number of immigrants from similar background in community
       3. economy of community
       4. presence of friends and family in community
     D. Customs and traditions
       1. familiarity with U.S. customs and traditions
       2. similarities and differences between native country and United States
     E. First-, second-, and third-generation immigrants and refugees

    IV. Immigrants' Contributions to U.S. Society and Culture
        A. Arts
           1. fine art
           2. music
           3. dance
           4. theater
        B. Food
        C. Religion
        D. Customs and traditions
        E. Language
        F. Technology, skills, methods of accomplishing tasks
        G. Architecture
    V. Current Events
        A. Current immigration policy
        B. Alien farm workers
        C. Sanctuary movement
        D. Implications of new Eastern Europe on U.S. immigration
        E. Racism
           1. segregated neighborhoods, schools
           2. discrimination
           3. reverse discrimination
        F. Bilingual education

SEQUENCE

Basically there are two obvious sequence choices: begin with the past and work forward, or begin with the present and work backward. I have chosen the sequence outlined above because it allows students to role-play immigrants' and refugees' lives in a natural sequence of events. In other words, students will study topics as they would come up in an immigrant's life, excluding the final subunit. However, other sequences are possible. In any of the possible sequences one could first explore U.S. laws and regulations pertaining to immigration and then study why people come to the United States, or vice versa.

    An alternative to the above sequence would be:

   I. Current Events
  II. Immigrants' Contributions to U.S. Society and Culture
 III. Why Come to the United States?
  IV. U.S. Laws and Regulations Pertaining to Immigration
   V. Factors for Success and Failure of Immigrants

This sequence begins with current events related to immigration. Studying current events would motivate students to explore present issues more deeply and the history behind these issues. One could also begin with immigrants' contributions to U.S. society and culture. This would motivate students to examine the backgrounds of individuals and groups of people who have affected American society and culture. However, I have chosen the sequence outlined in detail above because of the instructional foci I have selected to pursue and the fact that this sequence most closely follows an immigrant's own experience.

SUBUNIT ONE: WHY COME TO THE UNITED STATES?

Introduction

This subunit is three weeks long and is designed to familiarize students with the history of immigration and the experiences of immigrants. Students may begin this unit with a variety of background information about immigration, all of which will enrich class discussions. One must be prepared for students to bring misconceptions and misunderstandings about immigration to this unit. These can be discussed by the entire class as they come up. The topics studied in this subunit will be referred to continuously and reexamined throughout the unit. This subunit can be expanded to a more in-depth study of U.S. history as well as the study of immigration.

Instructional Foci

1. Brainstorm

2. "American Immigrants: Part 1," *Cobblestone*, December 1982, pp. 1–5

3. Interview family member to construct family tree showing where family members came from and where they settled

4. Keep journal of imagined experiences as if you are an immigrant

5. Guest speaker on experiences of immigrants, refugees, aliens

6. Research on immigrant group

ILOs

Cognitions: 1, 2, 6, 7
Cognitive Skills: 1, 2, 4, 6, 7, 8

General Teaching Strategies

The introduction of this unit will begin with a whole-class brainstorm on the topic of "Who Is an Immigrant?" and "Why Did Immigrants Come to the United States?" The teacher can expect students to identify several immigrant groups: English, Irish, Mexicans, and so on, as well as some of the reasons immigrants came to the United States: religious freedom, money, land, and so forth. Students will then read the article in *Cobblestone*, which gives a brief overview of immigration and introduces students to some key terms relevant to the study of immigration: *native, emigrate, immigrate, promised land*, and *melting pot*. A discussion about the terms introduced may follow the reading.

Over the course of the next few days, students will examine their own family heritage. Students will interview a family member or members to determine their own family heritage. With this information students will make a family tree, indicating where their ancestors came from and where they settled in the United States. Students will share their family trees with the class so students can get an idea of the diversity of backgrounds present in their classroom community. If many students have very similar family backgrounds, the teacher might challenge some students to create a family tree for another family with a heritage unlike their own. Students would have to interview a person from another family to gain information to make an accurate family tree. If this challenge is pursued, the family trees will then represent the diversity of the community in which the students live.

Having an understanding of their own ethnic heritage, students will choose an immigrant or refugee, real or fictitious, to impersonate or role-play for the next several days. To accurately impersonate an immigrant, students will need to conduct research on that particular immigrant group. Again, students may conduct research on an immigrant group of a different ethnic heritage than their own family. This research will be put together in the form of a research paper (the process is explained under "complex skill" on the preceding pages). The research project will extend for several weeks and, after a few days, will mainly be conducted during writing process time, not social studies. The research project is designed to enrich students' learning about immigration as well as give students experience in conducting research and writing a major research paper. Students will share information from their research project with other students throughout the unit.

As a part of the role-playing, students will keep a journal of the experiences and/or thoughts and feelings they might have as an immigrant. The teacher may guide some of these journal entries. For example, the teacher might ask students to close their eyes and imagine their journey to the United States and then have the students write about that experience. Throughout this subunit students will keep this immigrant journal, which will be collected periodically by the teacher, who may maintain a running dialogue with students in their journals.

Initially students will focus their research on the push and pull factors affecting the immigration of their chosen group of immigrants. In the second week, after students have conducted adequate research, the class will spend a few days making a chart listing the push and pull factors and discussing each of these and how they are relevant to particular immigrant groups.

In the third week, students will work in cooperative groups. Students will be grouped according to the region of the world from which their group of immigrants came: Northern and Western Europe and Scandinavia, Southern and Eastern Europe, Latin America, Asia. These cooperative groups will develop a presentation for the class in which they will give the class a sketch of the experiences of immigrants from that region of the world. The presentation will include characteristics and experiences of immigrants from the same region; what these people had in common, and how they were unique. The teacher or individual groups may require students to read background material prior to presentations. The information presented by the groups will be displayed on a bulletin board in the classroom for future reference.

Guest speakers presenting material on any of the topics covered in Subunit One on the "content outline" would be a welcome addition. Students would benefit a great deal from hearing the personal experiences of an immigrant or refugee.

It is suggested that the teacher hold students accountable for the information presented throughout this subunit by giving students some form of test or quiz or making assignments based on the information presented by other students, the teacher, and guest speakers. This will be discussed further in the "evaluation" segment of this unit plan.

SUBUNIT TWO: U.S. LAWS AND REGULATIONS PERTAINING TO IMMIGRATION

Introduction

In this subunit students will learn about the laws and regulations that affect immigration. The length of this subunit is one week. U.S. immigration laws have largely been reactionary. After an issue or problem has developed, the Congress has passed legislation to regulate immigration. Until the turn of the century, immigration was largely unregulated because of the need for workers and the abundance of resources in the United States. However, in the 1920s, legislation was passed to restrict immigration. The laws regulated immigration according to the national origin of the immigrant and were primarily aimed at keeping Southern and Eastern Europeans and Asians from coming to the United States in large numbers. Throughout the late 1800s and early 1900s, picture brides from Asia were common, particularly on the West Coast, where there were more Asian immigrants. As a result of World War II, in 1945 legislation was passed allowing brides of U.S. citizens entry into the United States. In 1952 the McCarran-Walter Act barred the entry of communists and gave preference to those who had special skills that would benefit the United States. This law was passed at a time when the fear of communism swept the United States. It was not until 1965 that the United States dramatically changed its immigration policy. This legislation abolished the national origins quota system, gave preference to family members of U.S. citizens, and limited the number of immigrants from the Eastern and Western hemispheres. In 1980, the Refugee Act addressed the problem of people seeking freedom from persecution in their native country. Students will be introduced to these laws that affect immigration, but the goal will not be to memorize the laws. The main objectives are for students to understand the relationship between immigration patterns and U.S. laws and to understand how immigration laws are connected to U.S. foreign policy.

Instructional Foci

1. Time line

2. Readings on periods of U.S. history relevant to major waves of immigration, such as "The Picture Brides of San Francisco," *Cobblestone,* January 1983, pp. 22–23

3. Role-play concept of "anchor"

ILOs

Cognitions: 1, 2, 5
Cognitive skills: 1, 2, 4, 6

General Teaching Strategies

To facilitate studying the history of immigration laws, students will construct a large time line. The teacher may give students the information, the students may gain some information from readings, or a combination of the two. The time line should include important dates relevant to immigration and a brief description of the laws and regulations. This time line should be posted around the walls of the classroom so it is visible to all students. Students will discuss the importance of these laws and how they affected immigration and immigrants' experiences in the United States. Discussions may be held in small groups or with the entire class.

An expansion of this unit could be to study the legislative process of how a bill becomes a law. Students could follow an immigration bill through the legislative process.

Since the 1965 legislation that placed a preference on relatives of U.S. citizens, the concept of an "anchor" in the United States has become very important. To illustrate the importance of an "anchor," several students could role-play an extended family trying to immigrate to the United States. One student would play the "anchor," or the family member who is a U.S. citizen whose status would allow other family members to legally immigrate. By acting out the process of immigration for that one family, students would physically see how this policy affects immigration.

SUBUNIT THREE: FACTORS FOR SUCCESS AND FAILURE OF IMMIGRANTS

Introduction

Though there are many different groups of peoples who have come to the United States, over the years many of the factors that affect the success and failure of immigrants have remained constant. In this subunit students will identify several factors that affect how immigrants "make it" in the United States. Students will also have the opportunity to study how immigrants struggle to maintain their own culture and assimilate. The length of this subunit is two weeks.

Instructional Foci

1. Debate
2. Brainstorm

3. Research customs and traditions of two countries that have sent a number of immigrants to the United States

4. Interview family members

ILOs

Cognitions: 1, 3, 4, 6, 7
Cognitive skills: 1, 4, 5, 6

General Teaching Strategies

This subunit will begin with a debate on "What is success and failure?" The point of this debate is for students to examine their own concept of success and failure and compare it to that of an immigrant. This debate will help students understand the immigrants' dilemma of maintaining their native culture and assimilating.

The class will then brainstorm what they think immigrants need to be successful as defined by the debate. After a list is compiled, students will select five to ten factors and spend the next few days writing about why they think these are important. If the teacher feels that the brainstorm did not adequately cover the factors presented in the "content outline," the teacher may make additions to the brainstormed list. Students will share what they have written and discuss the factors in small groups.

The second week, students will examine the similarities and differences between customs and traditions in the United States and two other countries of each student's choice. Students will pick five customs or traditions for two countries and briefly research them. Students will then compare and contrast these ten customs and traditions with U.S. customs and traditions. The class will create a list of foreign customs and their American equivalents and customs not practiced by most Americans. This list will be the focus of a class discussion about how immigrants' familiarity with U.S. customs and traditions and similarities between customs can affect the success or failure of immigrants. Students will also discuss the positives and negatives of both assimilation and the maintenance of native culture.

In the latter part of the second week, students will go back to their family trees and identify first-, second-, and third-generation family members. Students will then make a chart showing, for each generation, customs and traditions, characteristics (language, education, field of employment, etc.), and experiences. Information for the chart may be gained by interviewing family members. Students will compare their charts in small groups. Each group will create a set of generalizations that can be made about each successive generation of immigrants. These generalizations will be discussed by the entire class.

It is hoped that this subunit will give students an appreciation for immigrants' struggle between maintaining their own culture and assimilating. Students should also have an understanding of how and why characteristics of immigrant groups change and remain the same over the course of time.

SUBUNIT FOUR: IMMIGRANTS' CONTRIBUTIONS TO U.S. SOCIETY AND CULTURE

Introduction

The purpose of this two-week subunit is to familiarize students with immigrants' contributions to American society and culture. Many students may already know some ways immigrants have influenced American society. This knowledge will enrich class discussions.

Instructional Foci

1. Analyze immigrants' contributions to local community
2. Guest speaker from local ethnic group
3. Study famous immigrant or refugee who made contribution to U.S. society and culture
4. Cultural fair

ILOs

Cognitions: 1
Cognitive skills: 1, 3, 4

General Teaching Strategies

Students will begin this two-week subunit by examining the ethnic makeup of their own community. This information can be gathered using publications from the local government. An informal way to ascertain this information is to note the names of local businesses. For instance, in Northampton there are a number of businesses with Polish names. This reflects the number of people of Polish descent who live in Northampton. Students will then determine what cultural contributions various ethnic groups have made to the community. A guest speaker from a local ethnic organization will give students the opportunity to hear firsthand about an ethnic group's contributions to the community.

In the second week, students will study a famous immigrant and his or her contributions to American society. Students will choose an immigrant from a list compiled by the teacher. Students will write of the famous immigrant's contributions in the first person, as if they were that person. These writings will be shared with the class. The goal of this activity is that students will gain an appreciation of the wide variety and scope of immigrants' contributions to American society.

This subunit will culminate with a cultural fair complete with food, music, and dance from a variety of ethnic groups.

Throughout this unit the teacher should expose students to the variety of contributions ethnic groups have made to American culture. This can be done by displaying various ethnic groups' fine art, playing music, teaching dances, watching theater (possibly on video), looking at architectural influences, and teaching commonly used words that come from other cultures.

SUBUNIT FIVE: CURRENT EVENTS

Introduction

This one-week to ten-day subunit is designed to bring students up to date with current issues in immigration. It is assumed that throughout the unit students will be bringing in articles relevant to the study of immigration and that daily class discussions will be held around these articles. This subunit allows students to focus on current events. After studying immigration for eight weeks, students will be better prepared to learn about and discuss related current events.

Instructional Foci

1. Recent newspaper and magazine articles

2. Debate on alien farm workers

3. Debate on current immigration policy (liberal vs. conservative)

4. Create a scrapbook or publication of current events

ILOs

Cognitions: 1, 5, 6
Cognitive skills: 1, 4, 6

General Teaching Strategies

Students will begin this subunit by browsing through current events articles and categorizing the articles according to issues. These articles will serve as important sources of information for other activities. Class discussions may come up surrounding these articles. The teacher may select a few particularly interesting articles and structure a class discussion around those specific articles.

The next day, students will prepare for their debates. Students will be involved in one of two debates: alien farm workers or current immigration policy. The teacher will assign roles for the students to play and give students the necessary background information. The teacher will also outline the rules of the debates. Students are free to collect additional information that will help them in the debate. For each debate, the students who are not involved in the debate will serve as the judges. Discussions will follow the debates.

For the final project on immigration, students will create a scrapbook or newspaper around the theme of current events in immigration; the students or teacher may decide which is more appropriate. Individuals or small groups of students would be responsible for gathering information on different immigration issues: the sanctuary movement, emigration from Eastern Europe, racism, and bilingual education, to name a few. Students would be encouraged to use current events articles previously collected. Students would present material on that issue in writing and the written work would be compiled into a class newspaper or scrapbook. The finished product would then be shared with the entire class.

UNINTENDED LEARNING OUTCOMES

The most obvious outcome of this unit is that students will become disinterested in the subject of immigration. This disinterest can be combated by teaching stimulating lessons. For individuals who show a lack of interest, the teacher might find an area of immigration in which the individual is interested and allow that student to pursue study in that area.

It is possible that students will not understand or appreciate the complexities of immigration. If this proves to be the case, the teacher can make adjustments in the curriculum to simplify materials and assignments. Simplification will allow students to get a firmer grasp of concepts that can then be enriched with more complex materials and assignments.

Students who need a greater challenge can work on projects related to concepts currently being taught to the entire class.

Students who have poorer reading or writing skills may need to have assignments and readings adjusted to their abilities. This must be done on an individual basis.

Although highly unlikely, it is possible that students will not gain an appreciation for ethnic differences in this country and will see only their own experiences as acceptable. Students must understand the human element of immigration. It is not an "us" and "them" world; we are all people who share dreams and goals and have similar frustrations. If a tinge of racism enters the classroom, the teacher must address it promptly. It may help to have guests come to the classroom and speak about their own experiences as immigrants. This will bring some of the issues in immigration to a human level.

EVALUATION

Throughout the unit, the teacher will collect and evaluate students' written work. There are several places in this unit where the teacher might assign students written work. For example, the teacher might create an assignment to focus students' reading of an article. The teacher will also note individuals' contributions to class discussions. Evaluation should be based on students demonstrating comprehension of materials and concepts.

I am including a test covering material from Subunits One through Three as an example of the type of evaluation that can be done. This test is designed to evaluate students' knowledge in regard to the following three basic learnings:

Cognitions

Students will understand factors that pull immigrants to the United States and push refugees from their homelands.

Students will understand factors affecting immigrants' and refugees' success and failure in the United States.

Cognitive Skills

Students will compare and contrast characteristics of different immigrant groups.

Thorough, well-written answers will be evidence that students have moved toward accomplishing the desired learning outcomes. Other assignments throughout the unit will also provide the teacher with evidence of students' achievement of the previously mentioned ILOs. The test is to be started at school and completed at home. Students are free to use any material to help them answer the questions. Teachers should not feel that a test or quiz is required at the end of every subunit. Some of the projects completed during the subunits will provide the teacher with a more accurate picture of students' understanding.

TEST

You have two days to complete this test. You will work on it in school as well as at home. You may use any materials to help you answer the questions. This test should be worked on alone. You may ask *only* your teacher for help.

I. Your answers for the following questions should be written in complete sentences in paragraph form. You should provide evidence or details to support your statements. In both of your answers, you should consider push and pull factors affecting immigration.
1. How did immigrants from Northern Europe differ from immigrants from Eastern and Southern Europe?
2. What do Asian and Latin American immigrants have in common? How are they unique?
II. You are an immigrant, fleeing famine in your homeland, and coming to the United States in 1990. You are coming from a country very different from the

United States, with different customs and traditions, as well as language and food. Though you do not speak English, you have gone to college in your homeland. You worked as an elementary school teacher in the small farming town where you lived. You have little money and have brought just a small suitcase of personal belongings. You are not married. Your entire family has stayed behind, but you do have a friend with whom you went to school in your native country who now lives in Northampton. Your friend has told you that Northampton is a friendly town filled with people from all over the world. Your friend has already found you a job washing dishes at a local restaurant.

   Describe what you think your experiences will be like in the United States. Consider how you will both assimilate and maintain some of your own cultural traditions. Define success and how you will achieve that success. Remember, you are an immigrant!

POSSIBLE SOURCES

Cobblestone, December 1982, American immigrants: Part 1.

Cobblestone, January 1983, American immigrants: Part 2.

Cohen, Barbara, illustrated by Michael J. Deraney. (1983). *Molly's Pilgrim*. New York: Lothrop, Lee, & Shepard Books.

Freedman, Russell. (1980). *Immigrant kids*. New York: E. P. Dutton.

Shippen, Katherine B. (1950). *Passage to America: The story of the great migrations*. New York: Harper & Brothers.

Stein, R. Conrad, illustrated by Tom Dunnington. (1970). Cornerstones of Freedom, *The story of Ellis Island*. Chicago: Children's Press.

Tripp, Eleanor B. (1969). *To America*. New York: Harcourt, Brace, & World.

A METRIC MEASUREMENT UNIT FOR GRADES ONE AND TWO

Susan M. Etheredge

COMMENTS

This excellent example of a unit plan for young children has some features worth noting. The author includes an introduction in addition to a rationale. This was an excellent opportunity for her to express her thoughts on the unit immediately after planning it. ILOs are stated in order of priority and not by type of learning category. This has advantages and disadvantages. While readers get a good picture of the overall course emphasis, they do not ever get "talked through" the conceptual map or see the skill development sequence.

If the work is to be used by others, stating the ILOs by priority and by type of learning outcome is probably worthwhile.

The introductions to subunits and the description of general teaching strategies are easy to read and address themselves to sequence, emphasis, and children's thinking, although the use of the passive voice tends to obscure who is doing what in the classroom.

These are matters of central concern; they convey a sense of enthusiasm and they show evidence of thoughtfulness, of having grappled with difficult issues and decisions. They are characteristic of a plan that will be truly useful to teachers. A good plan captures something of the planner, something intangible but clearly recognizable in course designs such as this one.

RATIONALE

At one time junior and senior high school students learned metrics to aid them in their study of chemistry. It now seems imperative that the study of metrics should begin in elementary school classrooms to prepare students for the swing toward metrics that is reaching into every facet of American life. Metric conversion is seen in the goods we buy, the material we read (textbooks, newspapers, cookbooks, road maps, and signs), and the leisure activities we pursue.

Complete transition to the metric standard may or may not happen in the United States, but the influence that metric conversion has on our daily life provides sufficient reason for metric education in the elementary classroom. This unit plan, designed for first and second graders, introduces children to the concept of measurement in general and then, more specifically, to metric measurement.

Children at this age, although still somewhat egocentric, are beginning to show interest in the world around them and are ready to learn new things not directly related to themselves. The egocentricity still evident at this age can be appealed to in a study of measurement by using familiar topics, for example, height, weight, and body measurements or the weights and volumes of food and liquid children consume.

Six- and seven-year-olds just beginning to learn about measurement should acquire some basic knowledge about the need for standard units of measurement. They should know that they are learning a form of communication that enables people to understand one another. Above all, the children should have many practical experiences with linear, weight, volume, and temperature measurement. These experiences should combine actual measurement with estimation.

This metrics unit is designed to be taught separately from any teaching of our measurement system as it now exists. It is not to be taught as a comparative unit with the American system. Conversion from one system to the other is not at all important in this unit. I have found that there is less confusion and better understanding when metric measurement is taught separately from our present measurement system.

Throughout this unit, the children should become aware of the presence of metrics around them. They should begin to understand that they are learning a special language important to universal communication. Their study of metrics from unit to unit and year to year will become increasingly meaningful and valuable as they begin to relate it to their world outside of school.

CENTRAL QUESTIONS

1. What is measurement?
2. What do we measure?
3. How do we measure?
4. What are units of measurement?

INTRODUCTION

This metrics unit is designed for first and second graders. The unit can be adapted for any number of children, but the primary consideration would be the availability of measuring equipment. It is suggested that there be a centimeter ruler, a tape measure, and a meterstick for each child; a metric balance or scale for every two children; and a set of liquid measuring equipment for every two children. The suggested time block per day is about 40 minutes for actual teaching and practice. More time should be allowed on days when the children are expected to set up and put away their own measuring materials.

The prerequisites are few in number, but important: (1) The children should have a facility with numbers. They should be able to read and write numbers from 1 to 100 satisfactorily. For this reason, it is best, especially with a mixed first- and second-grade group, to plan this unit for the end of the year. They should also be able to compute simple addition and subtraction problems. (2) The children should have a clear understanding of the meanings of greater than, more than, less than, bigger than, larger than, smaller than, higher than, and lower than. (3) The children should have had some previous experiences and instruction in nonstandard measurement and informal measuring. This unit is designed on the assumption that the children have had experiences measuring with rods, books, clips, cards, balances, and so on (nonstandard forms).

This metrics unit is outlined into subunits. There are four subunits: Linear Measurement, Weight Measurement, Volume (Liquid) Measurement, and Temperature. There is also a "get ready" day outline to review briefly nonstandard measurement and to prepare the children for the first day's discussion.

The sequence of the subunits is intentional and serves a purpose. The child begins with a form of measurement that is the easiest to measure and read—linear measurement. Next come weight and liquid measurements, which are somewhat more difficult and abstract for young children just beginning a study of precise measurement. Finally, there is temperature, a form of measurement that the children do not really interact with in the same way they do with the other forms. The understandings in this subunit are the most abstract.

This sequence might be described as going from the concrete to the abstract. The understandings and the skills grow more complex and sophisticated as the unit progresses.

The closing statement in this introduction is a personal one. So often measurement units are taught with a pure skill emphasis. Children may become precise measurers, but they don't understand why they measure or even what can be measured. In designing this unit, the cognitive–psychomotor skills seemed to reoccur continually as high-priority learning outcomes. I was at first disturbed about this, thinking that some of the cognitions should receive first priority, but through the unit planning I came to the realization that for those final learning outcomes to happen the children would first have to understand many of the cognitions.

INTENDED LEARNING OUTCOMES FOR THE UNIT IN ORDER OF PRIORITY

1. *Cognitive–psychomotor skill.* The child should be able to measure in the metric units:
   a. measure and record length, width, height, and perimeter in metric units and state measure as whole units or combination of units—for example, 1 meter and 6 centimeters

b. measure, record, and compare weights of two or more objects and order up to three objects by weight

c. measure and record volume of a container using liter and milliliter, compare volume of two or more containers, and order up to three containers by volume

d. measure and record daily temperature, compare temperature of two or more days, and order up to three recordings by temperature

2. *Affect.* The child should have confidence in his or her ability to measure in the various metric units.

3. *Cognition.* The child should understand the concept of measurement.

4. *Cognition.* The child should know what a standard unit of measurement is.

5. *Cognition.* The child should understand the need for and importance of standard units of measurement.

6. *Cognitive skill.* The child should be able to explain what a standard unit of measurement is and why it is important.

7. *Cognition.* The child should be aware of the current uses of metric measurement in all areas of daily life: shopping, cooking, traveling, weather, work, recreation, and so on.

8. *Affect.* The child should appreciate the practical application of metrics in everyday life.

9. *Cognition.* The child should understand that the metric system is the system of measurement used by most countries in the world.

10. *Cognition.* The child should understand that we in the United States are presently using another form of measurement, but need to know (and possibly practice) the metric system since it is being used in the United States.

11. *Cognitive skill.* The child should be able to explain why he or she is learning metric measurement.

12. *Psychomotor–perceptual skill.* The child should be able to:

a. measure accurately with a centimeter ruler, a tape measure, a meterstick, and a trundle wheel to the nearest whole number

b. measure accurately with a balance scale using gram and kilogram weights to the nearest whole number

c. operate a metric scale, using the sliding weight, to the nearest gram or kilogram

d. read a metric scale

e. measure the volume of liquid, using metric spoons and flasks, always to the nearest milliliter or liter

f. read the thermometer in degrees Celsius, to the nearest whole degree

13. *Cognition.* (See also Figure D.1 on page 280.) The child should understand that we measure the following things:
    a. length, width, height, perimeter
    b. weight
    c. volume (liquids)
    d. temperature

14. *Cognition.* The child should understand the meanings of:
    a. length, width, height, perimeter (linear measurement)
    b. weight
    c. volume
    d. temperature

15. *Cognitive skill.* The child should be able to discuss what things are measured and define each term:
    a. length, width, height, perimeter
    b. weight
    c. volume
    d. temperature

16. *Cognition.* The child should know the basic units for the different measurement forms:
    a. centimeter, meter, and kilometer are all units for linear measurement
    b. gram and kilogram are units for weight measurement
    c. milliliter and liter are units for liquid volume measurement
    d. degrees Celsius are units for temperature measurement

17. *Cognitive skill.* The child should be able to name the basic units of measurement for each type of measurement:
    a. centimeter, meter, and kilometer for linear
    b. gram and kilogram for weight
    c. milliliter and liter for volume
    d. degrees Celsius for temperature

18. *Cognition.* (See also Figure D.1.) The child should understand what the word *precision* means and what tools are needed to measure precisely in metrics:
    a. centimeter ruler, meterstick, tape measure, and trundle wheel are used to measure the length, width, height, and perimeter of something
    b. scale and balance are used to measure weight
    c. measuring spoons, cups, and graduated flasks are used to measure liquid volume
    d. Celsius thermometer is used to measure temperature

19. *Cognitive skill.* The child should be able to identify which measurement tools are used to measure precisely a specific thing:
    a. centimeter ruler, meterstick, tape measure, and trundle wheel for linear measurement
    b. scale and balance for weight

FIGURE D.1 Conceptual map for "A Metric Measurement Unit for Grades One and Two."

*Numbers refer to ILOs stated in order of priority.

    c. measuring spoons, cups, and graduated flasks for liquid volumes

    d. Celsius thermometer for temperature

20. *Cognition.* The child should know the approximate amounts the following units represent:

    a. centimeter, meter, kilometer

    b. gram, kilogram

    c. milliliter, liter

    d. 0°C, 30°C, 100°C

21. *Cognitive skill.* The child should be able to represent the approximate value of these units either with "real-world" examples or physical demonstration:

    a. centimeter, meter, kilometer

    b. gram, kilogram

    c. milliliter, liter

    d. 0°C, 30°C, 100°C

22. *Cognition.* The child should understand what the word *estimation* means and what it means to estimate in measurement.

23. *Cognitive skill.* The child should be able to estimate measurement in the various metric units, within a reasonable scale for each unit.

24. *Cognition.* The child should understand what it means to compare, more specifically, to compare the results of an estimate and a precise measurement.

25. *Cognitive skill.* The child should be able to compare his or her estimations with precise measurements.

Note: Cognitions are also summarized in Figure D.1.

"GET READY" LESSONS AND DISCUSSION

This is a brief review of nonstandard units. As stated in the introduction, the children should already have had measurement experiences of the type described in the teaching strategy below. It is hoped that the children have acquired some knowledge from their earlier study of measurement. The purpose of the "get ready" lesson and discussion is to reactivate that knowledge and to prepare the children for the new information to follow.

ILOs

Numbers 3, 4, 5, 6, 9, 10, 11

Instructional Foci

Books, Cuisenaire rods, paper clips, pieces of string of various lengths, beans, pencils, straws, tiles, pieces of paper, file cards—any items you can use to measure something. Paper and pencil for each child.

Teaching Strategy

Each child will be given one item with which to measure. Most of the items are different. The teacher will tell them to use their item to measure the following things: the length of a chalkboard, a doorway, the top of a desk, and so on. They will record their measurement of each object.

A discussion will then follow. The ideas to be highlighted and emphasized are as follows: everyone got different answers—their measuring devices are called nonstandard units of measurement—everybody needs to use the same unit of measurement—otherwise we will have a confused group of people—won't understand each other—need for standard units—what are some standard units of measurement?—why do we need these standard units?—what is accurate communication?—why is it important?—awareness that there are two types of standard measurement units for accurate communication—metrics and the system we use now—we're going to study metrics—most of the world is using the metric system of measurement—we don't, but it is being used more and more in our country and we should understand it. This "get ready" activity should close with a discussion of "What Are We Doing When We Measure?"

SUBUNITS

The intended learning outcomes that will appear under each subunit are those particular to that subunit. At this time the ILOs that are common to all *four* subunits are 2, 3, 4, 5, 6, 7, 8, 9, 10, 11, 22, 23, 24, and 25.

The reader is asked to remember that the ILOs listed above are included in every subunit. The wording of these ILOs is of a general nature. It is up to the teacher to see that these learnings are reinforced and understood in the context of each subunit's topic or theme.

Subunit I: Linear Measurement

The concepts of length, width, height, and perimeter will be explored and defined in this unit. We will talk about length as the longest side of an object, width as the shortest side of an object, height as the distance from the bottom to the top of an upright object (often synonymous with length), and perimeter as the distance around an object. The metric units centimeter, meter, and kilometer will be introduced and used throughout the unit. The measuring tools presented will include the centimeter ruler, the centimeter tape measure, the meterstick, and the trundle wheel. Both estimation and precision will be discussed and stressed in this unit.

Intended Learning Outcomes: Numbers 1a, 12a, 13a, 14a, 15a, 16a, 17a, 18a, 19a, 20a, and 21a.

Instructional Foci: Centimeter rulers, centimeter tape measures, metersticks, trundle wheels; teacher-made posters with linear units and abbreviations written out; series of worksheets; classroom objects to measure (pencils, pens, books, paper clips, staplers, paper, file cards, blocks, crayons, and so on); Metric Measuring License (see page 285).

Teaching Strategy: The terms *length, width,* and *height* will be introduced and discussed. The children and teacher will spend time identifying the lengths, widths, and/or heights of various objects.

Then the standard metric units of linear measurement—centimeter, meter, and kilometer—should be presented. These units should be presented one at a time, not as a group. The organization and sequence is important here. First the centimeter should be introduced and discussed. Then the measuring tools to measure a centimeter should be presented. The estimation and measurement of items under 100 centimeters is necessary before presenting the meter. It is essential to perform the same sequence with the meter before discussing the kilometer.

The children should be given a frame of reference for each linear unit. For instance, a centimeter is about the width of your baby finger, the thickness of a slice of bread, or the width of a Popsicle stick. A meter might be the distance from the floor to a six-year-old's chin (use a meterstick to determine this), the width of a standard-size door, or the width of a newspaper opened up. A kilometer might be the distance from the school to the local movie theater or the YMCA—use a locality with which the children are familiar. These estimates will provide the children with some concrete, familiar ground before their actual measuring experiences begin. Teacher-made posters accompanied by pictures illustrating these metric units would be useful here.

The word *estimation* is to be defined and discussed. What does it mean to estimate? Why do we estimate? When might we make estimations? How do we estimate? Motivating questions at this stage might include: About how many centimeters long do you think this pencil is? About how many meters wide do you think this chalkboard is? Let the children actually use their pinkies and other visual or physical aids for rough estimates.

This will lead into the presentation of the linear measurement tools: the centimeter ruler, the tape measure, the meterstick, and the trundle wheel. The word *precision* should be introduced here. What does it mean to measure precisely? Why and when would we need precise measurements? Provide the children with hypothetical situations and ask, "Would it be better to estimate or measure precisely in this situation?"

Instruct the children in the use of each tool. Allow for many measuring experiences using classroom objects and any personal belongings the children may want to measure.

Worksheets should include both estimation and precise measurement and a comparison of results. How close was I? Did I estimate too much or too little? Actual problem solving using simple addition and subtraction could be integrated here. How many centimeters (meters) off was I? How much longer (wider) is the book than the paper? Perimeter should be introduced once the children have successfully estimated and measured lengths, widths, and heights.

Accurate measurement should be stressed. Estimation is of secondary importance. Accurate measurement, the ease with which it's done, and the written recording of measurements are of primary importance. An understanding of which measurement tool is best to measure various dimensions is also of high priority (use a centimeter ruler for a smaller length, a centimeter tape measure for distances around an object, a meterstick for a longer length, and a trundle wheel for very long distances). The children should also be able to measure and record distances as a combination of units, for example, 2 meters and 4 centimeters.

The Metric Measuring License is an activity that can be included in the complete Metrics Unit. (See the example on page 285.) It can act as a thread that runs through each subunit, unifying the Metric Measurement theme. It reflects the learnings of each subunit. The children work in pairs, helping each other with the measuring and recording of their personal data.

The centimeter and meter are worked with more often than the kilometer in this subunit. The kilometer is discussed in more abstract terms. The children and teacher may take a "Kilometer Walk" someday, but it is introduced as the unit used to measure very long distances, like a distance you may walk, run, drive, or fly. It can be used in the problem-solving sense—how many kilometers did Pat run if she ran 1 kilometer on Monday and 2 kilometers on Wednesday? Or, would you use meters or kilometers to tell someone how far it is to Amherst? The kilometer is to be taught in a more abstract way—there are no actual measurement experiences with the kilometer at this level.

The teacher should provide time for discussions of practical, real-life applications of linear measurement. Children should have ideas about possible situations when precise measurement would be essential and when estimation would be sufficient. They should understand clearly how precision is different from estimation.

The final lesson(s) should combine the three linear units: centimeter, meter, and kilometer. The children are to understand what unit and what tool is used to measure what linear dimension. The teacher is expected to check this understanding with observations of their interactions with the measuring equipment and their daily written and oral work.

Suggested time to spend on this subunit: five days, 30 to 40 minutes each day

Subunit II: Weight Measurement

What weight is and the way it's measured in the metric system are the topics of this subunit. We will talk about weight as the amount of heaviness something has. (See Figure D.2.) This type of measurement is to be contrasted with linear measurement. How are they different? How are they alike? The gram and kilogram are the measurement units introduced. Precision and estimation are important elements again in the subunit.

Intended Learning Outcomes: Numbers 1b, 12b, 12c, 12d, 13b, 14b, 15b, 16b, 17b, 18b, 19b, 20b, and 21b.

Instructional Foci: Balances, sliding weight scales, metric scales, weights of assorted sizes (grams and kilograms), dollar bill, nickel, piece of chalk, magic marker, golf ball, tennis ball, stick of butter, softball, loaf of bread, two-pound box of sugar cubes, pencils, paper, series of worksheets.

Teaching Strategy: This subunit will begin with a discussion of weight. What is weight? Does anyone know how we measure it? How is weight measurement different from linear measurement? How are they similar?

Metric Measuring License

For centimeter, meter, gram, kilogram, milliliter, liter, and degrees Celsius

cm = centimeter   m = meter   g = gram
kg = kilogram   ml = milliliter   l = liter

This license entitles _____, upon completion of the form below, to be an OFFICIAL METRIC MEASURER, authorized to measure, at any time, using OFFICIAL METRIC UNITS, anything that can be measured either with

OFFICIAL MEASURING TOOLS or by ESTIMATION:

height_____ arm spread_____ nose to fingertip_____ hand span_____

palm_____ thumb_____ index finger_____ middle finger_____

ring finger_____ pinkie_____ knee to floor_____ foot length_____

foot width_____ shoe length_____ shoe width_____ plain step_____

giant step_____ around head_____ around neck_____ around chest_____

around wrist_____ around waist_____ around thigh_____ around ankle_____

weight_____ weight of shoe_____ weight of relaxed hand_____

weight of favorite book_____ volume of lunch milk or juice_____

your body temperature_____ outside temperature today_____

age_____ years_____ signature_____ date_____

All of the measurements will change—keep your Metric Measuring License up to date!

FIGURE D.2   Metric Measuring License activity.

The gram is introduced as the basic unit of measurement of weight. Items that weigh various amounts are passed around for the children to hold: dollar bill (1g), nickel (5g), new piece of chalk (10g), large magic marker (25g), tennis ball (50g), stick of butter (100g), softball (200g), and a loaf of bread (500g). A chart is made with the children to record these amounts.

The children then estimate the weights of various objects under 500g using the above items to compare. They record their estimations.

The next lesson will be devoted to precision measurement. Gram weights are introduced and explained. The children are taught how to use a balance and sliding weight scale. They work in pairs or alone, depending on the number of scales and children. They weigh the objects they had previously estimated, record the precise weights, and compare their estimates with final results.

The kilogram is then introduced as the unit used for weights larger than a thousand grams. A two-pound box of sugar cubes, a kilogram weight, and any other items weighing about a kilogram are given to the children to handle. Estimation of items and precision measurement are again done, this time with the kilogram. Each child is weighed on a metric scale at this time.

The children will be asked to measure, record, and compare the weights of at least two or more objects and then order those objects by weight. They will also graph *or* order (heaviest to lightest) the weights of all the children in the group, providing that it does not cause any child undue embarrassment. They will also need to complete the sections of their Metric Measuring Licenses that apply to weight.

In order to relate metric weight measurement to the real world, the children will be asked to make a list of at least five packaged goods they can find in their homes that have a designated gram or kilogram weight. Together, the teacher and children can make a composite list. Discussion of weight application to other daily experiences is also important.

Suggested time to spend on this subunit: five days, 30 to 40 minutes each day.

Subunit III: Volume (Liquid) Measurement

Volume is the key word in this subunit. Volume will be presented as the amount of liquid that is needed to fill a particular amount of space. Amounts of water will be estimated, measured, and compared. The distinction between weight and volume will be an important point of discussion. Once again, estimation and precision will be emphasized. The milliliter and the liter will be introduced as the basic units of liquid measurement.

Intended Learning Outcomes: Numbers 1c, 12c, 13c, 14c, 15c, 16c, 17c, 18c, 19c, 20c, and 21c.

Instructional Foci: Measuring spoons, liter flasks, milliliter eye droppers, containers of various shapes and sizes, water table if possible, pencils, paper, series of worksheets.

Teaching Strategy: The first lesson will begin with a discussion of liquids the children drink. Containers (bottles, glasses) will be available for illustrative purposes. Do you usually drink this much orange juice? How many glasses of juice would we need to fill this bottle? Do you know how we measure liquids?

The distinction between solid weight measurement should be clarified in the children's minds. It should be demonstrated that we are not trying to find out how much the liquid *weighs,* but how much *space* it takes up in the container.

A milliliter will be introduced as a very small unit of liquid measurement. Together, with milliliter eye droppers, we will find out how many milliliters of water it takes to fill up various sizes of small containers. They will see that a common size cup is 250 milliliters. Precision measurement is stressed here.

The liter is introduced as the next unit of liquid measurement after the milliliter. The children will be told that it takes 1,000 of those milliliter drops to fill the 1-liter container. The children will be asked to estimate the amount of liters needed to fill various large-size containers, to precisely measure the amounts of liquids, and then to compare the volume of two or more containers, ordering up to three containers by volume. They will record their findings.

The children will look at home to see if they can find liquids packaged or bottled in milliliter and liter containers. A class list will be made. They will also complete the liquid volume section of their Metric Measuring Licenses.

Before starting the temperature subunit, the teacher and children will bake a sweet. They will follow a very simple recipe using both weight and liquid measurements.

Suggested time to spend on this subunit: four days, 30 to 40 minutes each—one day for the cooking activity.

Subunit IV: Temperature

Temperature—what is it? We will talk about temperature as the amount of hotness or coldness as measured on a definite scale. Degrees Celsius will be presented as the metric unit for measuring this amount. The Celsius thermometer will be introduced as the instrument, or scale, used to measure these degrees of hotness or coldness. Reference points on a Celsius thermometer will be established to help the children see the comparative nature of understanding temperature.

Intended Learning Outcomes: Numbers 1d, 12f, 13d, 14d, 15d, 16d, 17d, 18d, 19d, 20d, and 21d.

Instructional Foci: Indoor Celsius thermometer, outdoor Celsius thermometer, numerous Celsius thermometers—at least one to measure human body temperature—pencils, paper, series of worksheets, one large-scale model of a Celsius thermometer with "movable" parts.

Teaching Strategy: The topic of temperature will be introduced with a discussion of everything the children already know about it. What is temperature? How do we measure temperature? Why do we need to know temperatures?

The children will learn how to read a Celsius thermometer by using a large-scale model with movable parts that can be changed to many different temperature readings. We will talk about the different places thermometers can be used and the different types of thermometers (outdoor, indoor, freezer, refrigerator, meat, body, and so on).

Working in pairs or small groups, the children will take readings of various temperatures: outside, inside the classroom, a bucket of ice, a pot of boiling water, tap water (hot and cold), a refrigerator, a freezer, and body temperature. They will record their readings. Together the group will discuss their findings and will make a chart of the various readings. We will order them from coldest to hottest. We will talk about the degrees that represent very cold things, lukewarm things, and hot things. The following chart will then be presented.

−20°C	very cold
0	freezing
10	cool spring day
20	nice spring day
25	good room temperature

30	nice summer day
35	swimming weather
37	heat wave
40	normal body temperature
100	boiling water

A daily temperature reading will be taken. At the end of this subunit, the children will order the readings from hottest to coldest and will answer questions pertaining to them. On what day was it the hottest? the coldest? How much hotter was it on Tuesday than on Wednesday? They should work with five readings. The teacher will need to supply two of them since this is a three-day subunit.

As a final lesson, the children will need to give approximate temperatures in degrees Celsius for various situations. Here are a few examples. It's a hot summer day. How many degrees Celsius do you think it is? I want to make a cup of tea, but I need boiling water. How many degrees Celsius will the water need to be? If it's winter and there's ice on the ground, it's probably _____°C. What would you wear outside if the thermometer read 10°C?—20°C? What would you do outside if it was 25°C? How would you be feeling if your mom or dad took your temperature and it read 40°C? Those children who need to use the chart may do so.

The children should complete their Metric Measuring Licenses at the end of this subunit.

Suggested time to spend on this subunit: three days, 30 to 40 minutes each day.

Note: A final activity that might be interesting to try at the end of this subunit would be to construct a conceptual map with the children. Give them the headings What We Measure, How We Measure, and Need for Standard Units of Measurement. See what ideas they can come up with to fit under each heading. It may illustrate the structure of their thinking, the "chunks" of learning they've acquired from the unit, and the connections they have made among the "chunks."

UNINTENDED LEARNING OUTCOMES

1. The child who has already had some experiences with metric measurement or learns the material quickly may become bored and uninterested in the unit.

Possible solution: Enrichment! The child could learn more of the basic units in each measurement area: millimeter, decimeter, dekameter, milligram, and kiloliter. The child could begin doing some simple conversions within metrics. For example, 20 centimeters = _____ decimeters; _____ milliliters = 4 liters; 3,000 grams = _____ kilograms. The child could be exposed to a number of application problems that involve more advanced computational skills or reasoning, for example, How many meters of fencing are needed for a rectangular playground that measures 11 meters wide by 22 meters long? The height of a ceiling is 300 centimeters. How many meters is that?

The concept of area could be introduced and explored with square centimeters, square meters, and square kilometers.

2. A younger child in the group or a child who is not grasping the concepts may become frustrated and self-conscious because of unsuccessful attempts.

Possible solution: Remedial attention! Don't expect the child to learn all the measurement units presented. Allow the child to work only with the meter, gram, and liter. Stress measurement over estimation if that's the child's strength. Simplify the material. Pair the child with another slower learner so they may work together at their own pace rather than feel the pressure from a faster worker.

3. If a child has a good understanding of our present measuring system, he may want constantly to "talk conversion." This may confuse the child who is unable to understand that this is a measurement system unrelated to the one he or she already knows. The child may become frustrated with the teacher's unwillingness to compare centimeters with inches, for instance.

Possible solution: The teacher does not have to ignore the child's desire to know comparable amounts in our system. It can be done on an individual basis, so that the other children will not be confused with the information. The teacher should make it clear to the child that they are studying metrics as a measurement system by itself and are trying not to compare it with our system.

4. A child who consistently estimates poorly may feel as though he or she is not doing well or succeeding. Even though accurate estimation is not of the highest priority, it is included in many lessons. The child may feel like a failure if he or she is a poor estimator.

Possible solution: As stated in the remedial ideas section, deemphasize estimation with this child. Give the child more experiences with precision measurement. Have the child estimate more spacious dimensions that allow for "physical" aids—hands or feet, for example. Or allow each child to have examples (liter flask, kilogram weight) by their side for constant comparison. Allow the child to estimate with the help of concrete aids, rather than with mental visual pictures.

EVALUATION OF HIGH-PRIORITY INTENDED LEARNING OUTCOMES

Evidence of Main Effects of the Five High-Priority ILOs

1A–D. Cognitive–Psychomotor Skill

Evidence of cognitive skill/psychomotor skill: The child is given hypothetical situations and asked to solve them. Here are some examples:

Situation 1: There's a wall in my living room that is 2 meters long. I want you to measure that desk to see if it will fit against that wall. The child will have to figure out what measurement tool to use, measure the length of the desk, record the length, and then explain whether or not it will fit. (The desk should be straight-edged and easily measurable.)

Situation 2: I have three objects: an apple, a mug, and a golf ball. (Try to have items that weigh about the same as the gram weights.) I want you to measure them, write down the measurements, and then tell me which one is heaviest, next heaviest, and then lightest. The child will have to decide what measurement tool to use to find out how heavy or light an object is, weigh it, record it, and then order the objects by weight.

Situation 3: I have three containers: A, B, and C. They're all filled with different amounts of water. (The containers should all be different sizes, but not obvious as to how much liquid they hold.) I want you to measure each one, record the measurements, and then order them to show which container has the smallest amount to the largest amount. The child will have to choose the correct measuring instrument, measure the amount of water in each container, record, and then order them by volume.

Situation 4: I have three containers. One is filled with ice, one is filled with water that's been sitting here for awhile, and the last one is filled with very hot water. I want to know the exact temperature of the contents of each container and then I want you to order the temperatures from highest to lowest. The child will need to take a temperature reading from each container, record them, and then order the readings.

2. Affect

Evidence of affect (behaviors/actions): The child attacks the problems stated above in a confident, comfortable manner. The child doesn't hesitate when given measurement tasks; he or she doesn't need constant direction while measuring. The child is able to decide quickly what measurement tool is necessary to solve a problem. The child offers to help other children who are having difficulty with precision measurement or estimation. The child exhibits little difficulty in the recording of measurement results.

Circumstances: group activities in the classroom, written work, testing situation.

3. Cognition

Evidence of understanding: The child describes what sorts of things we measure, why we might want to measure these things, and how we measure each particular thing. The child is able to contrast the various types of measurement: linear, weight, volume, and temperature. The child is able to compare precision measurement with estimation.

4. Cognition

Evidence of understanding: The child is able to give examples of standard and nonstandard units of measurement. The child is able to categorize a list of words into standard units of measurement and nonstandard units of measurement.

5. Cognition

Evidence of understanding: The child should be able to explain, in his or her own words, why we need to have standard units of measurement. The child should be able to give examples of confusing situations when nonstandard units are used.

I would need to find	Unit I'd choose	Measuring tool I'd choose
length of this room		
outside temperature		
width of a book		
body weight		

FIGURE D.3   Assessment worksheet for units of measurement.

The daily written work and a final worksheet that would combine the four subunit topics of metric measurement would also be useful evaluative tools. Daily observation of the children interacting with the materials and the measuring equipment is the best way to assess the psychomotor–perceptual ILOs.

A final worksheet that combines linear, weight, volume, and temperature measurement would serve as a means to evaluate once again the children's learnings of some of the cognitions and cognitive skills. The worksheet could look like that shown in Figure D.3.

The following are some ideas for questions. Directions would be to choose the best estimate. They could be done orally for nonreaders or beginning readers.

1. The height of a ceiling in a home is:
   a. 3 meters
   b. 1 centimeter
   c. 4 grams

2. The length of an ant is:
   a. 5 meters
   b. 1 centimeter
   c. 2 liters

3. The weight of a newborn baby is about:
   a. 3 kilograms
   b. 30°C
   c. 500 milliliters

4. Your thermos might hold:
   a. 5 liters
   b. 30°C
   c. 500 milliliters

Actual learning outcome (ALO).   A change in a person's capability or state of mind that results from interaction with people, ideas, or objects. Changes such as physical injuries, physiological maturation, and those that are drug induced are excluded from this concept.

Affect.   An umbrella term for two types of intended learning outcomes: affective understandings and affective skills.

Affective skill.   A type of intended learning outcome dealing with the ability to behave in ways that reflect certain attitudes.

Affective understanding.   A type of intended learning outcome dealing with self-knowledge or knowledge about the interaction of self with others.

Assertion.   An idea that can be stated as a proposition, that is, asserting something to be true—facts, principles, generalizations. Assertions constitute one set of ideas for students to learn.

Central question.   One of the fundamental questions with which a course deals and which identifies the focus of the course.

Clustering ILOs.   The grouping of ILOs into unit-sized chunks.

Cognition.   An idea that is intended to be learned.

Cognitive skill.   The ability to use or apply cognitions.

Conception.   A type of cognitive intended learning outcome. Conceptions entail a way of looking at the world; that is, a person's theory or belief system regarding some set of phenomena.

Conceptual map.   A chart depicting the relationships among the important ideas with which a course deals. The map describes the organization of understandings in the course.

Curriculum.   An organized set of intended learning outcomes presumed to lead to the achievement of educational goals.

Curriculum development.   The process by which intended learning outcomes are selected and organized.

Educational goal.   A desirable attribute of a person (for example, literate, tolerant, or creative) that is expected to result from the educational process. These goals are "educational" (rather than societal or institutional) if they are achievable through learning.

Educational result.   A description of the kind of person that develops as a consequence of the complex interactive and cumulative effects of formal and informal education, as well as maturation. These may or may not correspond with the intended educational results, that is, the "educational goals."

Evaluation.   The collection and analysis of data for the purpose of making a judgment or rendering a decision.

Flowchart.   A diagram depicting the components of a complex skill in terms of subskills and understandings.

General teaching strategy.   The instructional events that are planned around an instructional focus for the accomplishment of ILOs. These strategies are described at a level more general than daily lesson plans but more specific than a list of materials to be used.

Goal setting.   The process by which goals are formulated.

Graphic organizer.   A visual illustration of verbal information. Graphic organizers highlight the structure or relationships inherent in the information being represented, often providing insight into these relationships not readily available in prose format. Flowcharts, pie charts, and family trees are familiar graphic organizers.

Instruction.   Providing experiences for learners with the intention of bringing about particular learnings.

Instructional focus.   A theme, problem, activity, stimulus, or vehicle for communicating ideas designed to facilitate the learning of a set of ILOs. They are termed "foci" because they serve as focal points for learning and lend coherence to a set of ILOs.

Instructional plan.   An outline for a course specifying its units and the means for teaching each unit. For each unit in the plan, intended learning outcomes for the unit, the unit rationale, and general teaching strategies should be described.

Instructional planning.   The process of forming and organizing unit-sized chunks of a course, specifying an instructional focus for each unit, and designing a set of instructional events around each focus.

Intended learning outcome (ILO).   Something that the student is expected to learn. A course's ILOs may consist of cognitions, cognitive skills, psychomotor–perceptual skills, or affects.

Interdisciplinary.   A curriculum or course that incorporates content from more than a single academic discipline. Typically, the distinct identities of the separate disciplines are fused. For example, a course in European Civilization might combine subjects such as history, geography, art, music, and literature.

Main effect.   An actual learning outcome corresponding to a course's ILOs.

Psychomotor–perceptual skills.   Physical or perceptual competencies and abilities intended to be learned.

Rationale.   There are two kinds of rationales: (1) *Course Rationale*, a statement justifying a course in terms of the course's educational goals. These goals are discussed in the context of the planner's conception of the learner, the society, and the subject matter. (2) *Unit Rationale*, a statement describing what a particular unit is about, how it builds on previous units, and how subsequent units build on it.

Sequencing principle.   The reason behind, or the basis for, ordering course units in a particular manner.

Side effect.   An unintended and often undesirable learning outcome resulting from a course's methods, materials, or organization, as well as other factors.

Skill.   A gross category of intended learning outcomes comprising the things a teacher wants students to be able to do as a consequence of instruction.

Understandings.   A gross category of intended learning outcomes including ideas a teacher wants students to acquire as a consequence of instruction.

Unit.   A coherent chunk of a course.

Value.   An ideal or a state of affairs toward which one or more persons has a high affective regard, for example, equality of educational opportunity.

INDEX